THE COBRA GODDESS
OF
ANCIENT EGYPT

Studies in Egyptology

Edited by: A. B. Lloyd

Professor of Classics and Ancient History, University College of Swansea

Editorial Adviser: A. F. Shore

Professor of Egyptology, University of Liverpool.

The Egyptian Temple
Patricia Spencer

**The Administration of Egypt in the
Old Kingdom**
Nigel Strudwick

**Corpus of Reliefs of the New Kingdom
from the Memphite Necropolis and
Lower Egypt Volume 1**
Geoffrey Thorndike Martin

**Problems and Priorities in
Egyptian Archaeology**
*Jan Assmann, Günter Burkard
and Vivian Davies*

Lost Tombs
Lise Manniche

**Decoration in Egyptian Tombs of the
Old Kingdom**
Yvonne Harpur

**Untersuchungén zu den
Totenbuchpapyri der 18. Dynastie**
Irmtraut Munro

The Monuments of Senenmut
Peter F. Dorman

The Fort Cemetery at Hierakonpolis
Barbara Adams

The Duties of the Vizier
G. P. F. van den Boorn

**A Glossary of Ancient Egyptian Nautical
Titles and Terms**
Dilwyn Jones

Land Tenure in the Ramesside Period
Sally L. D. Katary

Valley of the Kings
C. N. Reeves

Forthcoming:

The Private Chapel in Ancient Egypt
Ann H. Bomann

Akhenaten's Sed-Festival at Karnak
Jocelyn Gohary

A Bibliography of the Amarna Period
Geoffrey Thorndike Martin

After Tutankhamun
Edited by C. N. Reeves

Gods, Priests and Men
*Aylward M. Blackman
Compiled and edited by Alan B. Lloyd*

THE COBRA GODDESS
OF
ANCIENT EGYPT

Predynastic, Early Dynastic,
and Old Kingdom Periods

SALLY B. JOHNSON

Drawings by Victoria Solia

KEGAN PAUL INTERNATIONAL
London and New York

First published in 1990 by
Kegan Paul International Ltd
PO Box 256, London, WC1B 3SW, England

Distributed by
John Wiley & Sons Ltd
Southern Cross Trading Estate
1 Oldlands Way, Bognor Regis
West Sussex, PO22 9SA, England

Routledge, Chapman & Hall Inc
29 West 35th Street
New York, NY 10001, USA

The Canterbury Press Pty Ltd
Unit 2, 71 Rushdale Street
Scoresby, Victoria 3179, Australia

Printed in Great Britain by T.J. Press Ltd

British Library Cataloguing in Publication Data

Johnson, Sally B. (Sally Barber), *1921–*
   The cobra goddess of ancient Egypt.
   1. Egyptian religion, ancient period, Goddesses
   I. Title II. Series
   299'.31

   ISBN 0–7103–0212–6

Library of Congress Cataloging-in-Publication Data

Johnson, Sally B. (Sally Barber), 1921–
   The cobra goddess of ancient Egypt : Predynastic, Early Dynastic,
   and Old Kingdom periods / Sally B. Johnson.
   p. cm. — (Studies in Egyptology)
   Includes bibliographical references.
   ISBN 0–7103–0212–6
   1. Cobras—Religious aspects. 2. Goddesses, Egyptian. 3. Egypt—
   Antiquities. 4. Egypt—Religion. 5. Cobras in art. I. Title.
   II. Series.
   BL2450.C62J64 1990
   299'.31–dc20
                                    90–43046
                                    CIP

To my husband

C. Bedford Johnson

CONTENTS

LIST OF ILLUSTRATIONS

Frontispiece
Cobra detail from gold-encased bed canopy of Queen Hetep-heres I, Cairo CG 57711; photo courtesy of Boston MFA; reproduced with permission of Cairo Museum.

Chapter 1
Fig. 1, pryamid of Unas sarcophagus chamber, east wall; photo courtesy The Brooklyn Museum from Piankoff 1968, pl. vi; reproduced with permission of Princeton University Press.

Chapter 2
Fig. 2, live cobra with anatomical nomenclature; from R. A. Schwaller de Lubicz (photographs by de George et Valentine de Mire) 1982, pl. 107. Fig. 3, Egyptian cobra at the feet of a colossal statue; from Samivel and M. Audrian 1963, pl. 31. Fig. 4, detail, Hetep-heres I canopy; photo courtesy Boston MFA; permission of Cairo Museum. Fig. 5, detail of a living cobra; photo from Minton and Minton 1969; Fig. 6, Black-necked cobra; photo from Stidworthy 1971, p. 103. Fig. 7, Ringhals cobra; *ibid*., p. 102. Fig. 8, Indian cobra; photo from Whitfield 1984, opp. p. 454; permission of Marshall Editions Limited. Fig. 9, cobra skeleton showing movable neck ribs; photo from Stidworthy, 1971, p. 98; permission of Grosset & Dunlap. Fig. 10, cobra ventral scales; photo from Stidworthy 1971, p. 7; permission of Grosset & Dunlap. Fig. 11, cobra detail on Den's ivory tablet; drawing by Victoria Solia (hereafter VS). Fig. 12, 13, back and front views of cobra head from above; drawings by VS. Fig. 14, serpent head of Zer, Cairo JE 34915; drawing by VS. Fig. 15, Graeco-Roman gold snake head, CMA 1018.81 on exhibition at CMA, collection of Leo Mildenberg, cat. 163. pg. 180; photo courtesy The Cleveland Museum of Art; permission of L. Mildenberg and The Cleveland Museum of Art.

Chapter 3
Figs. 16-41, illustrations for **URAEUS TYPES WITH EARLIEST KNOWN EXAMPLES**; drawings by VS taken from photograph of appropriate Catalog entry.

Chapter 4.
Figs. 42-60: illustrations for **GLOSSARY OF DESCRIPTIVE TERMS**; drawings by VS.

Chapter 5.
Fig. 61, Amratian slate palette from Abadiyeh, Brussels MRAH E. 7062; photo courtesy Brussels Musées Royaux d'Art et d'Histoire; reproduced with permission of Institut Royal du Patrimoine Artistique. Fig. 62, Amratian bowl; Louvre E 27131, photo by C Bedford Johnson (hereafter CBJ); reproduced with permission of Musée du Louvre. Fig. 63, late Gerzean vase, Brooklyn 61.87; photo courtesy The Brooklyn Museum; reproduced with permission of The Brooklyn Musuem. Fig. 64, E. Berlin ÄMP 15129; reproduced with permission of Staatliche Museen zu Berlin, Hauptstadt der DDR, Ägyptisches Museum und Papyrussammlung. Fig. 65,

A-Group vase from Qustal in Nubia, Chicago OIM 24119; reproduced with permission of Chicago University, Oriental Institute Museum. Fig. 66, Gebel Tarif knife handle Cairo CG 14265; reproduced with permission of Cairo Museum. Fig. 67, drawing of detail, Brooklyn knife handle by VS. Fig. 68, side of Brooklyn knife handle with cobras, Brooklyn 09.889.118; photo courtesy The Brooklyn Museum; reproduced with permission of The Brooklyn Museum. Fig. 69, bronze sphinx protected by two uraei, Brooklyn 61.20; photo courtesy The Brooklyn Museum; reproduced with permission of The Brooklyn Museum Fig. 70, drawing of knife handle (MMA 26.7.1281) detail by VS. Fig. 71, "Carnarvon" knife handle, MMA 26.7.1281, Gerzean Period; The Metropolitan Museum of Art, purchase, Edward S. Harkness, Gift, 1926; photo courtesy MMA; reproduced with permission of The Metropolitan Museum of Art. Fig. 72, mace and drawing with detail of elephant and cobra, Cario JE 43883; photos from Firth 1929, fig. 8, pl. xviiia-c. Fig. 73, drawing of detail on two sides of comb handle (MMA 30.8.224) by VS. Fig. 74, one side of "Davis" comb handle, MMA 30.8.224, The Metropolitan Museum of Art, bequest of Theodore Davis, 1915; photo courtesy MMA; reproduced with permission of The Metropolitan Museum of Art. Fig. 75, drawing of detail, "Pitt-Rivers" knife by VS. Fig. 76, "Pitt-Rivers" knife handle., BM 68512; photo courtesy The British Museum; reproduced with permission of The British Museum.

Chapter 6.
Fig. 77, detail of Nagada Tablet, Cairo CG 14142; drawing by VS. Fig. 78-79, Nagada Tablet and drawing, Cairo CG 14142; photo from Garstang 1905, figs. 1, 3. Figs. 80-81, ventral and dorsal view of serpent head of Zer, Cairo JE 34915; photos courtesy Cairo Museum; reproduced with permission of Cairo Museum. Figs. 82-83, cobra detail and "Stela of the Serpent King", Louvre E 11007; photos by Chuzeville, Paris, Musée du Louvre; reproduced with permission of Musée du Louvre. Fig. 84, fragment of ivory inlay, London BM 32641; photo courtesy The British Museum; reproduced with permission of The British Museum. Fig. 85; ivory comb of Zet, Cairo JE 47176; photo from Englebach 1930, pl. viii. Figs. 86-87, drawings of uraeus on forehead and Wepwawet standard details of BM 55586 by VS. Fig. 88, ivory smiting tablet of Den, BM 55586; photo courtesy The British Museum; reproduced with permission of The British Museum. Fig. 89, name tablet of Den, BM 35552; photo courtesy The British Museum; reproduced with permission of The British Museum. Fig. 90, jar label of Semerkhet, BM 32668; photo courtesy The British Museum; reproduced with permission of The British Museum. Fig. 91, drawing of jar label, BM 32668; photo from Spencer 1980, cat. 461; reproduced with permission of The British Museum. Fig. 92, jar label of Qay-a, Philadelphia UPM 6880; photo courtesy University of Pennsylvania Museum; reproduced with permission of Philadelphia UPM. Fig. 93, drawing of jar label; photo from Petrie 1900, pls. xii-2, xvii-29. Fig. 94, vase fragment of Qay-a, BM 32672; photo courtesy The British Museum; reproduced with permission of The British Museum. Fig. 95, vase fragment of Qay-a, MMA 01.4.20, The Metropolitan Museum of Art, gift of the Egypt Exploration Fund, 1901; photo courtesy MMA; reproduced with permission of The Metropolitan Museum of Art. Fig. 96, vase fragment of Semti, BM 49278, photo courtesy The British Museum; reproduced with permission of The British Museum. Fig. 97, Dynasty II vase fragment, BM 35556; photo courtesy The British Museum; reproduced with permission of The British Museum. Fig. 98, drawing of sealing of Khasekhemuwy, BM 35592 by VS. Fig. 99, vase fragment of Kasekhemuwy, Cairo JE 55291; photo from Firth 1935, pl. 89, no. 16; reproduced with permission of Cairo Museum. Fig. 100, uraeus detail from Gebelein stela fragment; drawing by VS. Fig. 101, Gebelein stela fragment, Turin ME cat. supplement no. 12341; photo courtesy of Turin Museo Egizio; reproduced with permission of Museo Egizio. Fig. 102, ivory pin, Boston MFA 22.2526; photo courtesy Boston Museum of Fine Arts; reproduced with permission of Boston Museum of Fine Arts.

Chapter 7.
Fig. 103, Sa-nekht Sinai relief, Cairo CG 57101; photo by CBJ; reproduced with permission

of Cairo Museum. Fig. 104, drawing of relief, Cairo CG 57101; photo from Gardiner - Peet 1917, pl. iv. Fig. 105, relief from Gebelein, Cairo TL 20/1/21/7; photo by CBJ; reproduced with permission of Cairo Museum. Fig. 106, Zoser Sinai relief; photo from Gardiner - Peet 1917, pl. i-2. Fig. 107, detail of Zoser statue base, Cairo JE 49613; photo by CBJ; reproduced with permission of Cairo Museum. Fig. 108, Zoser *serdab* statue, Cairo JE 49613; photo from Firth 1935, pl. 29, 1. Figs. 109-110, north door lintel and detail, south tomb of Zoser; photos from Lauer 1962, pl. xxvii; reproduced with permission of Institut Français Archéologie Orientale du Caire. Figs. 111-112, Zoser boundary stela and detail, Cairo JE 52508; photos by CBJ; reproduced with permission of Cairo Museum. Fig. 113, detail, middle false door relief, south tomb, Saqqara; photo from Lauer 1962, pl. xxvii; reproduced with permission of Service des Antiquitiés Égyptienne, Cairo. Fig. 114, middle false door relief, south tomb, Saqqara; photo from Firth 1935, pl. 41. Fig. 115, south false door relief; photo from Firth *ibid.*, pl. 40. Fig. 116-17, Zoser cobra wall and detail; photos by CBJ. Figs. 118-19, Sneferu stela and detail, Cairo JE 89289; photos by CBJ; reproduced with permission of Cairo Museum. Figs. 120-21, Sneferu relief fragment and drawing of detail; photo from Fakhry 1961, pl. xixA, fig. 64; reproduced with permission of Service des Antiquitiés Égyptienne, Cairo. Figs. 122-23, Sneferu relief fragment and drawing of detail; photo from Fakhry 1961, pl. xviiiB, fig. 138; reproduced with permission of Service des Antiquitiés Égyptienne, Cairo. Fig. 124, cobra detail from Hetep-heres I bed canopy, Cairo CG 57711 (copy Boston MFA 38.873); photo courtesy Boston MFA; reproduced with permission of Cairo Museum. Fig. 125, Hetep-heres I furniture, Cairo CG 57711, JE 72030 (copy, Boston MFA 38.873, 39.746); reproduced with permission of Cairo Museum. Fig. 126a, b, right and left door-jambs of bed canopy, Cairo CG 57711; photos courtesy Boston MFA; reproduced with permission of Cairo Museum. Figs. 127, 129, 131, details on top, side, and end of Hetep-heres I wooden box, Cairo JE 72030; photos by CBJ; reproduced with permission of Cairo Museum. Figs. 128, 130, 132, drawings of details on top of box, Cairo JE 72030; photos from Reisner - Smith 1955, pl. ii. Fig. 133, drawing of detail, Cheops Sinai inscription; photo from Gardiner - Peet 1917, *op.cit.*, pl. ii-7. Fig. 134, Cheops relief reused at Lisht, MMA 22.1.19, The Metropolitan Museum of Art, Rogers Fund 1922; photo courtesy MMA; reproduced with permission of The Metropolitan Museum of Art. Fig. 135, drawing of detail from Cheop's relief by VS. Fig. 136, Cheops relief at Tanis; photo courtesy The Brooklyn Museum. Fig. 137, top view of Radedef head, Louvre E 12626; photo by CBJ; reproduced with permission of Musée du Louvre. Figs. 138-39, three-quarter and front views of Louvre E 12626; photos by Chuzeville, Paris, Musée du Louvre; reproduced with permission of Musée du Louvre. Figs. 140-141: front and side views of Radedef head, Cairo JE 35138; reproduced with permission of Cairo Museum. Fig. 142, top view of Chephren head, Cairo CG 14; photo by CBJ; reproduced with permission of Cairo Museum. Figs. 143-144, front and side views of Cairo CG 14; reproduced with permission of Cairo Museum. Fig. 145, top view of Chephren, Cairo CG 15; photo by CBJ; reproduced with permission of Cairo Museum. Fig. 146, seated statue of Chephren, Cairo CG 15; reproduced with permission of Cairo Museum. Fig. 147-49, top, side and front views, Cairo CG 41; photos by CBJ; reproduced with permission of Cairo Museum. Figs. 150-51 front and side view, Leipzig ÄMKMU 1946; photos courtesy Leipzig ÄMKMU; reproduced with permission of Leipzig Ägyptisches Museum der Karl-Marx-Universität. Fig. 152-53, three-quarter and front views, Cairo CG 39; reproduced with permission of Cairo Museum. Figs. 154-55, three-quarter and front views, Leipzig ÄMKMU 1949; photos courtesy Leipzig ÄMKMU; reproduced with permission of Leipzig Ägyptisches Museum der Karl-Marx-Universität. Figs. 156-57, side and front views, Boston MFA 21.351; reproduced with permission of Boston Museum of Fine arts. Figs. 158-159, royal head fragments, Leipzig ÄMKMU 1950, 1951; photos courtesy Leipzig ÄMKMU; reproduced with permission of Leipzig Ägyptisches Museum der Karl-Marx-Universität. Fig. 160, royal head fragment; photo from Hölscher 1912, fig. 94; formerly Leipzig ÄMKMU, destroyed World War II; reproduced with permission of Leipzig Ägyptisches Museum der Karl-Marx-Universität. Fig.

161, W. Berlin 15048; photo courtesy West Berlin ÄM; reproduced with permission of W. Berlin Staatliche Museen Preussinscher Kulturbesitz: Ägyptisches Museum. Figs. 162-163, top and front view of royal head fragment, Cairo JE 49692; reproduced with permission of Cairo Museum. Fig. 164, Great Sphinx at Giza; photo courtesy The Brooklyn Museum; reproduced with permission of The Brooklyn Museum. Fig. 165, uraeus head from Great Sphinx, BM 1204; photo by CBJ; reproduced with permission of the British Museum. Fig. 166, face detail of Great Sphinx; photo by CBJ. Fig. 167, uraeus hood detail, Great Sphinx; photo courtesy Archive Lacau; reproduced with permission of Centre Wladimir Golenischeff, Paris. Fig. 168: top view of Great Sphinx head; photo courtesy Archive Lacau; reproduced with permission of Centre Wladimir Golenischeff. Fig. 169, photogrametry drawing of top of Sphinx head; courtesy Mark Lehner; reproduced with his permission. Fig. 170, drawing of uraeus head from the Great Sphinx; photo from Vyse 1842, pl. A, fig. 1. Figs. 171-73: front, right side, and underside views of BM 1204; photos by CBJ; reproduced with permission of British Museum. Fig. 174, offering stand of Chephren, MMA 07.228.24, Rogers Fund 1907; photos courtesy New York MMA; reproduced with permission of The Metropolitan Museum of Art. Fig. 175, detail of stand (MMA 07.228.24); photo by CBJ with permission of The Metropolitan Museum of Art. Fig. 176, drawing of detail (MMA 07.228.24) by VS. Fig. 177, drawing of detail, Chephren stamped jar sealing by VS from Hölscher 1912, fig. 157. Fig. 178-80, Mycerinus statue in Cairo, top and side views of head, Cairo JE 40704; reproduced with permission of Cairo Museum. Figs. 181-82, Mycerinus Memphite statue, Cairo CG 42, and front view; reproduced with permission of Cairo Museum. Fig. 183, top view, Cairo CG 42: photos by CBJ; reproduced with permission of Cairo Museum. Figs. 184, 186-87, Mycerinus seated statue, front and side views of head, Boston MFA 09.204; photos from Reisner 1931, pls. 12-14; reproduced with permission of Boston Museum of Fine Arts. Fig. 185, top view of Mycerinus, Boston MFA 09.204; photo courtesy The Brooklyn Museum; reproduced with permission of Boston Museum of Fine Arts. Figs. 188-90, top, front, and three-quarter views of Mycerinus head, Cairo JE 40705; reproduced with permission of Cairo Museum. Fig. 191-92, left and right sides of Mycerinus throne, Boston MFA 09.202; photos courtesy Boston MFA; reproduced with permission of Boston Museum of Fine Arts. Fig. 193, one surface of Mycerinus gold seal, 19999; photo courtesy E. Berlin ÄMP; reproduced with permission of Staatliche Museen zu Berlin, Hauptstadt der DDR, Ägyptisches Museum und Papyrussammlung. Figs. 194, gold seal impression, E. Berlin ÄMP 19999; photo from Schäfer 1910. Figs. 195-96, three-quarter and side views of Shepseskaf (?) head, Boston MFA 09.203; reproduced with permission of Boston Museum of Fine Arts. Fig. 197, top view of Boston, MFA 09.203; reproduced with permission of Boston Museum of Fine Arts. Figs. 198-99, offering stand of Sethu and detail, Cairo CG 1298; photos by CBJ; reproduced with permission of Cairo Museum.

Chapter 8.
Figs. 200, 202, front and side views of Weserkaf head, Cairo JE 52501; reproduced with permission of Cario Museum. Fig. 201, top view of Cairo JE 52501; photo by CBJ; reproduced with permission of Cairo Museum. Figs. 203-04, Weserkaf relief and detail, Cairo JE 56600; photos by CBJ; reproduced with permission of Cairo Museum. Fig. 205, Sahura dyad, MMA 18.2.4, The Metropolitan Museum of Art, Rogers fund 1918; photo courtesy MMA; reproduced with permission of The Metropolitan Museum of Art. Fig. 206-07, side and top views of Sahura, MMA 18.2.48; photos by CBJ; reproduced with permission of The Metropolitan Museum of Art. Fig. 208, Sahura relief panel, Cairo JE 39533; photo from Borchardt 1910, fig. 15; reproduced with permission of Cairo Museum. Fig. 209, detail, JE 39533; photo by CBJ; reproduced with permission of Cairo Museum. Fig. 210, Sahura relief, Hamburg MKG 1925.63; photo courtesy of Hamburg MKG; reproduced with permission of Hamburg Museum fur Kunst und Gewerbe. Figs. 211-12, drawings of Sahura relief fragments; photos from Borchardt 1913, pls. 37, 38. Figs. 213-14, drawings of Sahura relief fragments; photos from Borchardt, *ibid*., pls. 32, 34, 42. Figs. 215-18, Sahura relief

fragments; photos from Borchardt, *ibid.*, pls. 64, 69, 70. Figs. 219-20, Sahura granite relief fragments; photos from Borchardt 1910, pl. 10 and fig. 58. Fig. 221-22, Sahura architrave fragment; photos from Borchardt 1910, fig. 29. Fig. 223-25, Sahura column and details, W. Berlin ÄM 343/67; photos courtesy of W. Berlin ÄM; reproduced with permission of W. Berlin Staatliche Museen Preussinscher Kulturbesitz: Ägyptisches Museum. Figs. 226-27, Sahura column titulary and drawing, Cairo JE 39527, 39529; reproduced with permission of Cairo Museum. Fig. 228, Sahura column, Cairo JE 39527; reproduced with permission of Cairo Museum. Figs 229-30, Sahura Sinai relief and detail, Cairo JE 38569; photos by CBJ; reproduced with permission of Cairo Museum. Fig. 231-34, Ne-user-ra seated statue, three-quarter, and front views of head, Cairo CG 38; reproduced with permission of Cairo Museum. Fig. 235, reconstituted statue of Ne-user-ra, Rochester MAG 42.54 and Cairo CG 42003; reproduced with permission of Cairo Museum and Rochester University Memorial Art Gallery. Fig. 236, profile of Rochester MAG 42.54; reproduced with permission of Memorial Art Gallery of the University of Rochester. Fig. 237, front view Rochester MAG 42.54; photo courtesy of Rochester MAG; reproduced with permission of University of Rochester Memorial Art Gallery. Figs. 238, double statues of Ne-user-ra, Munich ÄS 6794; reproduced with permission of Munich Staatliche Sammlung Ägyptischer Kunst. Fig. 239, left "older" and right "younger" details of Munich ÄS 6794; photos courtesy Munich ÄS; reproduced with permission of Munich Staatliche Sammlung Ägyptischer Kunst. Fig. 240, top views of Munich AS 6794; photos courtesy Munich ÄS; reproduced with permission of Munich Staatliche Sammlung Ägyptischer Kunst. Fig. 241, profile and front views of Byblos bust, Beirut B. 7395; reproduced with permission of the National Museum of Beirut. Fig. 242, front and profile views of bust of Ne-user-ra (?), Brooklyn 72.58; photos courtesy The Brooklyn Museum; reproduced with permission of The Brooklyn Museum. Figs. 243-44, large relief panel of Ne-user-ra, E. Berlin ÄMP 16100; reproduced with permission of Staatliche Museen zu Berlin, Hauptstadt der DDR, Ägyptisches Museum und Papyrussammlung. Fig. 245, drawing of Ne-user-ra relief fragment; photo from Bissing 1928, pl. 22 no. 352. Fig. 246-47, drawing of Ne-user-ra relief fragments; photos from Bissing 1928, pl. 1 no. 2, pl. 27 no. 425. Figs. 248, Ne-user-ra relief fragment, 17911; photo courtesy E. Berlin ÄMP; reproduced with permission of Staatliche Museen zu Berlin, Hauptstadt der DDR, Ägyptisches Museum und Papyrussammlung. Fig. 249, drawing from relief fragment, E. Berlin ÄMP 17911 by VS. Fig. 250, drawing of Ne-user-ra relief fragment; photos from Bissing 1928, pl.22 no. 352. Figs. 251-52, Ne-user-ra relief fragments, Munich Gl 185, 183; photos from Bissing *ibid.*, pl. 26, nos. 399, 403; reproduced with permission of Munich Staatliche Sammlung Ägyptischer Kunst. Fig. 253, Ne-user-ra relief fragment, Göttingen AIU Z.V.I-2t (1912); photo courtesy of Göttingen AIU; reproduced with permission of Archäologisches Institut der Universität, Göttingen. Figs. 254, drawing of Ne-user-ra column, Cairo JE 38664; photo from Borchardt 1907, pl. 13. Figs. 255-56, column details, Cairo JE 38664; photos by CBJ; reproduced with permission of Cairo Museum. Figs. 257-58, details of Ne-user-ra Sinai inscription, Cairo JE 38570; photos by CBJ; reproduced with permission of Cairo Museum. Fig. 259, drawing of Ne-user-ra Sinai inscription, detail, Cairo JE 38570; photo from Gardiner - Peet 1917, pl. vi. Fig. 260, drawing of Ne-user-ra relief fragment, Munich Gl. 181; photo from Bissing 1923, pl. 11 no. 27; reproduced with permission of Munich Staatliche Sammlung Ägyptischer Kunst. Fig. 261, drawing of part of Ne-user-ra *heb-sed* relief fragment, Cairo JE 57110; photo from Bissing 1923, no. 33b; reproduced with permission of Cairo Museum. Fig. 262, photograph of part of Cairo JE 57110; photo by CBJ; reproduced with permission of Cairo Museum. Fig. 263, drawing of Ne-user-ra relief fragment, Cairo JE 57115; photo from Bissing 1923, pl. 18 no. 44d. Fig. 264, Ne-user-ra relief fragment, Göttingen AIU Z.V.I-26 (1912); photo courtesy Göttingen AIU; reproduced with permission of Archäologisches Institut der Universität, Göttingen. Fig. 265, Ne-user-ra relief in Dresden with drawing, Dresden SKS Aeg 745; photo of relief courtesy of Dresden SKS; reproduced with permission of Staatliche Kunstsammlungen Skulpturensammlung; photo of drawing from Bissing 1923, pl. 15, no. 38. Fig. 266, Ne-user-ra relief fragment, E. Berlin ÄMP 20078; photo courtesy E.

314-15, drawings of Pepy II pyramid temple fragments and reconstructed scene from valley temple; photos from Jéquier *ibid.*, pls. 8, 10, 21; reproduced with permission of Institut Français Archéologie Orientale du Caire. Fig. 316, Pepy II tablet Cairo JE 62950; photo by CBJ; reproduced with permission of Cairo Museum. Fig. 317, Pepy II tablet Cairo CG 53836; photo from Quibell 1909, pl.v, no. 3; reproduced with permission of Cairo Museum. Fig. 318, Pepy II quartzite relief; photo from Jéquier 1927, pl. iii. Figs. 319-20, drawings of Pepy II relief fragments; photos from Jéquier 1938, pl. 36; reproduced with permission of Institut Français Archéologie Orientale du Caire. Fig. 321, drawing of Pepy II Sinai inscription, detail; photo from Gardiner - Peet 1917, pl. ix-17. Fig. 322, relief fragment and drawing of Queen Neith; photo from Jéquier 1933, pls. iv, v; reproduced with permission of Institut Français Archéologie Orientale du Caire. Figs. 323-24, drawings of Pepy II relief fragments; photos from Jéquier 1938, pls. 9, 42; reproduced with permission of Institut Français Archéologie Orientale. Fig. 325, Pepy II relief fragments and drawing; photos from Jéquier 1938, pls. 83, 84; reproduced with permission of Institut Français Archéologie Orientale du Caire. Fig. 326, drawing of Pepy II relief fragments; photos from Jéquier, *ibid.*, pl. 50; reproduced with permission of Institut Français Archéologie Orientale du Caire. Fig. 327, drawing of Pepy II relief fragment; Jéquier 1940, pl. 40; reproduced with permission of Institut Français Archéologie Orientale du Caire. Figs. 328-29, drawing of Pepy II relief fragments and reconstructed scene; photos from Jéquier, *ibid.*, pls. 30, 31; reproduced with permission of Institut Français Archéologie Orientale du Caire. Figs. 330-31, relief fragments of Amenemhet I, MMA 09.180.113, 08.200.10, The Metropolitan Museum of Art, Rogers Fund 1909 and 1908; photos courtesy MMA; reproduced with permission of The Metropolitan Museum of Art. Figs. 332-33, drawings of relief fragments and reconstructed scene using Pepy II relief fragments; photos from Jéquier 1938, pls. 50, 51; reproduced with permission of Institut Français Archéologie Orientale du Caire. Fig. 334, Pepy II cylinder seal impression, BM 2602; photo from Petrie 1917, pl. x no. 4; reproduced with permission of The British Museum. Fig. 335, obelisk of Vizier Prince Tety with *t3yty* detail, Cairo JE 63404; photos by CBJ; reproduced with permission of Cairo Museum. Fig. 336, falcon head with uraeus and feathered diadem, 3/4 and profile view Cairo CG 52701; photos from Vernier 1927, pl. lxi; reproduced with permission of Cairo Museum. Fig. 337, drawings of profile and front views of Cairo CG 52701; photos from Quibell 1900, pl. xliii. Fig. 338, diadem from Lahun, Dynasty XII, Cairo CG 52641; photo by CBJ; reproduced with permission of the Cairo Museum. Fig. 339, detail of Cairo CG 52701; photo by CBJ; reproduced with permission of Cairo Museum.

Chapter 11.
Figs. 340-494, drawings for **URAEUS CHRONOLOGY CHART** by VS taken from appropriate Catalog entries.

Chapter 12.
Figs. 495-655, drawings for **URAEUS TYPE CHART** by VS taken from appropriate Catalog entries.

ABBREVIATIONS

ACIO	*Actes du XXIe Congres International des Orientalistes*
Athens NAM	National Archaeological Museum, Athens
ASAE	*Annales du Service des Antiquités de l'Égypte*
ARCE	American Research Center in Egypt
BÄBA	*Beitrage zur Ägyptischen Bauforschung und Altertumskunde*
Beirut MN	National Museum of Beirut
BES	*Bulletin of The Egyptological Seminar*
E. Berlin ÄMP	Ägyptisches Museum und Papyrussammlung, Staatliche Museen zu Berlin, Hauptstadt der DDR
W. Berlin ÄM	Staatliche Museen Preussischer Kulturbesitz: Ägyptisches Museum,
BIFAO	*Bulletin de l'Institut Français d'Archéologie Orientale du Caire*
Bonn ÄSU	Ägyptologisches Seminar der Universität, Bonn
Boston MFA	Boston Museum of Fine Arts
BMFA	*Bulletin of the Museum of Fine Arts, Boston*
BMA	*Brooklyn Museum Annual*
BMB	*Brooklyn Museum Bulletin*
BMMA	*Bulletin of the Metropolitan Museum of Art*, New York
BMRAH	*Bulletin des Musées Royaux d'Art et d'Histoire*
CBJ	C. Bedford Johnson, Photographer
CdE	*Chronique d'Égypte*
CGC	*Catalogue General des Antiquites Egyptiennes du Musée du Caire*
Chicago OIM	Oriental Institute Museum, University of Chicago
Cleveland MA	Cleveland Museum of Art, Cleveland, Ohio
Dresden SK	Staatliche Kunstsammlungen, Skulpturensammlung, Dresden
Exp.	*Expedition: The University Museum Magazine of Archaeology/Anthropology, University of Pennsylvania*
GM	*Göttinger Miszellen: Beitrage zur Ägyptologischen Diskussion*
Göttingen AIU	Archäologisches Institut der Universität, Gottingen
Hamburg MKG	Museum fur Kunst und Gewerbe, Hamburg
IFAO	Institut Français d'Archéologie Orientale du Caire
ILN	*Illustrated London News*
JARCE	*Journal of the American Research Center in Egypt*
JE	*Journal d'entrée des antiquites égyptiennes du Musée du Caire*
JEA	*Journal of Egyptian Archeology*
JNES	*Journal of Near Eastern Studies*
Leipzig ÄMKMU	Ägyptisches Museum der Karl-Marx-Universtät, Leipzig
LdÄ	*Lexikon der Ägyptologie*, W. Helck, ed.
London BM	British Museum, London, England
London UCL	Petrie Museum, University College London
MMJ	*Metropolitan Museum Journal*
MDAIK	*Mitteilungen des Deutschen Archäologischen Instituts, Abteilung Kairo*
Montreal MFA	Museum of Fine Arts, Montreal, Canada

Mon. Piot	*Foundation Eugène Piot, Monuments et Memoires*
Munich ÄS	Staatliche Sammulung Ägyptischer Kunst, Munich
Munich Gl	Staatliche Sammlung Ägyptischer Kunst, Glyptotek, Munich
MRAH	Musées Royaux d'Art et d'Histoire, Brussels
New York MMA	The Metropolitan Museum of Art, New York
NARCE	*Newsletter of the American Research Center in Egypt*
Philadelphia UM	The University Museum, University of Pennsylvania, Philadelphia
PC	Private Collection
PM	B. Porter and R. Moss, *Topographical Bibliography of Ancient Egyptian Hieroglyphic Texts, Reliefs, Paintings* III-VII, 1934-1951; III, ed. rev. and augmented by J. Malek, 1974-1981
PT	*Pyramid Texts*
RdE	*Revue d'Égyptologie*
RSO	*Revista degli Studi Orientali*
Rochester MAG	University of Rochester Memorial Art Gallery, Rochester, N Y
SAE	Service des Antiquitiés Égyptiennes, Cairo
SÄK	*Studien zur Altägyptischen Kultur*
Turin ME	Museo Egizio, Turin, Italy
VS	Victoria Solia, drawings
Wb	A. Erman and H. Grapow, *Wörterbuch der Ägyptischen Sprache*, I-V, 1926-1931
ZÄS	*Zeitschrift fur Ägyptische Sprache und Altertumskunde*

ACKNOWLEDGEMENTS

Bernard V. Bothmer, Lila Acheson Wallace Professor of Egyptian Art and Archaeology, New York University, Institue of Fine Arts (retired Chairman of the Department of Egyptian and Classical Art, The Brooklyn Museum), has long believed that a study and catalog of stylistic development of the uraeus would be useful. His wish that one of his students would undertake the research and writing has inspired this undertaking. Without the stimulus of Professor Bothmer's teaching, his patient guidance, generous suggestions, careful correction, and constant assistance this attempt to fulfill his wish could never have been written.

James Romano, Associate Curator of Egyptian and Classical Art, The Brooklyn Museum, and Lecturer in the Art History Department, Queens College, whose knowledge and writing style I particularly admire, took time to read the manuscript and offered many helpful suggestions. Ogden Goelet, Research Associate, The Brooklyn Museum and Adjunct Professor of Near Eastern Languages and Literature, New York University, also read the work and offered advice and suggestions, particularly for Chapter I: Meaning and Importance of the Uraeus. He also drew hieroglyphs for the text, and I am especially grateful for his invaluable help.

I am also deeply indebted to Vivian Davies for accepting my original manuscript for publication. His efforts on behalf of this book go beyond those usually associated with the title of editor. Also, my thanks to Lynn Liebling who proof read the final typescript and offered suggestions.

Indispensible to research have been the Wilbour Library of Egyptology (Diane Guzman, Librarian), the remarkable Slide Collection and Photographic Archive of the Department of Egyptian and Classical Art (Victoria Solia, former Research Associate) at The Brooklyn Museum, and the library of New York University's Institute of Fine Arts. A stipend granted by The Brooklyn Museum's Bourse Jacques Vandier helped make it possible to study and photograph the Egyptian collections at the Louvre.

The following museums, their curators, and staffs have made photographs available, allowed and assisted us in photographing their monuments, and have given their permission to publish the photographs: at the the Ägyptisches Museum und Papyrussammlung, East Berlin, K-H Priese; at the Ägyptisches Museum, West Berlin, Jurgen Settgast, and Biri Fay; at the Boston Museum of Fine Arts, William Kelly Simpson, Edward Brovarski, Sue D'Auria, Rita E. Freed, Peter Lacovara; at the British Museum, T. G. H. James, W. V. Davies, Jim Putnam; at The Brooklyn Museum, Richard Fazzini, Robert Bianchi, James Romano, Victoria Solia; at the Wilbour Library in The Brooklyn Museum, Diane Guzman, Lillian Flowerman, Louise Capuano; at the Cairo Museum, Mohammed Saleh, Dya Abuou Ghazi, Galal el Sharawy, Siham abdel Raziq, and Hussein Ibrahim; at the Staatliche Kunstsammlungen, Skulpturensammlung, Dresden, Hans Rost; at the Archaologisches Institut der Universistät Göttingen, Göttingen, Klaus Fittschen; at the Museum fur Kunst und Gewerbe, Hamburg, Wilhelm Hornbostel; at Karl-Marx-Universtät, Leipzig, R. Krauspe; at the Montreal Museum of Fine Arts, David G. Carter; at the Louvre, Jean-Louis de Cenival, and Gennvieve Pierrat; at The Metropolitan Museum of Art, Christine Lilyquist, Henry G. Fischer, Peter Dorman (now at Chicago House and the Oriental Institute), Edna Russmann and Louis Kunsch; at Stattliche Sammlung Ägyptischen Kunst, Munich, Dietrich Wildung and Sylvia Schoske; at the

Musées Royaux d'Art et d'Histoire, Brussels, H. De Meulenaere; at Museo delle antichita egizie, Turin, Silvio Curto; at the Petrie Museum, Department of Egyptology, University College London, Geoffrey T. Martin and Barbara Adams; at the Pushkin Museum, Moscow, Svetlana Hodjash; at the Memorial Art Gallery of the University of Rochester, Rochester, N Y, Bret Waller; at The University Museum, University of Pennsylvania, Philadelphia, David O'Connor. I am also especially grateful to John L. Behler, Curator, Department of Herpetology, New York Zoological Society for his careful reading and correction of my chapter on the natural history of cobras.

Special thanks are also due to Paul Walker, Executive Director of the American Research Center in Egypt, Robert J. Wenke, and Nanette M. Pyne, Directors of ARCE in Cairo at the time of our work there, and Mai Trad for their help. I am grateful to Mark Lehner, Director, ARCE Sphinx Project, for sharing photographs, drawings, and knowledge.

Victoria Solia's sensitive drawings contribute immeasurably to what is essentially a visual book; I am grateful for her illustrations and for format suggestions which clarified the presentation.

Lastly, I am indebted to my family and Susie Thomas who have offered unfailing encouragement. Most especially, I would like publicly to thank my husband, C. Bedford Johnson, without whose support the work would have been impossible to accomplish. His skill as a photographer is acknowledged in the photographic credits by the initials, CBJ. From the top of ladders, stools, or whatever was available, he took innumerable, excellent photographs of the uraeus from above statues' heads. The unique results are essential to this study, as are many of his photographs of the uraeus in relief.

Sally B. Johnson
September 30, 1986

PREFACE: *Organization and Overview*

Organization and presentation of the data in *THE COBRA GODDESS of ANCIENT EGYPT*, Volume I, changed frequently as the book was being written; finally, it was decided to arrange the book in three parts. **Part I: PREAMBLE**, Chapters 1-4, contains information that pertains to uraei in all periods of Egyptian art history. It consists of: an introduction; a brief investigation of species and habits of cobras in nature; a brief summary of the religious and political significance and importance of the cobra goddess; the classification of uraei into eight different categories or types with illustrations of the earliest known occurrence of each; and an illustrated glossary of terms used to describe uraei in this study. **Part 2: HISTORY OF THE URAEUS**, Chapters 5-10, presents chronologically, by means of individual catalog entries, illustrations of locatable monuments, fragments, or objects depicting uraei through the end of Dynasty VI. Stylistic changes and variations of the cobra goddess from her first appearances in the late Predynastic and Early Dynastic Periods to the end of the Old Kingdom are discussed, with analysis and explanation, in this part of the book. Chapter 10 of this history section presents conclusions and a summary of uraeus chronology and types that occur in Egyptian art history until the end of the Old Kingdom. **Part 3: URAEUS CHARTS**, Chapters 11-12, with drawings, provide the reader with a visual summary of uraeus chronology and types as represented in Egyptian art from the Predynastic Period to the end of the Old Kingdom, c.4000-2195 B.C..

For sake of consistency, the chronology used is that of Jurgen von Beckerath;[1] spelling of kings' names is that of W. S. Smith and W. K. Simpson;[2] and the system of placing Dynasty III in the Old Kingdom, rather than in the Early Dynastic Period, is now used by most Egyptologists.[3]

Designation of material used in monuments, fragments, and objects is usually taken from the original publication of the piece. In some instances, personal observation has determined the material used. Where possible, measurements are given in meters, or centimeters, and are generally taken from previously published sources. A question mark (?) follows the identifiction of a sculpture or object when an inscription is lacking or when its attribution is not generally accepted. Appropriate notes and bibliography for each example and illustration are given in the catalog entries of the History section and are not necessarily found elsewhere, where details are used for illustration. Whenever applicable, the *Topographical Bibliography...* by B. Porter and R. Moss (*PM*) is cited by volume number, publication date, and page number; in those cases, only additional references are given. Careful drawings have been made by Victoria Solia from published reports (photograhs and line cuts), and from prints found in museum archives, or from photographs taken specifically for this study.

---

[1]1984, pp. 158-59 for dates of Dynasties; Beckerath, 1971, pp. 63-64 was used for the approximate length of each king's reign to give dates used in the Catalog.

[2]1981, p. 9.

[3]*e.g.*, Hayes, 1953, p. 2; Beckerath, 1984, p. 158.

The royal cobra goddess is a formidable subject. Vast are the number and variety of her representations; complex are the function, meaning, and significance of her religious and political symbolism. Errors of omission, commission, and classification are inevitable. Volume I, while in no way definitive or exhaustive, has attempted to catalog as many examples of the uraeus as possible from the earliest periods of Egyptian history and to analyse the stylistic development of the cobra goddess in these early periods of Egyptian art. "Earliest known" or "first preserved" are terms used to indicate the earliest examples my research has thus far uncovered; subsequent discoveries will no doubt change many of these. Although all relevant texts have been taken into consideration, mine is primarily an archaeological and art historical study.

Volume I of this study was undertaken in order to understand and recognize the types, styles, and iconography of the cobra goddess in Egyptian art of the Predynastic, Early Dynastic, and Old Kingdom Periods. Research has proved that each of these periods has a unique style of uraei; thus a knowledge of cobra goddess types, styles, and forms will be a useful dating tool as well.

CHRONOLOGICAL TABLE[4]

PREDYNASTIC, c.4000–3000 B.C
    Amratian (Nagada I)
    Early Gerzean (Nagada II)
    Late Gerzean (Nagada III)

EARLY DYNASTIC, c.3000–2670 B.C.

    DYNASTY I, c.3000–2820 B.C.
        Aha (Menes)
        Zer
        Den (Wedymu)
        Az–ib
        Semerkhet
        Qay–a

    DYNASTY II, c.2820–2670 B.C.
        Ra–neb
        Hetep-sekhemuwy
        Ny–neter
        Peribsen
        Sened
        Khasekhem
        Khasekhemuwy

OLD KINGDOM, c.2670–2195 B.C.

    DYNASTY III, c.2670–2600 B.C.
        Sa–nekht
        Neterkhet (Zoser)
        Sekhem–khet
        Kha–ba
        Neb–ka
        Huni

    DYNASTY IV, c.2600–2475 B.C.
        Sneferu
        Cheops (Khufu)
        Radedef
        Chephren (Khafra)
        Mycerinus
        Shepseskaf

DYNASTY V, c.2475–2345 B.C.
    Weserkaf
    Sahura
    Neferirkara
    Shepseskara
    Neferefra
    Ne–user–ra
    Men–kau–hor
    Isesy (Zedkara)
    Unas

DYNASTY VI, c.2345–2195 B.C.
    Tety
    Weserkara
    Pepy I
    Mernera
    Pepy II

---

[4]Dates are from Beckerath 1984, pp. 158–59; the spelling of kings' names is from Smith-Simpson 1981, p. 9; *v.s.*, n. 2–3.

MAP of EGYPT

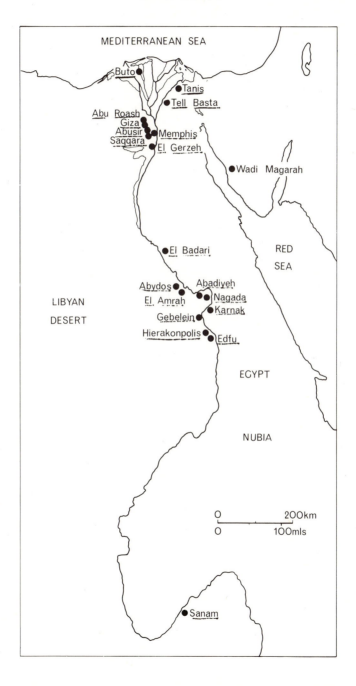

(Provenance sites of monuments, fragments, and objects discussed in Volume I are underlined.)

PART 1

PREAMBLE

•

INTRODUCTION

> "Life means spontaneous movement - essentially movement
> upwards - and this can be conceived in terms of a rearing serpent
> or a flower rising from the waters and opening its petals to reveal
> the first light."[5]

The cobra goddess, symbol of life, order, and legitimate kingship, appears as "a rearing serpent" in ancient Egyptian art from its inception.[6] A divine-royal cobra is the earliest palaeographically documented serpent symbol of any ancient mythology, literature, or art. Cobra goddesses are present in every period of Egyptian art history from Predynastic to late Roman times; and they appear in every aspect of its forms from minute objects of the so-called minor arts to monumental architecture. In addition, one could speculate that the cobra goddess of ancient Egypt was the cultural ancestress of the caduceus of ancient Greek mythology and modern medicine; Moses' brazen serpent on a staff with which he led the Israelites out of Egypt; and the serpent of the garden of Eden, where the powerful uraeus symbol is changed from one of female beneficence and protection of legitimate kingship to one of sin and seduction.[7]

While it is true that Egyptian literature and mythology, particularly of its later phases, is replete with harmful, enemy snakes, along with spells to ward off their evil, these noxious serpents are pictured and described very differently from the uraeus cobra.[8] With head raised and hood expanded, the uraeus snake is clearly a cobra. It is always a divine-royal symbol and a part of royal regalia, whereas enemy snakes are depicted as worm-like adders or as giant, dragon-like creatures.

The uraeus is so omnipresent in royal Egyptian art that it has been somewhat taken for granted and neglected by historians and philologists. Other major gods and goddesses of ancient Egypt who are shown in animal or human form have been the subjects of research in language and art; but a comprehensive study of the cobra goddess' first appearance and stylistic variations through the millennia of Egyptian art history has never been undertaken. There have been, however, several studies dealing with cobras carved on the headdresses of kings and queens to help date and identify uninscribed or usurped royal sculpture.[9]

---

[5]R. T. Rundle Clark 1978, p. 36.

[6]John Behler, Curator, Herpetology, The New York Zoological Society, (Bronx Zoo), New York, confirmed orally to the author in June, 1984 and in correspondence February, 1986, that the cobra is the only, "North African serpent that elevates the front third of its body and expands its cervical ribs (*i.e.* 'hood') when threatened".

[7]Jung 1976, pp. 96-103, *passim.*, where Jung discusses the snake as *archetype.*

[8]*i.e.*, *PT* (Utterance 242) Spell 247; Piankoff 1968, p. 99, pl. 70-247a.

[9]*e.g.*: Schäfer 1904, pp. 62-65; Engelbach 1928, pp. 13 ff; Evers 1929, pp. 21-28; Kriéger 1960, pp. 7 ff.; Lillesø 1975, pp. 137-46.

Since the earliest representations of the cobra in Egypt are two-dimensional, and subsequent cobra's in relief seem to precede or are at least closely related to those seen on royal three-dimensional sculpture, it became apparent at the outset that a study of the types and forms of the cobra goddess should begin with examples on early pieces of ivory, stone, and metal rather than with the earliest known uraei on royal sculpture, first preserved on Dynasty IV quartzite heads of Radedef. Royal Egyptian architectural relief is also replete with uraei, and it too is included, as are the uraei in the minor arts and cobras made to be worn as adornment. Study of the uraeus in Predynastic, Early Dynastic and Old Kingdom Periods shows that cobra goddesses appear in many forms with several different names. In the author's opinion, the evidence confirms that no matter what the uraeus is called, or where it appears, all representations of the divine-royal cobra are syncretic symbols for essentially one and the same omnipresent goddess.[10]

The consummate skill and artistry with which the Egyptians captured the essential humanity of men and women to insure their immortality was brought to bear as well upon vital representations of the natural world. Depictions of the cobra as the rearing serpent are always only a part of the artist's larger concept, yet he invariably captures the serpent goddess' alert, life-like qualities; her powerful, poised, and graceful symbolism contributes immeasurably to his whole design. Whether she is large, carved in high relief, almost three-dimensionaly, as a series of architectural elements on King Zoser's "Cobra Wall" at Saqqara (Cat. 24), or small, in low relief with elephants on late Predynastic handles (Cat.1-5), incised above a basket forming a part of the *nbty* title of Egypt's first king on the "Nagada Tablet" (Cat. 6), or on King Den's forehead on a small ivory plaque (Cat. 10), formed three-dimensionally as a tiny ivory pin (Cat. 16), or in relief and worn on the forehead of a king's statue (Cat. 30), the cobra goddess' presence in ancient Egyptian art always signifies life-giving, protective might.

---

[10]*v.i.*, discussion, p. 11 and Chapter 10: **CONCLUSIONS.**; also, see Martin 1985, *LdÄ* VI, pp. 864-69, for a recently published discussion of "Uraus".

1 MEANING AND IMPORTANCE OF THE URAEUS[11]

"Uraeus", the word used by Western scholars to describe the cobra worn by kings, is the Latinized form of the Greek. *ouraios*, undoubtedly taken from the ancient Egyptian word with cobra determinative, 𓈎𓏏𓆑, transliterated, *i'rt*, and translated "the Risen One".[12] In this study, "uraeus" or its plural "uraei" are used interchangeably with "rising" or "rearing cobra" or "cobra goddess" to describe representations of ancient Egyptian, divine - royal cobras.

Symbolic meaning of the cobra in Egytian art is inextricably associated with religion and written texts, whether these were incised on ivory tablets and stone vases, carved as a hieroglyph on stone walls and royal sculpture, or written in ink on mythological papyri. The cobra hieroglyph helps to illustrate that "...art and writing were one in ancient Egypt";[13] nuances of the meaning and function of the uraeus are found in ancient Egyptian inscriptions.

As Wadjet, the cobra is the goddess of Buto, or Pe, the ancient sanctuary in the Delta.[14] Her counterpart is the vulture, symbol for Nekhbet, goddess of Nekhen or Hierakonpolis, ancient sanctuary of Upper Egypt. The cobra and the vulture became symbols for unification of the country incorporated into the royal insignia as the *nbty*, 𓄿𓄿, "Two Mistresses",[15] title of kings; these two goddesses were female protectors and keepers of the crowns of the two lands. The vulture could be assimilated with the cobra; for example, the two uraei surrounding the solar disk (Cat. 60) were often interpreted as being Nekhbet and Wadjet. These goddesses were also mythical mothers of the king who suckled him at their breast[16] (Cat. 55, 70). The young, human female figure of Wadjet is often seen accompanying the king in Old Kingdom royal relief. She wears a vulture headdress with the head and hood of a cobra emerging from under the feathers to rise above her forehead (Cat. 67, 81, 89a, 100b, 102a). It has been said that Uto [Wadjet] and Nekhbet indicate for ancient Egypt the passage from a matriarchical to a patriarchical mode of thinking and that from the Middle Kingdom onward these matriarchical goddesses were denationalized and could be brought down from being divine assistants at the birth of the nation to mere midwives at the disposal of peasant women in labor.[17] Yet, the cobra goddess remained an effective symbol of royal-divine

---

[11]This Chapter is not meant to be a definitive philological or mythological study of the cobra goddess. It is offered only as a brief investigation of the meaning and importance of the cobra in Egyptian art to understand the iconography and stylistic development of the uraeus. I am deeply indebted to Ogden Goelet, the philologist, who not only offered many helpful suggestions for this chapter, but also drew the hieroglyphs throughout.

[12]Bonnet 1952, pp. 844-47; Posener 1962, p. 291.

[13]Fischer 1976, p. 31.

[14]See Redford 1983 for location and history of this site.

[15]Faulkner 1976, p. 129; Gardiner 1957, Sign-List V30, X1.

[16]*PT*, Utterance 221, Spell 198; Piankoff 1968, p. 69.

protection throughout pharaonic times.

All art "...is based on a sort of religious sense, a deep and unshakable seriousness....Every true work of art, great or small, is a 'symbol'....".[18] In ancient Egypt, art and language employed the same corpus of symbols.[19] Royal relief and sculpture, mythology, and its rituals were closely connected[20] and deeply serious. A complex mythology is evident in late Old Kingdom Pyramid Texts; but, in all probability, mythological or totemic symbolism is seen much earlier in the animals painted and incised on Predynastic pottery (Figs. 61-65) and carved on Predynastic ivory and gold (Cat. 1-5).[21] By Dynasty I the Egyptians most probably had a well developed creation myth which explained the formation of the universe, the eventual triumph of the first king, Horus, and the origins of divine monarchy. At the beginning of kingship in Egypt, these myths are expressed in the king's Horus and *nbty* titles on an ivory tablet from Nagada, the so-called "Nagada Tablet", c.3000-2925 B.C. (Cat. 6).[22] The cobra goddess is prominent here and in many early depictions of Egyptian mythology and kingship.

The cobra's importance is explained by the *Bremner-Rhind Papyrus*,[23] a fourth century B.C. document whose archaizing language is one of several indications that the papyrus had a prototype in the Middle Kingdom or earlier. It contains two versions of the Heliopolitan creation myth that help to clarify certain Old Kingdom Pyramid Texts and Eleventh Dynasty Coffin Texts. In both versions of the myth, Atum, while formless in the primeval waters, delivered an utterance which gave form to the visible world. He created Shu, "air", and Tefnet, "moisture", by spitting out or masturbating into the waters;[24] then he sent his eye to bring back Shu and Tefnet. When his eye had found and returned "air" and "moisture", primordial unity of divine power was attained. However the eye became enraged when it saw that it had been replaced by a "brighter one", the sun. The eye magically transformed itself into a rearing cobra with expanded hood, "...so I promoted it to the front of my face, so that it could rule the whole world.".[25] Thus the cobra or eye, with the feminine *t* ending in hieroglyphic texts, became female power, personified - the might that was used to protect gods against formlessness in the abyss of chaos and kings against evil enemies in the created world. The god of creation appeased the eye, which had become a cobra, by placing it on his forehead as the uraeus, *i' rt* [Iaret],[26] "the Risen One", who guards the crown. The pacification of the cobra thus marked the establishment of monarchy, and the uraeus became the protective symbol of legitimate kingship and unity.[27] In the Pyramid Texts the cobra goddess is called

---

[17]Beltz 1982, p. 160.

[18]Schafer-Baines 1974, p. 37.

[19]Fischer 1973, pp. 7-25; Fazzini 1975, pp.xxiii-iv.

[20]Morenz 1973, p. 6

[21]Breasted 1912, pp. 4-5; also, *v.i.*, Cat. 1, p. 51.

[22]See I.E.S. Edwards 1971, pp. 11-15, and the sources he cites for full discussion of identity of the Nagada Tablet king, as well as Early Dynastic mythology.

[23]British Museum 10188; Jankuhn 1974, p. 32 for a bibliography of this papyrus.

[24]*PT* 1248 a-d; Morenz 1973, p. 163.

[25]Faulkner 1933, pp. 22 ff..

[26]Transliterations of Egyptian hieroglyphs are placed within [brackets] and spelled with vowels inserted to allow a make-shift pronunciation of Egyptian hieroglyphs.

[27]Bonnet 1952, pp. 733-35, 844-47; Clark 1978, p. 90.

wrt [Weret], "the Great One" or *wrt-ḥḳ3* [Weret-hekaw], "Great of Magic"[28] who rises on the forehead of Horus (the king). In the titulary of kings on royal relief, the cobra goddess on a *nb*,  , "basket", above the *t*, , "bread loaf", means "mistress or lady".[29] Associated with the Horus title of kings, the cobra goddess is usually supported by the *w3ḏ*,  , "papyrus",[30] of her name, Wadjet; she presents to the king's cartouche and Horus name the *w3s*,  , scepter and *šnw*,  , the signs for "dominion" and "infinity or the circuit of the sun",[31] "enclosure" or "cartouche",[32] thereby legitimizing his crown and sovereignty (Cat. 28, 58b).

Words in Middle Egyptian, the classical dialect, which designate the uraeus or cobra goddess in her many aspects, along with their derived words,[33] indicate an essentially positive attitude toward her. For example, in addition to *ỉ‘rt* [Iaret], derived from the verb, *ỉ‘r*, and its later form, *‘r*, "ascend", "rise", or "mount up",[34] there are the following beneficent names for the uraeus:

 *sby* [Seby], "guide serpent" derived from the verb *sbỉ*, "watch over" "attain";[35]

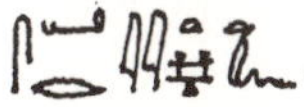 *s‘ryt* [Saryet] from the verb *s‘r*, "cause to ascend", "make to rise in rank";[36]

 *tpt* [Tepet], root noun *tp*, "head"; derived from adjective, *tpy*, "principal foremost",[37] also, "one belonging to the head", *i.e.* the cobra on royal and divine heads.

Another word for "uraeus serpent" is:

 *3ḫt* [Akhet], additional meaning, with appropriate determinative, "eye of the god", "fertile land", "flame", "what is good, profitable, useful"; the root word, *3ḫ*, means "spirit", "be, or become, a spirit", "glorious", "splendid".[38]

Among the names for the cobra goddess are:

 *w3ḏt* [Wadjet], the cobra goddess Edjo;[39]

---

[28]Faulkner 1969, p. 49; Piankoff 1968, pp. 69-70, pls.49-52, Utterances 220, 221.

[29]Faulkner 1976, p. 129; Gardiner 1957, Sign-List V30, X1

[30]Faulkner, *op.cit.*, p. 129; Gardiner, *op.cit.*, Sign-List M13.

[31]This definition provided by a reader of my manuscript who wishes to remain anonymous.

[32]Faulkner, *op.cit.*, pp. 54, 268; Gardiner, *op.cit.*, Sign-List S40-41, V9.

[33]Shennum 1977, p. 165, *passim*..

[34]Faulkner, *op.cit.*, pp. 11, 45; *Wb.*I, p. 42,1-4.

[35]Piankoff 1968, p. 45; Faulkner, *op.cit.*, p. 219; *Wb.*III, p. 433,1. Also see Cat. 86e for use of this name in *PT* of Unas.

[36]Faulkner, *op.cit.*, p. 214; *Wb.*IV, p. 33,20.

[37]Faulkner, *op.cit.*, p. 296; *Wb.*V, p. 293,8.

[38]Faulkner, *op.cit.*, p. 4; *Wb.*I, p. 16,16-18.

[39]Gardiner 1957, p. 560, Sign-List I13.

W3dyt [Wadjyet], "the Two Cobra Goddesses", "the two Serpent Goddesses of U. and L. E.";[40] the name is derived from the root word, w3d, "green, fresh fortunate, happy, hale, sturdy", as well as, "papyrus";

wrt [Weret], "Great One", epithet of the uraeus and of goddesses;

wrt-ḥk3w [Weret-hekaw], "Great of Magic", epithet of goddesses, crowns, and the uraeus;[41]

nsrt [Nesert], "Royal Serpent"; root word, nsry, "flame of uraeus", used with the preposition r, "against" the "king's enemies", also, nsr, nsrt, "flame";[42]

rnnt [Renenet], "Nurse Goddess"; root words, rnn, "rejoice", "caress", "bring up", nurse"; "wet nurse";[43]

rnnwtt [Rennewtet], "Harvest Goddess";[44]

tfnt [Tefnet], "Eye of Re",[45] also "moisture", the primeval daughter of the creator god, Re or Atum.[46]

The cobra goddess is also addressed as "the Eye of Horus", protectress of the pharaoh and loyal to Horus. In her other aspect of Tefnet or "moisture", she was "the Eye of Re" and his daughter as well. In the *Book of the Dead*, Chapter XVII, the "Eye of Re", who is probably again Tefnet, appears as Hathor, or Hathor-Sakhmet.[47] During the Late Period, goddesses with lioness heads normally represent the goddess Wadjet.[48] Wadjet is eventually assimilated with all goddesses, and the cobra hieroglyph becomes the determinative at the end of the word,   , ntrt, "goddess".[49]

From Egyptian inscriptions on walls (Fig. 1), coffins, and papyrus, we learn that the cobra goddess was fiercely protective, and, although she was loved and loving, she was also fearsome and vindictive to enemies. The earliest preserved, written expression of these qualities occurs in the Saqqara pyramid of the Dynasty V monarch, Unas.

---

[40]Faulkner, *op.cit.*, p. 56; *Wb.*I, pp. 268,17, 269,1-2

[41]Faulkner, *op.cit.*, p. 64; *Wb.*I, p. 332,1.

[42]Faulkner, *op.cit.*, pp. 139-40; *Wb.*II, p. 335,8.

[43]Faulkner, *op.cit.*, pp. 150-51.

[44]Faulkner, *op.cit.*, pp. 150-51; *Wb.*II, pp. 436,11-17, 437,2-18; see, also Broekhuis 1971, pp. 1-20 for a detailed discussion of Rennewtet and her "qualities".

[45]Faulkner, *op.cit.*, p. 298; *Wb.*V, p. 299,5-6.

[46]Morenz 1973, pp. 162-63, 270.

[47]Bakry 1969, pp. 177-80, fig.1, pl. 1.

[48]Bothmer 1949, pp. 121 ff.; James 1982, pp. 156 ff..

[49]Faulkner 1976, p. 142; Gardiner 1957, Sign-List, I12-13.

Fig. 1, pyramid of Unas sarcophagus chamber, east wall.

Pyramid Text 396 (Utterance 273) has been translated by Piankoff[50] as follows:

> The Kas of Unas are behind him,
> His maidservants are under his feet,
> His gods (protecting him) are over him,
> His Uraei {Iarwet}[51] are on his head.
> The guide-serpent {Sebi} of Unas is on his brow,
> She who perceives the soul (of the enemy),
> She whose fire is effective;
> The might of Unas is for his protection."

In Pyramid Texts 196-198 (Utterance 221), the crown of Lower Egypt is addressed as follows:[52]

> "O Net (crown of Lower Egypt), O Inu,
> O Great One! {Weret}
> O Great of Magic, {Weret-hekaw}
> O Nesert!
> Inspire fear before Unas as fear before thee,
> Inspire dread before Unas as dread before thee,
> Inspire awe before Unas as awe before thee,
> Inspire love for Unas as love for thee!
> Let him rule at the head of the living,
> [Let him be powerful] at the head of the spirits,
> Let his knife be firm against his enemies!
> O Inu, [thou camest forth from him,
> He came forth from thee].
> The Great Ikhet {Akhet}[53] [has given thee birth]
> Ikhet-Utet {Akhet-wetet} has adorned thee,
> The Ikhet-Utet has given birth,
> The Great Ikhet [has adorned thee],
>   for thou art indeed Horus who fought to
>   protect his eye."

From the Middle Kingdom "Hymns to the Diadem",[54] c.1650-1550 B.C., we have an excerpt from a hymn to the crown of Upper Egypt:

> "Praise to thee, O Eye of Horus, that didst
>   cut off the heads of the followers of Seth.
> She trod them down (?),
> She spat at the (foes) with that which came
>   forth from her - in her name of 'Mistress

---

[50]1968, p. 45, pl. 28 with permission of Princeton University Press; see Cat. 86 for illustration and discussion of cobra goddess names found in Pyramid Texts from the pyramid of Unas.

[51]{} contain transliterations of the hieroglyphs as they appear in Piankoff's text, *ibid.*, spelled with vowels inserted for vocalization.

[52]Piankoff 1968, p. 69, pls. 49, 50, 51 with permission of the Princeton University Press.

[53]"Ikhet" and "Akhet" represent different vocalizations of the same word, and "Akhet" is the author's preference. The Egyptians themselves did not have a strictly consistant orthography for the sign, 🦅 , in the Pyramid Texts, where the name of the cobra goddess is rendered both as 3ḫt and i3ḫt (see Cat. 86c, and 86h).

[54]Erman-Blackman 1966, p. ll.

of the Atef-crown'.
Her might is greater than that of her
foes - in her name of 'Mistress of might'.
The fear of her is instilled into them that
defame her - in her name of 'Mistress of fear'.
O (king N.), thou hast set her on thine head,
that through her thou mayest be lofty,
that through her thy might may be great....
Thou abidest on the head of (king N.),
and shinest forth on his brow - in this
thy name of 'Soceress'...."

To awaken the royal serpent, the following chant was probably sung by Egyptian women or priestesses:

"Awake in peace! Great Queen, awake in peace;
thine awakening is peaceful.
Awake in peace! Snake that is on the brow of
(king N.), awake in peace; thine awakening
is peaceful.....
Awake in peace! Upper Egyptian snake, awake
in peace; thine awakening is peaceful.
Awake in peace! Lower Egyptian snake, awake
in peace; thine awakening is peaceful.
Awake in peace! Renenutet, awake in peace;
thine awakening is peaceful.
Awake in peace! Uto with splendid..., awake
in peace; thine awakening is peaceful.
Awake in peace! Thou with head erect, with
wide neck,[55]
Awake in peace; thine awakening is peaceful...."[56]

Ancient Egyptian writing and mythological representations indicate that the cobra image had many aspects and names. Ancient Egyptian art depicts them all as a rearing serpent, the divine-royal uraeus cobra. Although her form is employed in a variety of ways - eight different uses or types of cobra symbol can be distinguished in the Old Kingdom alone - she is always shown alertly aroused and poised. Whether she is on the king's forehead, a part of his titulary, or represented as decorative ornament, the uraeus, "the risen one", is consistently associated with Horus, the king. Whatever she is called, she can be perceived as the cobra goddess who is also mother, wife, sister, or daughter. Her raised head and expanded hood are threatening and powerful; she is, nevertheless, primarily a protective, beneficent, and nurturing symbol.

The Egyptians who created representations of the uraeus believed that the living spirit of the snake was contained within their finished work.[57] It was, of course, from keen observation of the cobra in nature that they drew inspiration for depicting the serpent as an ever-living, effective goddess. To understand and appreciate their work, a brief discussion of the natural history of the cobra is useful.

---

[55]Erman inserted a footnote here saying, "The angered snake which raises itself erect and puffs out its throat; the royal serpent is always thus depicted."

[56]*ibid.*, p. 11.

[57]Schäfer-Baines 1974, p. 38; Smith-Simpson 1981, p. 15.

2 THE COBRA IN NATURE

The Egyptian cobra (*Naja haje*) and Egyptian desert cobra (*Walterinnesia aegyptia*) are indigenous to Egypt; Black-necked (*Naja nigricollis*) and Ringhals cobras (*Hemachatus haemachatus*) are found in Central and South Africa; the King cobra (*Ophiophagus hannah*) does not range beyond Southeast Asia; Indian cobras (*Naja naja*) are also Asian, found from the Transcaspian Region eastward to Indonesia and north into southern China.[58] These living cobras have markings which correspond to various depictions of the uraeus in Egyptian art (*i.e.*, ventral and dorsal scales, head plates, wide bands on their hoods).

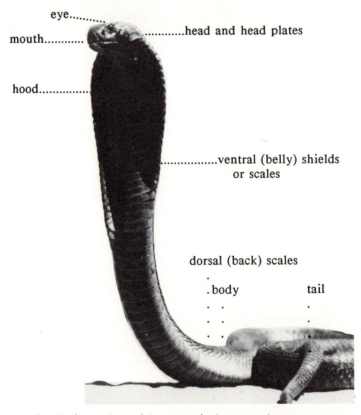

Fig. 2, live cobra with anatomical nomenclature.

---

[58]Behler, correspondence, February, 1986; *v.s.*, INTRODUCTION, n. 6.

Ancient Egyptian artisans, close observers of nature, used these cobra forms and markings in representations of the cobra goddess in relief and on sculpture. A photograph of a large Egyptian cobra, taken at Karnak (Fig. 2), shows the nomenclature used in this study to identify the various parts of its anatomy.

The Egyptian Cobra (Fig. 3) lives mostly in arid country; its presence in temples and tombs is well attested by native populations and visiting archaeologists for most regions of Egypt.[59] Its chief prey is rodents and toads, and with this diet, these cobras can grow up to nine feet in length. "In spite of its size and the large amount of venom it secretes, the Egyptian cobra is not troublesome to humans and few fatalities have been known....Death from cobra bites is much less painful and frequent than from bites of those adders known as asps."[60]

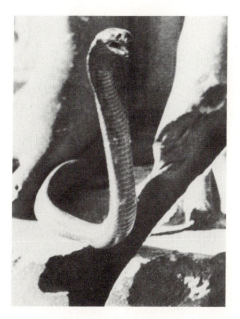

Fig. 3, Egyptian Cobra at the feet of a colossal statue.

Large Egyptian cobras look much like King cobras (Fig. 8), largest of all poisonous snakes. However, since the King cobra does not range beyond Southeast Asia, it probably is not the species represented with late Predynastic elephants and worshiped with awe (Cat. 1-5). A King cobra can be as long as fourteen feet and is able to raise its head five to six feet before it strikes. According to Behler, "Most often, they behave calmly until disturbed and then quickly retreat. The animals are routinely gathered as food items ... and it is really a very rare event when someone is bitten."[61]

---

[59]*e.g.*, Weeks 1983, p. 5, "...a cobra seen in the crawl space [tomb of the Three Princesses, tomb 1 in spur D at the Theban necropolis] made it impractical to proceed."; and in conversation with the author in Jan., 1984, Kent Weeks said he, personally, had seen four cobras during the mapping of the necropolis.

[60]Stidworthy 1971, p. 101.

[61]Behler, *op.cit.*

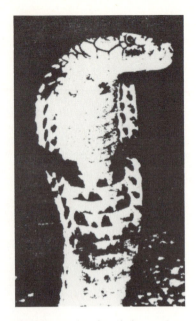

Fig. 4, detail, Hetep-heres I canopy.   Fig. 5, detail of a living cobra.

A photograph of the head and hood of a living cobra shows head plates, dorsal and ventral scales, and hood markings common to both Egyptian and King cobras (Fig. 5).   Wadjet embossed and engraved on Queen Hetep-heres I's gold encased bed canopy (Fig. 4; Cat. 27), depicts naturalistic details corresponding to these markings.

Black-necked (*Naja nigricollis*) and Ringhals cobras (*Hemacha-tus Haemachatus*) are found in Central and South Africa.[62] Relatively small, the Black-necked or Spitting cobra (Fig. 6) averages three to four feet in length. It is not aggressive, although, like the Ringhals, it can spit potent venom as protection.[63] The Ringhals cobra (Fig. 7) averages three to four feet, but some reach lengths of six to eight feet. It, too, protects itself by spitting venom. The poison duct in the fang turns outward at its end; when annoyed the snake leans back and ejects venom by muscular pressure to a distance of six to eight feet. It aims at the eye region, causing burning, agonizing pain and, in severe cases, permanent blindness.

The Asian or Indian cobra is found from the Transcaspian Region eastward to Indonesia and north into southern China.[64] It averages four to five feet in length, and preys chiefly on rats. It is a wide ranging snake of which several sub-species can be distinguished. Some show a V-shaped marking on the front of the hood, as well as bands or rings on the ventral scales (Fig. 8).

Cobras expand their hoods when they are frightened or annoyed. They have long, movable ribs in the neck region which provide for distention of the skin when air is inflated from the lungs. A cobra skeleton shows the long, movable neck ribs of the expandable hood in Figure 9.[65]

---

[62]Behler, *op.cit.*.

[63]Stidworthy, *op.cit.*, pp. 102-03.

[64]Behler, *op.cit.*.

[65]Stidworthy 1971, pp. 97-98.

Fig. 6, Black-necked cobra.

Fig. 7, Ringhals cobra.

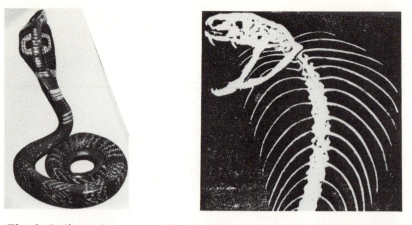

Fig. 8, Indian cobra.   Fig. 9, cobra skeleton showing movable neck ribs.

Invariably there is a single, horizontal row of ventral (front or belly) shields or scales, each corresponding to and covering a single vertebra (Fig. 10). These are clearly incised in early Dynasty I representations of the cobra goddess appearing on the "Stela of the Serpent King" (Cat. 8) and the ivory name tablet of King Den (Fig. 11; Cat. 11). Thereafter, ventral scales are frequently shown as horizontal lines by Egyptian artisans, or drawn as small, parallel, horizontal trapezoids.

Fig. 10, cobra ventral scales.   Fig. 11, detail on Den's ivory tablet.

The head of a live cobra is covered with large scales or plates, while the remainder of the body surface is covered with small, convex scales known as dorsal (back) scales[66] (Figs. 12, 13). Egyptian craftsmen also indicated these markings; they often used cross-hatching to show serpent scales, as on a fragmentary, Dynasty I, ivory serpent head from King Zer's tomb (Fig. 14; Cat. 7) and on a Graeco-Roman snake head from a gold bracelet, now in the Cleveland Museum of Art (Fig.15).[67]

Like all snakes, the cobra sheds its skin and is "reborn" at least once a year, giving rise to the belief in its immortality.[68] The cobra is found in all types of country, often

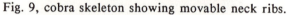

[66]Harrison 1972, pp. 22-24; Stidworthy 1971, pp. 7, 15.

[67]CMA 1018.81, coll. Leo Mildenberg; Kozloff 1981, p. 180, cat. 163.

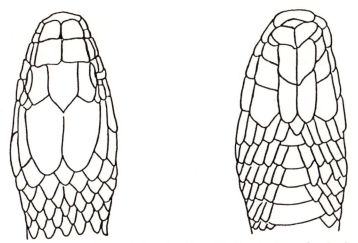

Fig. 12, back view of cobra's head.   Fig. 13, front view of cobra's head.

near human dwellings, which causes it to be a danger to human life, although only one in ten cobra bites is fatal.[69] In dry seasons, or dry places cobras are rarely far from water. The yearly flood of the Nile usually flushed out cobras in great numbers, and the Egyptians found "...a direct connection between the reptiles and the fertility bestowed by the innundation. The Nile itself was pictured as originating in a great cave where its guardian spirit, a serpent, controlled the level of its waters."[70]

   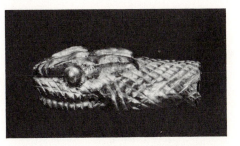

Fig. 14, serpent head of Zer.   Fig. 15, Graeco-Roman snake head.

The illustrations above of an Egyptian cobra at Karnak (Fig. 3) and of a Ringhals or Spitting cobra (Fig. 7) show the snakes poised, with hoods erect and expanded, mouths open, fangs visible, ready to strike. However, there is not one known depiction of the uraeus in Predynastic, Early Dynastic or Old Kingdom art which shows the snake with its mouth aggressively open at the moment of striking. [71] This fact supports the thesis that the ancient Egyptians thought of the cobra goddess as primarily benificent - a poised, powerful, and protective ally who did not attack unless provoked, yet could be deadly to her enemies.

Minton and Minton[72] are husband and wife herpetologists who have written about the

---

[68]Minton and Minton 1969, p. 195.

[69]Stidworthy 1971, p. 98.

[70]Minton and Minton 1969, pp. 151-52; Kakosy 1981, pp. 255-60, pl. 43.

[71]Later representations of fire spitting cobras as a determinative hieroglyph, ⳬ   , show

feelings of man toward serpents. They say that all people, ancient and modern, universally respect and fear, covertly love, and intensely hate the snake. Probably because of these feelings, serpents are a part of religion and myth for all people who live, or have lived, close to the soil; in all cultures the snake is an important image. In ancient Egyptian art the cobra is always present as a part of mythological or politico-religious iconography. Arkell[73] has suggested that cobra goddesses of ancient Egypt had their "...origins in a primitive belief that the female ancestor (also of course associated with fertility or vitality) appears in the form of a snake." This belief survives today among the Bari tribe of the southern Sudan.

---

drops of venom falling from a closed mouth.

[72]1969, p. 197

[73]1933, pp. 175-76

3 URAEUS TYPES: *Earliest Known Examples*

By the end of the Old Kingdom, c. 2150 B.C., representations of the cobra goddess had evolved into eight categories or symbol types associated with royalty and divinity. Since several types undergo distinctive variations and changes, they have been sub-divided according to style. All eight types and their subdivisions are related to one another in form and symbolism.[74] In relief, each uraeus has the outline of an upright cobra with a small, oval head projecting forward and shown in profile; a long, distended neck region rises from the body to form a widely expanded hood, depicted frontally. The earliest examples of the uraeus, however, represent the hood in profile, as seen from a side view; therefore, one cannot see the expanded hood of cobras depicted in the Predynastic and Early Dynastic Periods. Cobras first appearing as uraei in the late Predynastic Period are shown with elephants, leading processions of animals (Cat. 1-5). They were, perhaps, totems for tribes who inhabited the regions of Pe or Buto in the Delta where Wadjet is said to have had her origins.[75] However, beginning with the establishment of monarchy, c. 3000 B.C., it is apparent that the cobra goddess, as uraeus, had become an important part of ancient Egyptian state religion and written mythology.

Political overtones of the creation myth are supplied when the cobra goddess is understood as Wadjet, symbol of Lower Egypt; the vulture goddess, Nekhbet, as symbol of Upper Egypt; and the falcon god, Horus, son and earthly counterpart of the creator god, as symbol for the king who unites the "Two Lands". Representations of Wadjet, the cobra goddess, are always closely associated with Horus, the falcon, or king.

Priests, scribes, architects, and artisans of the king's entourage created the concepts and forms for at least eight different uses and ways of depicting uraei-cobra goddesses. Beyond the immediacy of their aesthetic appeal, these representations of the serpents were meant to be hieroglyphs, visual mythology, to be read and interpreted by literate priests and scribes for the illiterate masses, who were doubtessly awed and impressed by their pictorial symbolism.

The first known occurrences of these eight basic types of uraei and their stylistic variations are illustrated in this chapter by drawings. (Examples of all uraei used in this study were drawn for use in the charts of PART 3: Chapter 11, **URAEUS CHRONOLOGY CHART** and Chapter 12, **URAEUS TYPE CHART**, where each cobra goddess is shown chronologically under the appropriate king and dynasty and, again, according to type with stylistic variations or subdivisions.)

---

[74]See discussion, p. 11; also, Chapter 10: **CONCLUSIONS**.

[75]*v.s.*, see n. 10.

TYPE I. WITH ANIMAL OR DEITY SYMBOLS

A. With Elephant;
Late Predynastic, c. 3200 B.C.,[76]
Brooklyn knife handle (Cat. 1-5)

Fig. 16

Cobras on this and other handles are the earliest preserved serpents which are clearly cobras with rising heads and hoods.[77]

B. With Deity Symbol
Dynasty V, Sahura,
Granite column.

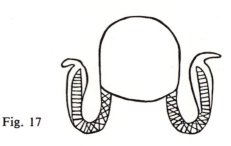

Fig. 17

A sun disk, symbol of the god Ra, is depicted with pendent uraei at its sides (Cat. 60).

Type II. IN DIVINE AND ROYAL NAMES

A. On Basket in *nbty* Name[78]
Dynasty I, c. 3000-2970 B.C.
Nagada Tablet (Cat. 6)

Fig. 18

Incised hieroglyphic <u>d</u> cobra, above *nb*, basket, is part of the earliest preserved *nbty* name of a king.

---

[76]An even earlier cobra preceding an elephant is probably represented on a Nagada I, rhomboid, slate palette, from Abadiyeh, Brussels MRAH E. 7062; *v.i.*, Fig. 61; however, the abstract Z-shape cannot be unquestionably identified as that of a cobra.

[77]*v.i.*, Chapter 5, Cat. 1.

[78]Gardiner 1957, p. 73, Sign-List I/13; Beckerath 1984, pp. 13-21.

B. Detailed Hieroglyphic _d_ above Facade[79]
Dynasty I, Zet (Wadji), c. 2925-2915 B.C.
Ivory comb; "Stela of the Serpent King" (Cat. 8-9a,b).

Fig. 19

The _d_ forms of Wadjet in Horus titles of this king are unique.

C. Detailed Double Loop Uraeus above _nbw_ and _šnw_[80]
Dynasty I, Den, c. 2915-2865 B.C.
Name plaque (Cat. 11).

Fig. 20
The only example of the "Golden Horus" title uraeus;
with head and hood in profile, body of double loops;
cobra goddess is shown above hieroglyphic signs, _nbw_,
"gold", and _šnw_, "enclosure" or "infinity".

**D. Undetailed, Double Loop;   Wadjet Offers _w3s_ Scepter and _šnw_
to Cartouche of King**
Dynasty IV, Queen Hetep-heres I, c. 2600-2575 B.C.
Faience inlay on wooden box (Cat. 28a, b.).

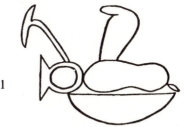

Fig. 21

Wadjet presents the _w3s_ scepter, "dominion" and _šnw_, "enclosure" or
infinity" to the cartouche of King Sneferu.

---

[79]Beckerath 1984, pp. 7-13, fig. 1.

[80]Gardiner 1957, Sign-List, S/12, V/9; Beckerath 1984, p. 23.

E. With Falcon above Horus Name
Dynasty IV, Chephren, c. 2540-2515 B.C.
Mud sealing (Cat. 43).

Fig. 22

Cobra goddess precedes falcon atop Horus name of king.

F. Determinative in Names of Cobra Goddess
Dynasty V, Unas, c. 2365-2345 B.C.
Pyramid Texts (Cat. 86e)

Fig. 23

Cobra goddess without basket at end of name, Sebi, "Guide Serpent".

Type III. ON ROYAL OR DIVINE HEADDRESS IN RELIEF

A. On Forehead of Plain Headdress
Dynasty I, Den, c. 2915-2865 B.C.
Smiting plaque (Cat. 10).

Fig. 24

First preserved uraeus on forehead of a king.

B. Entwined On Diadem
Dynasty IV, Sneferu, c. 2600-2575 B.C.
Relief fragment (Cat. 26a, b).

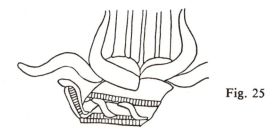

Fig. 25

Uraeus entwined on diadem worn beneath the feather and horn crown.

C. Coiled on King's Headdress
Dynasty V, Sahura, c. 2467-2455 B.C.
Relief fragment (Cat. 55).

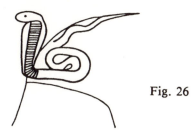

Fig. 26

Coiled uraeus encloses small loop; long undulating body shown on king's forehead.

D. On Feathered Headdress of Goddess
Dynasty V, Ne-user-ra, c. 2445-2415 B.C.
Relief panel (Cat. 67).

Fig. 27

Wadjet in human form wears uraeus emerging from an elaborate, vulture headdress.

E. On Feathered Headdress of Queen
Dynasty VI, Queen Neith, c. 2276-2195 B.C.
Relief fragment (Cat. 104).

Fig. 28

F. Pendent from Sun Disk Above Deity
Dynasty VI, Pepy I, c. 2323-2283 B.C.
Relief fragment (Cat. 92).

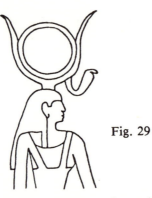

Fig. 29

Uraeus hangs from the horned sun disk of Hathor.

Type IV.   ON STANDARD

A. Wepwawet Standard
Dynasty I, Den, c. 2915-2865 B.C.
Smiting Plaque (Cat. 10).

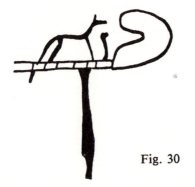

Fig. 30

Cobra goddess precedes canine god on standard in front of the king.

B. Wadjet Standard
Dynasty IV, Queen Hetep-heres I, c. 2600-2575 B.C.
Faience inlay on wooden box (Cat. 28c).

Fig. 31

Wadjet, entwined with papyrus umbel on standard, faces cartouche of
King Sneferu.

Type V. ARCHITECTURAL ELEMENT

A. On Wall
Dynasty III, Zoser, c. 2655-2635 B.C.
Cobra Wall (Cat. 24).

Fig. 32

Frieze of uraei is carved almost three-dimensionally at the top of Saqqara
chapel wall.

B. In Relief atop Hieroglyph, *t3yty*
Dynasty IV (?),
Offering stand of Vizier Sethu (Cat. 51).

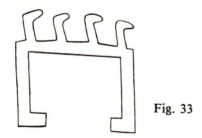

Fig. 33

A series of four cobras is atop the hieroglyph, *t3yty*, a vizierial title.

Type VI. ON ROYAL CLOTHING
Dynasty VI, Pepy II, c. 2276-2193 B.C.
Painted plaster on wooden plaque (Cat. 100a).

Fig. 34

Uraei decorate lower edges of king's sash.

Type VII. SCULPTURE

A. Ivory
Dynasty I, Zer, c. 2970-2925 B.C.
Ivory serpent head (Cat. 7).

Fig. 35

Though fragmentary, this head shows large head plates and dorsal scales   of a cobra.

B. Stone
Dynasty VI, Tety, c. 2345-2323 B.C.
Model Sistrum (Cat. 88).

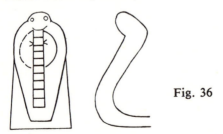

Fig. 36

Cobra carved in three dimensions with falcon on top of calcite sistrum; details incised on head and body of cobra goddess.

C. Gold
Dynasty VI (?)
Uraeus on diadem of "Golden Falcon" (Cat. 112).

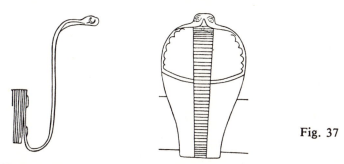

Fig. 37

Heavy, cast gold uraeus attatched to diadem worn on head of falcon; details engraved on head and hood of cobra.

Type VIII. ON ROYAL HEADDRESS IN SCULPTURE

A. On *Nemes*
Dynasty IV, attributed to Radedef, c. 2550-2540 B.C.
Two quartzite heads from statues (Cat. 30, 31)

Fig. 38

First preserved uraei on royal sculpture are found on these heads; worn on foreheads of the king's plain *nemes*.

B. On Short Cap or Wig
Dynasty IV, attributed to Shepseskaf, c. 2487-2480 B.C.
Calcite head (Cat. 50).

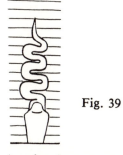

Fig. 39

A uniquely preserved cobra head is intact on the uraeus worn on a striated wig or cap.

C. On Diadem
Dynasty V (?), unknown prince or king, c. 2415-2345 B.C.(?)
Limestone head (Cat. 78).

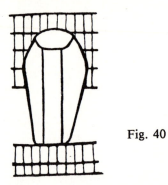

Fig. 40

This is the first and only preserved sculpture of the Old Kingdom to wear a valanced wig with diadem and uraeus.

D. Cavity; Uraeus Missing; Form Undetermined
Dynasty V (?), unknown king, c. 2415-2345 B.C.(?)
Calcite head (Cat. 79).

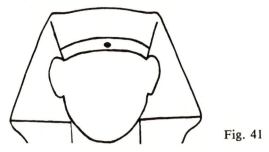

Fig. 41

Hole at center of *nemes* frontlet no doubt once held the uraeus.

4 GLOSSARY AND ILLUSTRATION OF DESCRIPTIVE TERMS

^^

Fig. 42, *body* of three, open curves

body = **uraeus body and tail excluding the head and hood.**

^^

Fig. 43, single *coil* of body.   Fig. 44, *coil* containing a loop.

coil = **circular or oval ring or spiral;** *coil* **is the term used when the circular form occurs alone, and when it contains other forms within the** *coil.*

^^

Fig. 45, five, full bodied, semi-compressed *curves.*

curve = **turn or bend.**

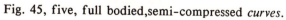

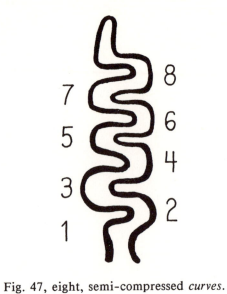

Fig. 46, six, compressed *curves*.   Fig. 47, eight, semi-compressed *curves*.

curve = **turn or bend** (continued).

∧∧

Fig. 48, *entwined* on a standard.   Fig. 49, *entwined* on a diadem.

entwined = **twisted around an object.**

∧∧

Fig. 50, hood in *front* view (characteristic of most uraei).

front = **the part of something that faces forward.**

∧∧

∧∧∧

Fig. 51, *hanging* from a horned disk.

hanging = **suspended from above and not attatched below; used interchangeably with pendent.**

∧∧∧

cranial bone structure.........................

large head scales...   ....eye and lids.

                                                        ...forked tongue.

                                                        ....jaw and mouth.

Fig. 52, *head markings.*

head markings = **details taken from the cobra head in nature and shown on Egyptian relief and sculpture.**

∧∧∧

Fig. 53, *hieroglyphic d̠ uraeus.*

hieroglyphic d̠ uraeus = **a rising cobra with its head, hood, and body shown in profile view; expanded hood is not visible.**

∧∧∧

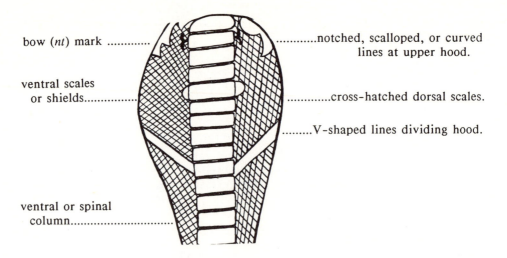

bow (*nt*) mark ....

ventral scales
    or shields...............

ventral or spinal
    column..............................

...........notched, scalloped, or curved
            lines at upper hood.

.............cross-hatched dorsal scales.

.........V-shaped lines dividing hood.

Fig. 54, *hood markings*.

hood markings = **details observed on cobra hoods in nature and depicted on uraei throats in
            profile view at begining of Dynasty I; shown in front view in reign of King
            Zoser and thereafter.**

Fig. 55, *interlaced* serpents.

interlaced = **united by passing over and under each other; woven together.**

Fig. 56, body forms double *loops*.   Fig. 57, solid, double *loops*.

Fig. 58, double *loops* with body passing under, then through back loop from behind.

loops= **oval figures formed by the uraeus body crossing itself.**

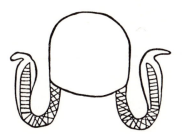

Fig. 59, uraei *pendent* on a sun disk.

pendent = **hanging cobra or cobras.**

Fig. 60, head and throat or hood seen in *profile*.

profile = **a side view or outline.**

serpent = **a snake, especially a large or poisonous one.**

snake = **any of a wide variety of limbless reptiles with an elongated, scaly body and a tapering tail; some species have a poisonous bite.**[81]

tail = **tapered back end of the uraeus body.**

thick = **fat bodied, plump or fleshy.**

thin = **slim bodied, lean, slender.**

uraeus = **any and all depictions of cobras in ancient Egyptian art; the only species of snake able to raise and expand its hood and head high above its body,**[82] **it is represented on royal relief and sculpture; word derived from the ancient Egyptian,**

, *i* rt **[Iaret], "the Risen One" (feminine), via the Greek,** *ouraios.*

---

[81]Snake and serpent are used interchangeably.

[82]J. L. Behler, *v.s.*, n. 2.

PART 2

HISTORY OF THE URAEUS, c.3200–2157 B.C

5 PREDYNASTIC SERPENTS; LATE PREDYNASTIC URAEI, c. 4000-3000 B.C.

PREDYNASTIC SERPENTS, c.4000-3200 B.C.

A rhomboid slate palette,[83] found by Petrie at Abadiyeh, is incised with a Z-shape preceding an elephant decorated with triangular forms of the Amratian Period (Fig. 61). It is difficult to be certain that the Z is an abstract representation of a risen cobra and is therefore the first example of a uraeus (Type IA2), but the form in front of the elephant does seem to be an even earlier example of the cobra type preceding elephants on the knife, comb, and mace handles of late Predynastic times (Cat.1-5; Type IA).

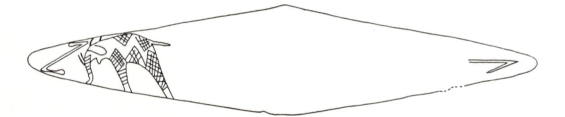

Fig. 61, Amratian slate palette from Abadiyeh.

Among the earliest, probable representations of serpents in ancient Egypt are those painted in buff on the red polished ware of the Amratian Period or Nagada I, c.4000-3500 B.C., and in red on the buff ware of the late Gerzean Period or Nagada III, c.3200 B.C.. Long, winding curves are represented on the pottery of both periods. Often interpreted as water, these rounded curves with heads are more likely to represent large serpents. Since none of these curving lines is represented with a raised hood or neck region, they cannot be identified as uraeus cobras.

An Amratian bowl from Gebelein, now in the Louvre (Fig. 62), shows a serpent stretched out in a V-shape with multiple curves; it fits between triangular forms painted on the inside of a shallow, oval bowl. There is only one snake represented, rather than two whose tails meet, since there is only one raised head with what appears to be the detail of an eye.

---

[83]Now in Brussels MRAH E. 7062; Petrie 1901b, pls. vii-98, v-B102; *BMRHA* 1935, p. 134, fig. 5; Baumgartel 1955, p. 12, fig. 2.

Fig. 62, Amratian bowl, Louvre E 27131.

There is no doubt that a serpent is represented, attacked by large birds, on an A-Group vase (contemporary with Nagada II)[84] found in Nubia (Fig. 63), and now in Chicago at the Oriental Institute Museum.[85] The snake's long, single curve form is not unlike that of the

Fig. 63, A-Group vase from Qustal in Nubia, Chicago OIM 24119.

hieroglyphic _d_ cobra of Dynasty I's King Zet (Cat. 8); since the heads and throats of the snakes on this vase are not really raised, it cannot be proved that these are representations of cobras in profile view, attacked by an ancient, Nubian bird.

On a late Gerzean vase in The Brooklyn Museum from near Akhmim[86] (Fig. 64), there are snakes shown beneath aardvarks. The oval heads at the end of their horizontal, undulating bodies leave little doubt that large serpents are represented. Three similar but longer snakes, whose bodies are formed in fourteen curves, are placed as vertical, dividing elements on a late Gerzean vase in East Berlin, German Democratic Republic (Fig. 65). These serpents are

---

[84]Amiet 1972, no. 486, illustrates a stamp seal from Susa of approximately the same date where a series of these birds are shown above and below two entwined serpents. I am indebted to J. Romano for this observation and reference.

[85]To be published in _The Oriental Institute: Nubian Expeditions_, ed. Bruce Williams.

[86]Bothmer 1974b, pp. 16-17.

Fig. 64, late Gerzean vases, Brooklyn 61.87;   Fig. 65, E. Berlin ÄMP 15129.

behind a scorpion and giraffes. The last of the giraffes has a short, four curve serpent
vertically preceding it.

Fig. 66, Gebel Tarif knife handle, Cairo CG 14265.

Large serpents curving around one another on the gold-cased, Gebel Tarif knife handle
formerly in Cairo[87] (Fig. 66) are the chief design elements on one side. However, these
snakes, seen from above, are not represented like the interlaced cobras on Predynastic handles
(Cat. 1-3). They do not raise their necks or heads and their bodies are thicker and heavier.
They appear to resemble pythons[88] which are not found in Egypt,[89] more than cobras.

---

[87]*PM* IV 1962, p. 106; Mundkur 1983, Chap. 4, "The Serpent as Sexual Symbol", pp. 180 ff.,
fig. 82, where the author says that depictions of interlaced serpents are symbols of fecundity.

[88]Keimer 1947, pp. 28-36.

[89]Behler, Curator, Herpetoloty New York Zoological Society (Bronx Zoo), written
communication to the author, February, 1986.

LATE PREDYNASTIC URAEI, c.3200-3000 B.C.

CATALOG 1

Brooklyn knife handle
From Abu Zeidan,
  south of Edfu
Late Predynastic,
  c.3200-3000 B.C.
Ivory and flint:
  L. 9.8cm, W. 5.8cm
Brooklyn 09.889.118
(Type IA1)

Fig. 67, Drawing of detail, Brooklyn knife handle.

The Brooklyn knife has a carved ivory handle showing registers of animals on each side. On the surface without the boss, a series of elephants is depicted on, or beside,[90] interlaced serpents in the first register from the top (Figs. 67, 68). The long necks and heads of the snakes are raised in the manner of cobras. They project forward, leading the procession,

Fig. 68, side of Brooklyn knife handle with cobras, Brooklyn 09.889.118.

followed by a series of similarly carved elephants and cobras. Rows of birds, felines, and other quadrupeds are shown in the succeeding registers. The Brooklyn knife handle is one of five (CAT. 1-5) late Predynastic objects with similar representations of animals.[91]

---

[90]Hofmann 1970, p. 623.

[91]Keimer 1947, pp.27-28.

Cobras with elephants are the earliest known, certain depiction of the uraeus; they are the only uraei preserved from the Predynastic Period. Each example of this first type, **(Type I: With Animal or Deity Symbol; A. With Elephant; 1. Two Interlaced Uraei)**,[92] shows the snakes under or beside elephants[93] with two raised cobra hoods and   heads represented in profile view. Since cobras are the only serpents which can raise and hold their bodies as high as approximately one-third of their length,[94] they must be the reptiles represented on these late Predynastic handles.

Keimer[95] and Churcher[96] tentatively suggest that because of the size and lack of visible hoods or other means of identification, these serpents, interlaced under elephants, are pythons; Benedite,[97] however, correctly identified the reptiles as cobras. Like the elephants, they are shown in profile view; therefore the expansion of the uraeus hood is not visible. The first example of a uraeus on a king's forehead occurs on a relief of Den, Dynasty I (CAT. 10); it too is shown in profile, as are all examples of Dynasties I and II[98] uraei but one.[99]

Fig. 69, Bronze sphinx, with two uraei, Dynasty XIX, Brooklyn 61.20.

Numerous scholars refer to the snakes as being "trampled upon" by the elephants. If this were so, surely the characteristically observant and realistic Egyptian artisan would have shown the cobras - or pythons, for that matter - with their heads turned toward the elephants

---

[92]*v.i.*, Chapter 12: **Uraeus Type Chart** lists and compares all examples of Type I.

[93]Hofmann 1970, p. 623.

[94]Behler, *v. s.*, n. 2; Stidworthy, *op. cit.*, p. 97.

[95]1947, pp. 29-36.

[96]1984, p. 155; *v.s.*, p. 48, n. 86.

[97]1918, p. 229.

[98]*v.i.*, CAT. 6-13, 16.

[99]The *nbty* title cobras of King Khasekhemuwy, late Dynasty II, (Cat. 14-15) show the expanded hood of the cobra in front view without detail.

in an attacking or defensive position. Plainly, these first uraei are not conquered, subjugated, or even struggling with the elephants. Their heads are jutting out and their hoods are protectively raised as they lead the procession. Rather than fighting the elephants, they are supporting, aiding, and defending them.

W. C. Hayes[100] says, "The motif is clearly more than mere decoration, and it has been suggested that the animals were totems or emblems of a confederation of prehistoric Egyptian clans or districts...." This totemic explanation can be combined with the concept of divine power and might, attributed to the cobra goddess in Old Kingdom Pyramid Texts, to provide the most plausible description of their proud portrayal on these handles.

They seem to be conceptually related to the two cobras which flank the disk of the sun god, Ra, on Dynasty V and VI reliefs (CAT. 60, 74, 92, 93), as well as to uraei flanking a sphinx, whose representations are frequently seen in New Kingdom relief and bronzes (Fig. 69).

Bibliography: *PM* V 1962, p. 205; de Morgan 1909, p. 272; de Morgan 1926, p. 42, fig. 39; Keimer 1947, pp. 27-28, fig. 25; Hofmann 1970, p. 623, pl. a; Bothmer 1974b, p. 18; *Archéologie comparée* 1982, pp. 100-01; Needler 1984, pp. 136, 268-271, cat. 165; Churcher in Needler 1984, pp. 152-168.

---

[100]1953, pp. 27-28, fig. 82.

CATALOG 2

"Carnarvon" knife handle
Provenance not known
Late Predynastic, c.3200 B.C.
Ivory: L. 11.5cm.
New York MMA 26.7.1281
(Type IA1)

In the middle or second of three registers there is an elephant above or beside two interlaced cobras whose heads and hoods are raised at the front of a procession of

Fig. 70, drawing of "Carnarvon" knife handle detail.

animals (**Type IA1**). It is curious that on the other four, late Predynastic, ivory handles the elephant and cobras are in the first register, while here the first register depicts a series of long legged, large billed birds; the third is filled with long horned cattle and calves. Once more, cobras with the elephant are clearly in the lead.

Fig. 71, "Carnarvon" knife handle, MMA 26.7.1281.

Bibliography: Bénédite 1918, pp. 1-15, 225-41, fig. 2, pls. i-iii; Keimer 1947, p. 28, fig. 27; Vandier 1952, pp. 540-42, fig. 361; Hayes 1953, pp. 27-28; Hofmann 1970, pl. 1,c.

CATALOG 3

Mace handle
From near Seyala, Nubia
Late Predynastic, c.3200 B.C.
Gold-encased wood:
   H. approx. 20.8cm.
Cairo JE 43883
(Type IA1)

Firth[101] found a mace handle,
encased with gold and decorated
with animals incised on its
surface. In the drawing we
see interlaced cobras, engraved
with cross-hatching on their
bodies; dots on their raised
heads indicate eyes (Fig. 72).
Once again cobras with an
elephant at the top of the
mace handle appear to lead
a procession of animals.
There are a giraffe, long-
legged bird, and other animals
represented singly spaced
on the slim column of gold.

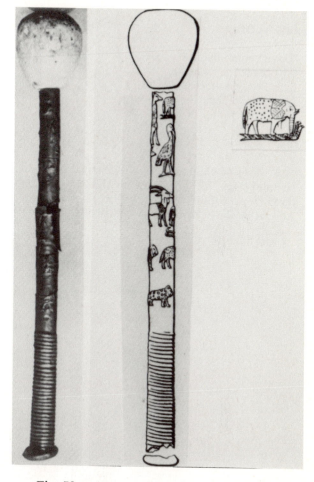

Fig. 72, mace and drawings, Cairo JE 43883.

Bibliography: Firth 1929, pp. 204-08, fig. 8, pl. xviiia-c; Kantor 1944, pp. 127-3l, fig.
   13; Keimer 1947, p. 28, fig. 29.

---

[101]1929, pp. 204-08, pl. xviii a-c, where an inserted note says this mace handle disappeared
from the Cairo Museum in 1920.

CATALOG 4

"Davis" comb handle
Provenance not known
Late Predynastic, c.3200 B.C.
Ivory: H. 5.5cm.
New York MMA 30.8.244
(Type IA2)

Fig. 73, drawing of detail, "Davis" comb handle.

A series of animals in five registers cover both surfaces of the so-called "Davis Comb Handle" (Figs. 73, 74). On each side, the top register is composed of three elephants above three single cobras whose raised necks and heads jut out to lead the procession (**Type I: With Animal or Deity Symbol; A. With Elephant; 2. Single Uraeus**).

Fig. 74, one side of "Davis" comb handle, MMA 30.8.244.

Bibliography: Capart 1905, p. 78; Maspero 1911, p. 25, fig. 40; Bénédite 1918, pl. xxxiii; Schäfer and Andrae 1925, pl. 179; Keimer 1947, p. 28, fig. 28; Vandier 1952, pp. 544- 46, fig. 365; Hayes 1953, pp. 27-28, fig. 20; Hofmann 1970, p. 623, pl. 1,b.

CATALOG 5

"Pitt-Rivers" knife
From Nagada (?)
Late Predynastic, c.3200 B.C.
Ivory and flint
London BM 68512
(Type IA2)

Fig. 75, drawing of detail, "Pitt-Rivers" knife handle.

As on the Brooklyn knife, registers of animals decorate this ivory knife handle. An elephant with a single cobra is again seen in the first register at the top on the side without the boss (Figs. 75-76).[102] Here, however, the figures are not well preserved. The single lines, visible under the elephants, can be supposed to have represented a single cobra **(Type IA2)** since the knife handle is in all respects so similar to the Brooklyn (CAT. 1), "Carnarvon" (CAT. 2), and "Davis" (CAT. 4) handles.

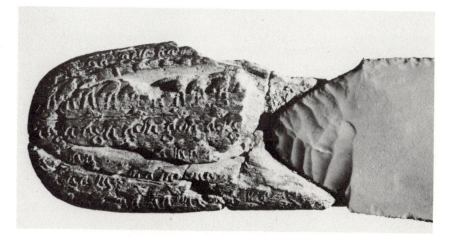

Fig. 76, "Pitt-Rivers" knife handle, BM 68512.

Bibliography: Petrie and Quibell 1886, pl. lxxvi; Bénédite 1918, p. 227, fig.1; Keimer 1947, pp. 27-28, fig.26; Hofmann 1970, p. 620, fig. 1; Edwards 1955, p. 1061.

---

[102]On the boss side of the knife, the serpent head is not delineated, but appears to be a part of an aardvark. It is doubtful that an elephant and cobra are depicted on this side of the knife.

6 EARLY DYNASTIC URAEI, DYNASTIES I-II, c.3000-2670 B. C.

CATALOG 6

Nagada Tablet
From Nagada
Dynasty I, c.3000 B.C.
Ivory
Cairo CG 14142
(Type IIA1)

Fig. 77, detail of Nagada Tablet.

The first preserved *nbty* title of a king occurs on an incised ivory plaque from Nagada (**Type II: A. On Basket in *nbty* Name**). Since the cobra goddess is always shown on a basket as a part of the king's *nbty* title, the representation of the uraeus in this context is important to the study of her origins and forms. Schäfer[103] well describes the early hieroglyphic $\underline{d}$ form of Wadjet,

> "This image, which was formerly thought to show a jumping snake,
> should probably be interpreted as follows: the snake is lying in
> a broad coil on the ground with just its head raised."[104]

Shown here above a basket, this earliest known example of the hieroglyphic $\underline{d}$ cobra being used in the titulary of a king is attributed, appropriately, to the first king of Dynasty I. In her first association with royalty the cobra goddess is represented by a simple line drawing. She is a part of the so-called *nbty*, "two ladies", epithet of the king.[105] The other "lady", Nekh-bet, the vulture goddess of Upper Egypt, precedes the cobra, and both are shown here in profile view, above baskets. These figures form the feminine, dual hieroglyphic word,

, *nbty*, translated "The Two Mistresses" or "Ladies".

Wadjet, the cobra goddess of Lower Egypt, is represented in the form of a hieroglyphic, $\underline{d}$, which shows the cobra in side view; her body and tail are curved in an arc behind her head and rigidly raised throat or hood (Figs. 77-79).

Gardiner suggests that the tablet probably belonged to Menes, founder of Dynasty I, and that this first use of the *nbty* title, preceding the Horus title of King Aha (Menes),[106] symbolizes the unification of the "two lands" and the dual protection of the vulture goddess of

---

[103]1974, p. 145, n. 97.

[104]*v.s.* Figs. 6, 7 for drawings of actual cobras in a similar position.

[105]Gardiner 1957, p. 73; Beckerath 1984, pp. 13-21 for a recent discussion of this title.

[106]I.E.S. Edwards 1971, pp. 11-15 for full discussion of identity of king named on this tablet.

Upper Egypt, Nekhbet, and the cobra goddess of Lower Egypt, Wadjet. The Greeks called Wadjet Buto or Uto, names of the Delta city where she was originally worshiped.

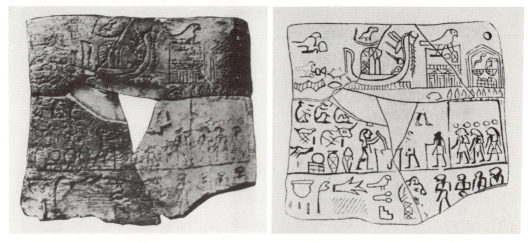

Fig. 78, Nagada Tablet, Cairo CG 14142.   Fig. 79, drawing of Nagada Tablet.

Bibliography: *PM* V 1962, p. 118; de Morgan 1897, p. 167, fig. 149; Garstang 1905, pp. 61-64, fig. 1-3; Emery 1939, pp. 5-6, 32 ff.; Vandier 1952, pp. 827 ff., fig. 556.

CATALOG 7

Serpent head
From Abydos
King Zer, c.2970 B.C.
Dynasty I
Ivory: H. 8cm.
Cairo JE 34915
(Type VIIA)

Fig. 80, ventral view and Fig. 81, dorsal view, Cairo JE 34915.

According to Petrie,[107] who found this object, it represents the small head of a snake in ivory, "carefully carved". If the serpent represented is a cobra, this is the earliest known three-dimensional representation (**Type VII: Sculpture; A. Ivory**). Petrie[108] also found a spoon which has a handle in the form of the head and cross-hatched body of a snake, but the head and hood of the spoon handle are not clearly identifiable as those of a cobra. However, the fragment pictured above represents large scales on the head and the beginning of cross-hatched dorsal scales of the neck region like those depicted on the cobra of King Zet's stela (CAT. 8). Since it is fragmentary, the form and function of the piece is difficult to determine.

Bibliography: *PM* V 1962, p. 78.

---

[107] 1901, p. 23, pl. vi-2.
[108] and others 1913, pl. xxii-15.

CATALOG 8

"Stela of the Serpent King"
From Abydos
King Zet (Wadji)
Dynasty I, c.2925-2915 B.C.
Limestone: W. 65cm.
Louvre E 11007
(Type IIB)

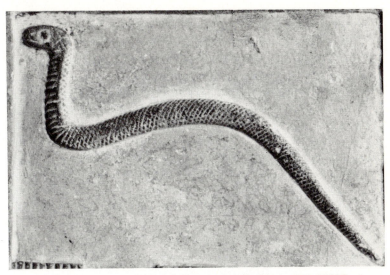

Fig. 82, cobra detail, Louvre E 11007.

The most prominent find from the royal cemetery at Abydos is undoubtedly the limestone stela dominated by a falcon in raised relief, symbol of the god Horus. He surmounts a rectangle containing the facade of a palace.[109] Above it the name of King Zet is carved in a gracefully curved hieroglyphic _d_ form of the cobra goddess whose body tapers to a pointed tail (**Type II: In Royal Names; B. Detailed Hieroglyphic _d_ above Facade**). This type of uraeus cobra is found only in the Horus titles of King Zet. The "Serpent King", "The Horus Cobra", "King Djet", or "King Wadji" are the various names given to Dynasty I's fourth king. Since the _t_ of Djet[110] is a feminine ending, and the king was presumably male, this cobra has created problems of translation for Egyptologists.[111] Fortunately, art historians need only emphasize that, here, early in Dynasty I, c.2880-2870 B.C., the first, great work of Egyptian art appears.

The work is carefully done with every naturalistic detail in place. Commonly used in later Dynasties, these details are shown here for the first time. Markings on the cobra include: the circle for an eye; incised, large head plates; ventral scales on the hood, indicated by fine horizontal lines; cross-hatching to show the small dorsal scales on the body and tail. The way in which the sixteen ventral scales are incised at the front of the snake's neck, with the smaller, cross-hatched scales at the back, suggests that the artisan meant to depict the cobra entirely in profile.   Therefore, the inflated hood of the raised neck region is not shown (Fig. 82). The fact that the neck is raised indicates that the cobra is not in repose, as Schäfer suggests.[112]   The uraeus cobra, placed in a rectangular space which may represent the courtyard of the king's palace,[113] is carved in medium high relief. The whole is in pleasing

---

[109]Kaplony, in _LdÄ_, "Horusname", p. 59, describes the rectangle as the palace complex of the king - the courtyard seen from above here contains the cobra in profile behind a facade, or palace wall shown in section - with Horus perched on top of the rectangle, as on a falcon's perch.

[110]Transliterated as Zet by Smith-Simpson 1981, p. xxiv.

[111]Vergote 1961, pp. 355-65, for a summary of this problem, as well as his interpretation.

[112]Schäfer 1974, p. 11.

proportion on a sizable slab of limestone; yet the form of the cobra is the same, $\underline{d}$, hieroglyph as that found on he small, rudimentary "Nagada Tablet" of approximately one century earlier (CAT. 6).

Fig. 83, "Stela of the Serpent King", Louvre E 11007.

Bibliography: *PM* V 1962, pp. 82-83.

---

[113]See n. 109. Kaplony curiously omits this Dynasty I example; Beckerath 1984, pp. 7-13, fig. 1, discusses this early use of the Horus name and calls the cobra space an inner room or courtyard.

CATALOG 9

Ivory Representations
  of Zet (Wadji)
From Abydos
Dynasty I
a. Ivory inlay: H. 3.2cm., W. 1.5cm.
   London BM 32641
b. Ivory comb: H. 7.5cm., W. 4.cm.
   Cairo JE 47176
   (Type IIB)

a. Fig. 84, fragment of ivory inlay,
     BM 32541.

   a. Although the incised ivory inlay is
broken and very small (Fig. 84), it shows
the same design as the large limestone stela
of King Zet (CAT. 8). The same
hieroglyphic $\underline{d}$ cobra goddess is shown, not
as a simple line drawing, but deeply
incised, a fully formed serpent. There are
at least two other small fragments found
by Petrie which show Zet's name using
similar forms and displaying the same
skillful attention to design and
execution.[114]

   b. On an ivory comb in Cairo, at the
center of a more complicated composi-
tion, there is, again, a hieroglyphic $\underline{d}$
cobra signifying Zet's Horus name (Fig.
85). Above the Horus falcon, atop the
rectangle containing the building facade
and cobra goddess, wings support a boat
carrying another falcon. In addition, the
Horus name is flanked by $w3s$ scepters,
and there is an $'n\underline{h}$ in front of the cobra.

b. Fig. 85, ivory comb of Zet, Cairo JE 47176.

Bibliography: a. Spencer 1980, p. 65, cat. 467 pls. 50, 54; b. *PM* V, 1962, p. 55.

---

[114]Petrie 1900, pls. x-8, xiii-4

CATALOG 10

Tablet with smiting scene
Probably from Abydos
King Den (Wedymu),
    c.2915-2865 B.C.
Dynasty I
Ivory:
    H. 4.5cm., W. 5.4cm.
London BM 55586
(Types IIIA1, IVA1)

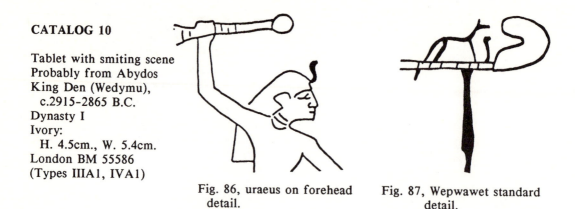

Fig. 86, uraeus on forehead
    detail.

Fig. 87, Wepwawet standard
    detail.

To the best of our knowledge, the earliest occurrence of the uraeus worn on a king's forehead occurs on this small, incised ivory label or tablet in the British Museum (Figs. 86, 88). It was first published by Spiegelberg[115] and has been illustrated frequently since. However, only W. S. Smith[116] mentions this uraeus as the first to be worn by a king. The

Fig. 88, ivory smiting tablet of Den, BM 55586

cobra rises high above the king's head, apparently attached at his forehead (**Type III: On Royal and Divine Headdress in Relief; A. On Forehead of Plain Headdress; 1. Hood in Profile High above Royal Head**). It is clear that the uraeus is fighting along with the king and defending him. Alert and ready to strike, the raised hood and body are formed in a single curve whose contours seem to depict a slightly expanded hood.

This tablet also represents the earliest known Wepwawet standard with uraeus cobra (Figs. 87, 88).[117] A cobra goddess is shown in the same form as that of the uraeus on the king's

---

[115]1897, pp. 7-11.

[116]1946, p. 129, where he calls this object the "Berlin plaque".

headcloth (**Type IV: On Standard; A. Wepwawet Standard; 1. Cobra Represented in Profile Facing** $šdšd$). The standard carries a canine god, and the cobra goddess, with raised head and hood in side view, behind a $šdšd$,[118] a bag, or sail-like protruberance on a platform at the top of a long pole (Fig. 87). Classification of this type of uraeus could also be **Type I: With Animal or Deity Symbol**, but since it is invariably carried on a standard with the canine god, it is classified separately.

Wepwawet, the "Opener of the Ways"[119] is the name given to the jackal, or wolf god. He seems to have been connected with the king's victory in battle and with victory over death. As "leader of the gods", Wepwawet, with the cobra goddess on his standard, opened royal processions, preceding the king.[120] The cobra goddess who slaughtered and "spat at foes", "cut off the heads of the followers of Seth", and was named "Mistress of Fear", "Mistress of Might"[121] was a fitting and obvious choice for the female companion of the warlike god, Wepwawet, who also "opened the ways" to the eternity of the necropolis. The Wepwawet standard precedes Den who is shown smiting a Bedouin; the accompanying inscription reads, "First time of smiting the East.".[122]

Bibliography: Spencer 1980, p. 65, cat. 460, (with bibliography) pls. 49, 63; *PM* V, 1962, p. 84.

---

[117]Gardiner 1957, Sign-list E18, 19; standards with *sdsd* and one with *sdsd* and canine god but no uraeus are carried in front of the king on the Narmer palette.

[118]Faulkner 1976, p. 274.

[119]Gardiner 1957, Sign List E/18; Faulkner 1976, p. 60.

[120]Faulkner 1969, pp. 170, 181, 203, 206, 215, 244, 314, *PT* Utterances 483, 505, 535, 539, 555, 556, 594, 734; James 1971, pp. 117, 140; Morenz 1973, pp. 173-74, 271; Clark 1978, pp. 128-31.

[121]*v.s.*, p. 16.

[122]Spencer 1980, p. 65, cat. 460, pls. 49, 63.

CATALOG 11.

Inscribed name tablet
From Abydos
Den (Wedymu)
Dynasty I
Ivory: H. 6.0cm., W. 5.6cm.
London BM 35552
(Type IIC)

Here, opposite the Horus
name of Den, the cobra
goddess appears with her
hood raised above a double
looped body.[123] She sits
above the signs for *nbw*,
"gold"[124] and, *šnw*,
"infinity" or "enclosure".
This form of uraeus (**Type
II: In Royal Names; C.
Detailed, Double Loop
above** *nbw* **and** *šnw*) is
represented by only one
example and is part of a
title of Den incised on

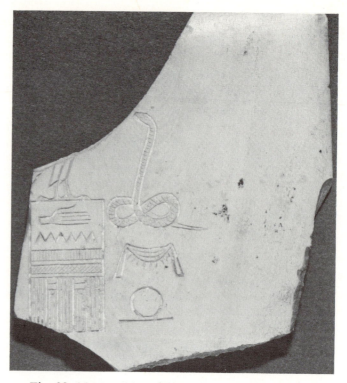

Fig. 89, Name tablet of Den, London BM 35552.

a small ivory tablet.[125] Den, the fifth king of Dynasty I, followed Zet, the "Serpent King",
and the cobra on his tablet displays the same attention to naturalistic detail
as that on Zet's stela (CAT. 8).

The cobra head is tilted up and the throat, or hood, rises very tall and erect (Fig. 89). As
on Zet's stela, the expansion of the uraeus hood is not shown, but horizontal lines of the
ventral scales are again at the front of the hood shown in profile view, and dorsal scales are
indicated on the body. Seen for the first time, double loops with the tail crossing behind
them, are represented as if seen from above, just as they are on the later, Dynasty II cobra
of Khasekhemuwy's *nbty* title, illustrated below (CAT. 14, 15), and on most uraei in relief
thereafter.

This vertical composition of a detailed cobra goddess above the hieroglyphic signs for
"gold" and "enclosure", facing the Horus name of Den, makes, as Schäfer[126] noted, "...a highly
finished ...." picture.

Bibliography: Spencer 1980, p. 65, cat. 466, pls. 50, 54 (with bibliography).

---

[123]Spencer 1980, p. 65, cat. 466.

[124]Faulkner 1976, p. 129.

[125]Beckerath 1984, pp. 21-25 for his discussion of "Der Gold-Titel".

[126]1974, p. 145, n. 97.

CATALOG 12

Inscribed labels
From Abydos
a. King Semerkhet
    Dynasty I
    Ivory: H. 3.4cm., W. 3.9 cm.
    London BM 32668
    (Type IIA2)

b. King Qay-a
    Dynasty I
    Ivory: H. 2.0cm., W. 3.1cm.
    Philadelphia UPM E. 6880
    (Type IIA2)

a. An ivory, oil jar label or tablet, now in the British Museum, is inscribed with the names of Semerkhet. To the left of an incised, vertical, red-painted, dividing line, the cobra of Semerkhet's *nbty* title is profiled behind a vulture; the incised hieroglyphs are painted black. A single coil of the cobra body, with tail hanging over the back edge of the basket, is a new development, seen for the first time on these plaques (**Type II: In Royal Names; A. On Basket in *nbty* Name; 2. Single Coil; Hood in Profile**). This form of the uraeus seems to combine the <u>*d*</u> hieroglyph (Type IIA1) with that of Den's cobra rising from its double coil (Fig. 89; Type IIC).

a. Fig. 90, jar label of Semerkhet, BM 32668.

a. Fig. 91, drawing of jar label.

b. In the tomb of Qay-a at Abydos, Petrie found an ivory plaque very similar to Semerkhet's but incised with Qay-a's names. Here, too, the *nbty* title cobra has a single coil body (Type IIA2), but in this example it has no tail.

b. Fig. 92, jar label of Qay-a, UPM E. 6880.   b. Fig.93, drawing of jar label.

Bibliography: a. Spencer 1980, p. 65, cat. 461, pls. 49, 54 (with bibliography). b. *PM* V 1962, p. 86; Petrie 1900. pls. xii-2, xvii-29.

CATALOG 13

Inscribed vase fragments
From Abydos
Dynasties I, II

a. Qay-a
    Gray marble: H. 12.2cm., W. 6.5cm.
    London BM 32672 (Fig. 94)
    (Type IIA2)

b. Qay-a
    Limestone: H. 5.1cm., W. 3.2cm.
    New York MMA 01.4.20 (Fig. 95)
    (Type IIA1)

c. Dynasty II, King? Merpabia in palimpsest
        under incised names of Semti and Irynetjer
    Rock crystal: H. 5.6cm., W. 6.5cm.
    London BM 49278 (Fig. 96)
    (Type IIA1)

d. Dynasty II names of Peribsen,
        Raneb, and Ny-netjer
    Volcanic ash: H. 5.0cm., W. 9.5cm.
    London BM 35556 (Fig. 97)
    (Type IIA2)

Many stone vase fragments with inscriptions of Dynasty I and II kings were found at Abydos and Saqqara. The fragments illustrated here are from Abydos and were found by Petrie. They are representative of two types which show the *nbty* title cobra (Type IIA-1, 2).

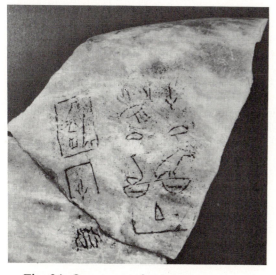

a. Fig. 94, Qay-a vase fragment,
      BM 32672.

b. Fig. 95, Qay-a vase fragment,
      MMA 01.4.20.

   a. A marble fragment found in the tomb of Qay-a has a *nbty* title cobra with a very long neck and a single coil body formed by an incised line. Its type is the same as that on Qay-a's ivory label (CAT. 12b; Type IIA1).[127]

---

[127]Pittsburg, Carnegie Museum of Natural History 1917.338 is another vase fragment of Qay-a found by Petrie with a similarly formed *nbty* name cobra.

   b. The cobra in this *nbty* title of Qay-a, seen on a fragment now in New York, shows a
simple, long necked version of the hieroglyphic *d* type, incised in a simple line (Type IIA-1).

c. Fig. 96, Semti vase fragment,
    BM 49278

d. Fig. 97, Dynasty II vase fragment
        BM 35556

   c. On a rock crystal fragment in the British Museum, the names of Semti and Irynetjer
have been incised over the name of Merpabia in palimpsest. The *nbty* title cobra is another
hieroglyphic *d* variation, leaning back with a long neck and a high, curved body (Type IIA-1).

   d. A volcanic ash fragment from the tomb of King Peribsen, Dynasty II, has a partially
erased text giving the name of Raneb on the right, as well as that of Ny-netjer, inscribed at
the left. The *nbty* cobra is a single coil type (Type IIA2); however, there is a horizontal line
within the coil indicating, perhaps, a compressed double loop.

Bibliography: a. Spencer 1980, p. 42, cat. 272 (with bibliography), pls. 23, 26; b.
   Petrie 1901, pl. viii-6; Hayes 1953, p. 37, fig. 26; c. Spencer 1980, p. 42, cat. 271,
   pls.23,26; d. *PM* V 1962, p. 8l; Spencer 1980, p. 42, cat. 275, pl. 26.

CATALOG 14

Inscriptions of Khasekhemuwy,
   c.2705-2670 B.C.
Dynasty II

a. Sealing
    From Abydos
    Clay: H. 8.0cm., W. 9.0cm.
    London BM 35592
    (Type IIA3)

b. Vase fragment
    From Saqqara
    Diorite:
      H. 4.5cm., W. 12.2cm.
    Cairo JE 55291
    (Type IIA3)

a. Fig. 98, drawing of Khasekhemuwy
sealing, BM 35592.

b. Fig. 99, vase fragment of Khasekhemuwy,
Cairo JE 55291.

a. On this clay mud seal is found the first depiction of the *nbty* title cobra with an expanded hood shown frontally (**Type II: In Royal Name; A. On Basket in** *nbty* **Name; 3. Double Loop; Hood in Front View**). It occurs on a mud sealing and vase fragment of Dynasty II's King Khasekhemuy (CAT. 14a, b). A stela fragment, attributed to late Dynasty II,[128] also shows this well developed form of Wadjet on her basket, and, therefore, probably also belongs to Khasekhemuy's reign (CAT. 15).

In each of these examples the body of the uraeus is formed in double loops, with tail hanging over the edge of the basket (Figs. 98, 99), thereby achieving the characteristic form of the *nbty* title cobra by the end of Dynasty II.

Like the serpent on Den's name label (CAT.11), the cobra goddess rises from a double looped body, but here the tail hangs over the edge of a *nbty* basket.

b. A similar *nbty* title cobra is seen on a Khasekhemuwy diorite vase fragment found by Firth at Saqqara. Incised double loops support an inflated hood, shown frontally and a head which looks straight ahead in profile view (Type IIA3).

These are the representations to which Schäfer[129] refers when he says that the puffing of the hooded cobra is first represented in Dynasty II, "...when 'Egyptian' art originated." Khasekhemuwy's inscribed fragments with the *nbty* title are the first to show the side view of the head, followed by a front view of the hood, and either a profile or top view of the body.

---

[128]Curto 1953, pp. 105-124; Scamuzzi 1963, pl. viii.

[129]1974, p. 145, n. 97.

Developed by the end of Dynasty II, this form of the cobra goddess is used with variations throughout the millenia of royal Egyptian inscriptions.

Bibliography: a. *PM* V 1962, p. 87; Spencer 1980, p. 56, cat. 397. pl. 35; b. *PM* III 1978, p. 403; Firth 1935 ii, pl. 89-16, i, pp. 18, 121.

CATALOG 15

Stela fragment
From Gebelein
King Khasekhemuwy (?)
Dynasty II
Limestone:
  H. approx. 85cm.
  W. approx. 45cm.
Turin ME;
  Cat. supplement no. 12341
(Type IIA3)

Fig. 101, stela fragment, Turin ME.

Fig. 100, uraeus detail on stella.

Although the cobra[130] and vulture are not next to one another in the *nbty* title, both goddesses are shown on this fragment behind the striding figure of a king wearing a garment with the bull's tail;[131] the uraeus on a basket is at the lower left; the vulture on a standard rather than a basket, is above her to the right. Their forms are almost indentical to the cobra and vulture depicted in the *nbty* titles of Khasekhemuwy's inscriptions (CAT. 14a, b); an attribution to his reign seems reasonable.[132] Like the uraeus cobra in Khasekhemuwy's mud sealing and vase fragment, the elongated hood is expanded and shown frontally; the body of the serpent bends in a large loop behind the base of the hood, then crosses itself, and forms a small loop in front of the hood (Type IA3), just as it does in the Khasekhemuwy inscriptions.

Bibliography: Smith 1946, p. 137; Curto 1953, pp. 105-124, no illus.; Scamuzzi 1964, pl. viii.

---

[130]Scamuzzi 1963, pl. viii, calls this, "...the hieroglyph of asps rearing up in a basket...", but it is clearly a single uraeus cobra, not adders or asps, depicted on a basket.

[131]Smith 1946, p. 137; Scamuzzi 1963, pl. viii.

[132]Smith, *op.cit.*, compares this relief to those of Zoser from Heliopolis and Sa-nakht from Wadi Maghara, Sinai (Cat. 17); however, the forms of the hieroglyphs most resemble those from the reign of Khasekhemuwy.

CATALOG 16

Ivory pin
From Zawiyet el-Aryan
Dynasty II, c.2820-2670 B.C.
Ivory: H. 14.7cm.
Boston MFA 11.2526
(Type VIIA)

A minuscule raised cobra head and neck carved in the round at the top of a small pin, although not as large as King Zer's serpent head (CAT. 7), is the second example of a uraeus sculpted in ivory (Type VIIA). It was found at Zawiyet el-Aryan and is attributed to Dynasty II.

Similar to pins or *kohl* sticks of the New Kingdom,[133] the form of the cobra goddess, carved in the round, is like that of the Dynasty IV Wadjet standard on Queen Hetep-heres I's curtain box (CAT. 28c). Here, Wadjet is at the top of the three-dimensional pin instead of a papyrus standard made of faience inlay.

Fig. 102, ivory pin, MFA 11.2526.

Bibliography: Appel 1946, fig. 46; Dunham 1978, p. 20; Brovarski 1982, cat. 272, p. 221.

---

[133]*e.g.*, Boston MFA 00.713; Brovarski 1982, p. 272.

7 OLD KINGDOM URAEI, DYNASTIES III-IV, c.2670-2475 B. C.

CATALOG 17

Fragment of relief
From Wadi Maghara, Sinai
King Sa-nekht (Nebka),
  c.2670-2655 B.C.
Dynasty III
Sandstone: H. 0.33cm.
Cairo CG 57101
(Type IVA)

Fig. 103, Sa-nekht Sinai relief, Cairo CG 57101.

A large relief fragment commemorating the king's expedition to Sinai, shows a Wepwawet standard with a cobra between the šdšd and the canine god (Type IVA). Černý,[134] describing this standard, says, "...Upwawet [is] represented in the usual fashion as a wolf on a standard, the foremost extremity of which ends in a curious bulging object known as the shoshed (šdšd); behind the latter is an uraeus, erect and with the head thrown back.". Similar in fashion to the cobra on Den's "smiting plaque" standard (CAT. 10), the representation of the uraeus is here more fully developed, in well executed, raised relief on a larger scale. As before, the standard precedes the king who, in this instance, stands alone and wears the White Crown, without the uraeus.[135] The cobra goddess rises on the standard with head tilted upward above a thick hood shown in profile. Detailed markings are not visible on the animals.

---

[134]1955, p. 55.

[135]The uraeus is not shown on the White Crown until the Middle Kingdom.

Fig. 104, drawing of Sa-nekht relief.

Bibliography: *PM* VII 1962, p. 34.

CATALOG 18

Relief fragment
Probably from Gebelein
King Sa-nekht (Nebka)
   or King Neterkhet (Zoser)
   c.2670-2635 B.C.
Dynasty III
Limestone: H. 19.2cm.
Cairo TL 20/1/21/7
(Type IVA)

   This relief fragment depicts a Wepwawet
standard carved in a style similar to that of
Sa-nekht's relief representation from Sinai
(Cat. 16): the cobra goddess is in the same
full, profile form with an elongated neck
(**Type IVA**). Although equal to the best of
the fine low relief found in Dynasty IV[136]
and similar to the style of Zoser's reliefs at
Saqqara (CAT. 23), the quality of cutting,
modeling, and detail forming the canine
and cobra on the Wepwawet standard are
here not as fully developed as on the
Zoser monuments.

Fig. 105, relief from Gebelein,
Cairo TL 20/1/21/7.

Bibliography: Smith 1946, pp. 137-39, pl. 30d.

---

[136]Smith 1946, p. 139.

CATALOG 19

Relief representation
From the Wadi Maghara, Sinai
King Neterkhet (Zoser)
Dynasty III
  c.2655-2635 B.C.
Sandstone
In situ
(Type IIIA1)

Fig. 106, Zoser Sinai relief.

   Taken from squeezes made early in this century for the Egypt Exploration Fund,[137] the drawing of this sandstone relief shows the king wearing a uraeus. It is in the same form **(Type IIIA1)** as that first seen in Dynasty I on the forehead of Den (CAT. 10) and appears here in its second, preserved example.

   Since there is no line separating the uraeus and the king's forehead, the cobra appears to be part of the royal head or headcovering as its body pushes straight out horizontally. Like Den's plaque, the uraeus is shown in profile view (Fig. 106). The cobra throat and head jut out and up at the top of the king's forehead in raised relief.

   Petrie[138] says that, "...the work is very rudely and slightly cut, and it will not photograph intelligibly.", and Smith,[139] "The king wears one of the early examples of the uraeus on his forehead, but otherwise it is not remarkable.".

Bibliography: *PM* VII 1962, p. 340; Petrie 1906, p. 44; Gardiner - Peet 1917, pl. i-2;
   Smith 1946, p. 132; Cerny 1955, p. 25.

---

[137]Gardiner - Peet 1917, pl. i-2.

[138]1906, p. 44.

[139]1946, p. 132.

CATALOG 20

Serdab statue base
From Saqqara, step pyramid
Neterkhet (Zoser)
  Dynasty III
Limestone: H. of base, 18.0cm.
Cairo JE 49613
(Type IIA4)

Fig. 107, detail of statue base, Cairo JE 49613.   Fig. 108, Zoser *serdab* statue.

The base of Zoser's well known seated statue, now in Cairo, displays Wadjet as part of his *nbty* title. Cobra goddesses shown on Zoser's monuments (CAT. 20-24) are the first to show fully developed, detailed, naturalistic forms (**Type II: In Royal Name; A. On Basket in** *nbty* **Name; 4. Double Loop; Hood Front View; Eye and Ventral Scales Detailed**). They occur only a few years after the reign of Khasekhemuwy at the end of Dynasty II when the cobra goddess first begins to show a frontal, expanded hood and double looped body (CAT. 14-15) without detail. *Nbty* title cobras of Zoser's monuments (CAT. 20-22) show Wadjet on her basket with a double loop body. Unlike the Khasekhemuwy examples, the body curves forward from behind double loops, crosses in front of them, and ends with a curved tail hanging over the basket's edge (Fig. 107). In bold relief, naturalistic details include: cranial structure of the head, eye and mouth, separation of the head and flared hood, ventral shields, narrow waist, plump body, and thin, tapered tail. The modeled head and eye are seen in profile; a fully expanded hood with ventral scales is shown frontally; and a double looped body and thin tail are seen from a side view.[140] These details are indicated by, "...very slight but telling gradations of the surface.",[141] modeled on the statue's limestone base.

---

[140]New York, MMA 11.150.31, illustrated by Hayes (1953, p. 6l, fig.38) as a "stone sculptor's model" and thought to belong to Zoser, is probably a later period's copy of Zoser relief. When the vultures and cobras of the two pieces are compared, it is seen that the proportions of their heads, the vulture necks and cobra hoods, and cobra coils are quite different. In addition, the model does not show the *nbty* baskets; also, no other sculptors' models exist from the Old Kingdom.

Like the craftsmen who made Zet's stela (CAT. 8) and Den's ivory name label (CAT. 11) three hundred years earlier, the artisan added details keenly observed from the cobra in nature.[142] However, on Zoser relief, as on that of Khasekhemuwy - late Dynasty II and thereafter - the cobra is shown, similar to the human figure in relief, with the head in profile; the hood, like the human torso and shoulders is shown frontally; and the remainder of the body, like human legs, is shown in side view.[143] This form of the cobra goddess is the prototype for its appearance in *nbty* titles of kings after Zoser, and is a type continually used, with minor variations, until the end of ancient Egyptian art.

Bibliography: often illustrated; Firth 1935 II, pl. 29-1; *PM* III 1978, p. 414.

---

[141]Smith 1946, p. 139.

[142]*cf*. Figs. 2-4, 10.

[143]Schäfer - Baines 1974, p. 98, for discussion of depiction of the human figure on Egyptian relief.

CATALOG 21

False Door lintel
From Saqqara,
 step pyramid, south tomb,
 north door frame of room II
Neterkhet (Zoser)
 Dynasty III
Limestone
In situ
(Type IIA4)

Fig. 109, detail, north door lintel, south tomb of Zoser.

Fig. 110, north door lintel, room II, south tomb of Zoser.

Neterkhet's (Zoser's) *nbty* title cobra is also shown at Saqqara as part of his titulary on the lintels of false door frames.[144]   Three of these doors are in room II of the south tomb. Pictured here are the north false door frame and its lintel. In the inscription on the lintel, the sedge plant and bee of the *n-sw-bty* title[145] and the vulture and cobra of the *nbty* name (Fig. 110) are shown twice as they face the central hieroglyph of the lintel.[146] The cobra goddess' form is detailed in the same way as that on Zoser's seated statue base (CAT. 19), but is modeled here in fine low relief (**Type IIA4**) and shows a double loop body of slightly thicker proportions.

Bibliography: *PM* III 1978, p. 409; Lauer 1976, p. 97, pl. 100.

---

[144]G. Haeny in *LdÄ*, "Scheintur", p. 571; although earlier scholarship refers to these doors and niches as "doors" and "stele", the terms "false doors" and "false door reliefs" seem more apt.

[145]Gardiner 1957, p. 73.

[146]Schäfer 1933, p. 3, fig. 2-c.

CATALOG 22

Boundary stela
From Saqqara,
   Great South Court
Neterkhet (Zoser)
   Dynasty III
Limestone: H. 23cm.
Cairo JE 52508
(Type IIA4)

Fig. 111, Zoser boundary stele.

A fragment of a columnar, gray limestone boundary stele is one of several found in the Great South Court of Zoser's pyramid complex at Saqqara. It is inscribed with the names of Neterkhet (Zoser) and his daughters Hetep-her-nebti and Intkaes. The *nbty* cobra goddess, on her basket, is carved in the the form of Zoser's other relief inscriptions (**Type IIA4**); here, she appears behind a falcon, crowned with double plumes and horns, who stands above the rectangle containing the Horus name of the king. As Smith[147] says, however, writing about the stele, "The sculptor of the boundary stelae of the princesses...indulged in little modelling and there is a sparseness of inner detail."

Fig. 112, detail of Zoser boundary stele, Cairo 52508.

Bibliography: Smith 1946, p. 138; *PM* III 1978, p. 407.

---

[147]1946, p. 138.

CATALOG 23

False door, relief of
  Neterkhet (Zoser)
Dynasty III
From Saqqara, step pyramid,
  south tomb, room II
Limestone
In situ
a. Middle false door
b. South false door
    (Type IVA2)

a. Fig. 113, detail, middle false door relief.

a. Fig. 114, middle false door relief.

The three false door reliefs found in small rooms or niches behind doors and lintels in Zoser's south tomb, room II, show almost identical Wepwawet standards preceding life-size representations of the king (Figs. 113-15). Superlative, low relief modeling shows the uraeus between the *šdšd* and a slim Wepwawet, as on Den's small "smiting plaque" (CAT. 10), Sanekht's Sinai relief (CAT. 17) and limestone relief fragment, possibly from Gebelein (CAT. 18). At Saqqara, the cobra goddess is only faintly visible, and is not mentioned in most publications. The form and details of the serpent's head and hood are much like those of Zoser's *nebty* name cobras on the door lintels (CAT. 20); but on this Wepwawet standard (Figs. 113-115) the long, slim body and tail of the cobra goddess stretch out in a rounded form between, and clearly not under, the front legs of the canine (**Type IV: On Standard; A. Wepwawet Standard; 2. Detailed Hood in Front View Facing** *sdšd*; **Body Between Legs of Canine**).

a. On the middle false door relief in the south tomb, Zoser is shown wearing the Red Crown of Lower Egypt and the falcon on the rectangle above his Horus title wears the White Crown.

b. The king wears the White Crown of Upper Egypt on all these false door reliefs at Saqqara, except the middle one in room II where he wears the Red Crown (Fig. 114). There are no uraei on any of these crowns, a circumstance which prevails throughout the Old Kingdom.

b. Fig. 115, south false door relief.

Bibliography: often illustrated; *PM* III 1978, p. 409; Lauer 1976, pl. xii.

CATALOG 24

Cobra Wall
Saqqara, reconstructed east facade
  of south tomb chapel
Neterkhet (Zoser)
Dynasty III
Limestone: H. of uraei
  approx. 25cm.
In situ
(Type VA)

Fig. 116, Cobra Wall.

The cobras in a frieze of uraei
from the uppermost course of the
east facade of Zoser's south tomb
chapel at Saqqara. They are the
first preserved uraei used as
architectural elements,(**Type V:
Architectural Element; A. On
Wall**). Restored by Lauer[148] from
pieces scattered at its base, the top
course of the paneled wall consists
of blocks of limestone carved to
represent uraei, three/fourths in the
round and almost three-dimensional.
The large, triangularly oval heads
are modeled to show the bone
structure of the skull; they jut out,
in the round, tilted upward, above
expanded hoods. A ventral column
with horizontal trapezoids marking
the ventral shields is modeled in
slightly higher relief and ends in

Fig. 117, detail of cobra wall.

a pointed triangle under the lower jaw of the serpents, just as it does in nature.[149]

It has been suggested that the cobra frieze symbolizes the Buto burial which took place in the mastaba.[150] Quibell[151] says that this type of frieze is probably represented two-dimensionally on the *pr*-sign, "chapel", in the hieroglyph *t3yty*.

Research thus far indicates that there is no stone, architectural frieze of cobras preserved, after Zoser's Cobra Wall, until that of a large, black granite cobra at the Louvre,[152] from the Dynasty XVIII temple of Amenhotep III at Sanam in Upper Nubia.

Bibliography: *PM* III 1978, p. 408; Lauer 1976, p. 94, pl. 95.

---

[148]1976, p. 94.

[149]*v.s.* Figs. 4, 13.

[150]Ricke 1944, p. 105, fig. 44.

[151]In Firth 1935, p. 11; *v.i.*, Cat. 51.

[152]E 17392.

CATALOG 25

Stela of King Sneferu
From Dahshur, southern complex,
  subsidiary pyramid
Sneferu, c.2600-2575 B.C.
Dynasty IV
Limestone: h. 3.30m.
Cairo JE 89289
(Type IIA4)

Fig. 118, Sneferu stela, JE 89289.

   The form of the cobra goddess in
Sneferu's *nbty* name on this tall stela (**Type
IIA4**) is similar to the finely modeled uraeus
on Zoser monuments (CAT. 20-22), but
here Wadjet is represented on a much larger
scale. Her height is the same as that of the
seated king's double crown behind her. The
cobra head is tilted upward with a large eye
and modeled eye socket; the hood is concave on each side of the raised relief of
the ventral column which is less wide than
on the Zoser cobras; also, the column is
marked with many more, fine, horizontal
lines indicating ventral shields. The work is
accomplished in "...low relief of striking
delicacy.".[153]
   Similarly formed, but damaged and
fragmentary, cobras appear as part of
Sneferu's *nbty* names in his valley temple at
Dahshur[154] and on his large sandstone relief
from Sinai.[155]

Bibliography: PM III 1981, p. 882.

Fig. 119, detail of Sneferu stela.

---

[153]Edwards 1977, p. 103.

[154]Fakhry 1961, figs. 120, 125.

[155]Cairo JE 38568; Gardiner - Peet 1917, pl. ii-5.

Fig. 120, Sneferu relief fragment.

CATALOG 26

Painted relief fragments
From Dahshur, valley temple,
    southern pyramid complex
Sneferu
Dynasty IV
Painted limestone
Present location not known[156]
(Type IIIB)

Fragments of limestone from the valley temple of Sneferu's south pyramid show the first preserved occurrence of the "...feather crown of Horus..."[157] with diadem and entwined uraeus,[158] (**Type III: On Royal or Divine Headdress in Relief; B. On Diadem**).

The king wears a short, valanced wig with echeloned, stylized curls and over it a diadem or fillet around which a uraeus is wound on each fragment (Figs. 120-121). The cobra head in profile and hood shown frontally rise up and out from the king's forehead. The hood is modeled and painted to indicate details of the ventral column and the horizontal ventral scales. Fakhry says, "...[the] band...has remains of a yellow color."[159]

Another fragment from the same location, with the head and hood of the uraeus missing, also depicts the feathered and horned crown above a diadem with entwined uraeus, "...a part of the lotus shaped edge of the ribbon is also preserved.".[160] It appears that a ribbon, or diadem, of gold with "lotus shaped" ends is here represented in relief

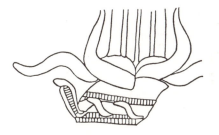

Fig. 121, drawing of Sneferu fragment.

---

[156]Illustrated by Fakhry 1961, pl. xixA, fig. 64; pl. xviiiB, fig.138.

[157]Fakhry 1961, p. 82.

[158]See Barta 1984, pp.7-8 for the most recent analysis of the meaning of this crown with its uraeus. On his relief from Sinai, Cairo JE 38568, Sneferu wears the double feather and horn crown without the diadem and uraeus.

[159]Fakhry, *op.cit.*, p. 85.

[160]*ibid.*, p. 126.

Fig. 122, Sneferu relief.   Fig. 123, drawing of Sneferu relief.

(Figs. 122, 123). No color was preserved on the cobras. The diadem with uraeus encircles the king's head and is separate from the cap-like crown with double feathers, ram, and cow horns worn on top of the king's head.   Fakhry says that the crown signifies a "...combination of Horus, Khnum, and Hathor."[161] It is curious that he omits Wadjet, the protective cobra goddess worn on the diadem below the crown, from this list of symbols for deities.

Bibliography: *PM* III 1981, pp. 877-78; Fakhry 1961, pp. 82-126, pls. xviiiB, xixA, figs. 64, 138, 144, 148.

---

[161]*ibid.*, p. 82.

Fig. 124, cobra detail on bed canopy.

CATALOG 27

Cobra details in gold
From Giza
Queen Hetep-heres I,
  Wife of Sneferu
Dynasty IV
Gold: H. (of cobra) 7.5cm.
Cairo CG 57711
  (copy, Boston MFA 38.873)
(Type IIA4)

The design and execution of the gold *nbty* title cobras on Queen Hetep-heres I's gold-cased bed canopy have a "...beauty perhaps never excelled in Egyptian art."[162] The cobra forms are similar to those on Sneferu (CAT. 25, 26) and Zoser (CAT. 20-23) monuments, but here the hood, depicted frontally, rears back even more and additional details are shown. A variation of the *nbty* title cobra, this is the first detailed example of the type (**Type II: In Royal Name; A. On Basket in *nbty* Name; 5. Double Loop; Tail through Back Loop from Front**).

Wife of Sneferu, mother of Cheops, and matriarch of Dynasty IV, Hetep-heres I's monuments indicate that she was a woman of exquisite taste and a style-setter of high standards. The cobra goddesses of Sneferu's *nbty* titles, on the inside, lower, front of her bed canopy's corner posts, display the most beautifully detailed uraeus that has thus far been found (Fig. 124). These details, embossed and engraved on sheet gold include: the goddess' forked tongue; an eye with modeled eyelids and eye socket; large head plates; notched upper edges inside the hood; rectangles, marking twenty ventral scales with the fifth scale enlarged; a V-shaped band dividing the upper hood; cross-hatched dorsal scales over the entire body; and a thin tail which slips through the back loop from the front. Most of these details are seen here for the first time; the forked tongue and eyelashes are not depicted again in the Old Kingdom. The elegant serpent seems to be the standard for its type of uraeus in relief for the remainder of the Old Kingdom. The details and design of the goldsmith's work show remarkable craftsmanship and artistry applied to close observation and knowledge of the cobra in nature (Figs. 2, 5-10, 12-13). Wadjet's representation on Hetep-heres I's gold-cased bed canopy is never surpassed in the beauty of its forms or in the skill of their execution.

---

[162]Smith 1946, p. 148; Beckerath 1984, p. 15, fig. 2.

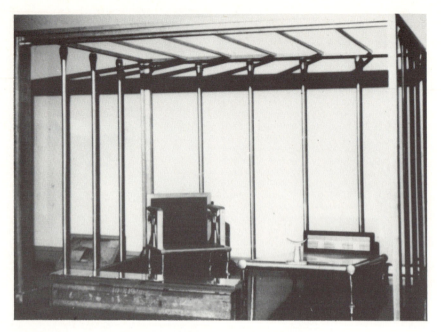

Fig. 125, Hetep-heres I furniture.

Fig. 126a, right door-jamb
of canopy.

Fig. 126b, left door-jamb
of canopy.

Bibliography: *PM* III, 1974, p. 180.

CATALOG 28

Faience inlays on wood box
From Giza
Hetep-heres I
Dynasty IV
Faience on wood
Cairo JE 72030;
  (copy Boston MFA 39.746)
a. Wadjet on top of box
b. Wadjet on sides of box
    (Type IID1)
c. Scene on end of box
    (Type IVB1)

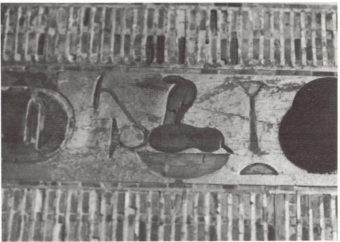

a. Fig. 127, detail on top of box.

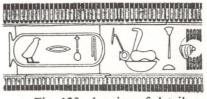

a. Fig. 128, drawing of detail.

a. One of the faience inlays
on top of the box shows the cobra
goddess sitting on her basket with
šnw sign and *w3s* scepter. Wadjet's
hood is seen seen frontally, without
detail, surmounted by a head seen in
side view, not tilted up. The double
loop of the body is shown in a solid
form hitherto unknown **(Type II: In
Royal Name; D. With *w3s* Scepter
and *šnw*;**[163] **1. Solid Double Loops,
without Detail).** It is the first
example of an Old Kingdom type of
uraeus which offers the scepter and
cartouche to the king's titles. Wadjet sits on a basket which in later variations is supported by
papyrus. Here, the *w3d,* "papyrus plant", , and *t*, "bread loaf", ⌒ , of her name, Wadjet,
are behind her in each of her appearances on the box. Type IID is usually associated with the
Horus or "Golden Horus" title of kings.[164]

b. The same form of the cobra appears on each side of the box, behind Sneferu's cartouche
with the *šnw* sign alone; and, again, her name, Wadjet, is behind her (Figs. 129-30).

c. On one end of Hetep-heres I's box the carved wood holds a scene in faience inlay. At
its right edge is the first known Wadjet standard **(Type IV: On Standard; B. Wadjet
Standard; 1. Undetailed; Hangs in Three Solid Loops with Six Curves).** Behind the king's
Horus name, the cobra at the top of the standard faces the seated king who wears a boatman's
fillet without uraeus (Figs. 131-32). Wadjet's head and expanded hood rise from the top of a
papyrus stalk, whose horizontally bent umbel is at the front of the standard with its looped
stem at the back, worn around Wadjet's neck. Shown in three solid loops, the body hangs
down on the standard pole which seems to be a papyrus stem. Her name is written in
hieroglyphs above her head. Very little of the once bright colors of the faience remains.

---

[163]Gardiner 1957, Sign-List R/19, V/9.

[164]*v.s.*, Fig. 21; Gardiner 1957, p. 72.

The shape of the standard is similar to the Dynasty II ivory pin of Catalog 16. An upright standard, surmounted by the Wadjet cobra, continues to be used in royal inscriptions of Dynasties V and VI (CAT. 59, 108), in the Middle Kingdom, and throughout Egyptian history.

b. Fig. 129, detail on side of box.

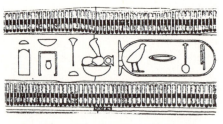

b. Fig. 130, drawing of detail.

c. Fig. 131, scene on end of box.

c. Fig. 132, drawing of scene.

Bibliography: PM III 1974, p. 180.

CATALOG 29

Uraei in *nbty* titles of
King Cheops, c.2575-2550 B.C.
Dynasty IV
a. Sandstone inscription
   Wadi Maghara, Sinai[165]
   (Type IIA4)
   Now destroyed
b. Limestone relief
   From Lisht
   New York MMA 22.1.19
   (Type IIA4)
c. Inscription on red
      granite
   At Tanis
   In situ
   (Type IIA4)

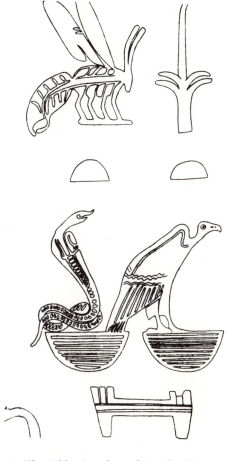

a. Fig. 133, drawing of detail, Cheops'
   Sinai inscription.

The only representations of the cobra goddess preserved from the reign of Cheops are those of his *nbty* title in inscriptions. Three examples show essentially the same form of *nbty* title cobra as that of Sneferu on his stela (CAT. 25), but Cheops' cobras have narrower hoods.

a. According to Černý,[166] Cheops' Sinai relief at the Wadi Maghara no longer exists, but, fortunately, squeezes were made and drawings from them published. Here, the cobra goddess and other hieroglyphs seem to have been "...engraved with much care and attention to detail.".[167] A drawing in Gardiner and Peet (Fig. 133),[168] shows Cheops' Sinai relief with an elaborately marked cobra goddess. The serpent's head is pointed, with mouth and eye indicated; ventral shields and dorsal scales are shown by what appear to be large and small dots; a long, thin head tilts upward; and an open mouth seems to be depicted. The cobra's slim body is in a compressed double loop with the tail crossing in front and hanging down over the basket's edge (**Type IIA4**).

b. On the limestone block from Lisht, in The Metropolitan Museum of Art, New York, the head is modeled to show an eye and jaw, but there is no cranial bump (Fig.134-35). The cobra of this Cheops *nbty* title is modeled in fine, low relief. The spinal column is in slightly higher relief; thin horizontal lines mark the ventral shields. The body seems to form multiple

---

[165]Gardiner-Peet 1917, pl. ii-7.

[166]1955, p.57

[167]*ibid.*

[168]1917, pl. ii-7

b. Fig. 134, Cheops relief reused at Lisht.   b. Fig. 135, drawing of relief detail.

loops, and the tail passes in front of the loops (**Type IIA4**).

c. At Tanis, in the eastern Delta, a granite block, which most probably comes from Cheops funerary temple at Giza,[169] also shows Cheops' *nbty* title (Fig. 136). This granite example is carved in deep sunk relief in which the details of the uraeus are unmarked (**Type IIA4**); but in contour it is the same type as those from Wadi Maghara and Lisht.

c. Fig. 136, Cheops relief at Tanis.

Bibliography: a. *PM* VII 1951, pp. 340; b. Goedicke 1971, pp. 27-28, no. 9; c. Ricke 1970, pp. 31-32.

---

[169]Ricke 1970, pp. 31-32.

CATALOG 30

Head of a statue
From Abu Roash
Attributed to King Radedef,
  c.2550-2540 B.C.
Dynasty IV
Red quartzite: H. 28cm.
Louvre E 12626
(Type VIIIA1b,2a,3a)

Quartzite heads from
statues of Radedef are the
first sculptures to show the
uraeus cobra. The serpent is
carved in high relief on a
plain *nemes*, (**Type VIII: On
Royal Headdress in Sculpture;
A. On** *nemes*).
Seen from the side on the

Fig. 137, top view, Louvre E 12626.

Louvre example, there is a small nodule remaining from the back part of the cobra head; it is
not difficult, mentally, to reconstruct the forward part projecting out in the round (**Type
VIIIA1: Uraeus Head; b. Remains of Damaged Head**), as it does on the head of Shepseskaf
(?) which displays the only intact and attached uraeus head from the Old Kingdom (CAT. 50).

The expanded hood of the cobra lies back along the forehead of Radedef, rising from the
upper edge of a *nemes* frontlet to the top of his brow (**Type VIIIA2: Uraeus Hood; a.
Unmarked Ventral Column; Begins at Upper Edge of Frontlet**); the hood of the

Fig. 138, three-quarter view.

Fig. 139, front view

snake viewed from the side is slightly thicker at its top than at its base. A ventral column is indicated by deeply incised, vertical lines; ventral scales are not shown (Fig. 138). Beyond the remnants of the head, the body of the cobra (Fig. 137) is carved in full, rounded, high relief; it winds in three open curves and has a long, tapered tail ending just beyond the crown of the king's head (**Type VIIIA3: Uraeus Body; a. Full Bodied; Three Open Curves**).

Bibliography: *PM* III, 1974, p. 2.

CATALOG 31

Head of a statue
From Abu Roash
Attributed to Radedef
Dynasty IV
Red quartzite: H. 14cm.
Cairo JE 35138
(Type VIIIA2a,3a)

The uraeus is also found on the king's red quartzite head in Cairo, one-half the size of the Louvre head. It was inaccessible for this study and could not be photographed from above; however, the uraeus seems to follow the same form as that on the larger head in the Louvre except that there appears to be no part of the cobra head remaining.

Bibliography: *PM* III 1974, p. 2.

Fig. 140, front view, Cairo JE 35138.

Fig. 141, side view.

CATALOG 32

Statue of King Chephren,
   c.2540-2515 B.C.
From Giza, Chephren valley temple
Dynasty IV
Diorite (gneiss): H. 1.68m.
Cairo CG 14
(Type VIIIA2a,3b)

Fig. 142, top view, Cairo CG 14.

   This is one of two (CAT. 32, 33)
complete, seated statues of hard stone
inscribed with the name of Chephren, found
at Giza, and wearing the uraeus on a *nemes*.
Both are adorned with the cobra goddess
carved in low relief. Here, on the statue
with the falcon, the rounded top of the
expanded cobra hood reaches to the top of
the king's forehead rising from the upper
edge of his *nemes* frontlet. Unmarked, the
uraeus ventral column is modeled in flat relief (**Type VIIIA2a**).

   The head of the cobra is missing. Winding in four open curves with a finely tapered tail
(Fig. 142), the cobra body ends at the center back of Chephren's head in front of the falcon
(**Type VIIIA3b: Slim Bodied; Four Open Curves; Low Relief**). As Smith noted, "...one feels
that all superficial ornament has been eliminated, and a restrained richness in dress and
decoration has been subordinated to the imposing form of the royal figure.".[170]

Fig. 143, front view.

Fig. 144, side view.

Bibliography: PM III 1974, p. 22.

---

[170]Smith 1946, p. 36.

CATALOG 33

Statue of Chephren
From Giza, Chephren valley temple
Dynasty IV
Schist: H. 1.20m.
Cairo CG 15
(Type VIIIA2e,3b)

   The slightly smaller, schist statue of
Chephren, also from Giza, has a uraeus
similar to that of CATALOG 32. Here,
however, the uraeus hood is based at the
lower edge of the frontlet; also, the hood
surface is flat and unmarked by a ventral
column (**Type VIIIA2e: Unmarked Ventral
Column; Begins at Lower Edge of Frontlet**).

Fig. 145, top view, Cairo CG 15.

Fig. 146, seated statue of Chephren, Cairo CG 15.

Bibliography: PM III 1974, p. 22.

CATALOG 34

Statue of Chephren
From Mit Rahina
Dynasty IV
Calcite: H. 77cm.
Cairo CG 41
(Type VIIIA1b,2c,3e)

On the Mit Rahina statue of
Chephren the uraeus appears in a
style entirely different from those on
the king's statues sculpted in harder
stone (CAT. 32, 33). The cobra
hood is worked in more detail;
also, it rises higher and, therefore,
appears to be more prominent.

Fig. 147, top view, Cairo CG 41.

A small portion of the uraeus head remains standing out at the top of the king's forehead
(**Type VIIIA1b**), thus adding to the height of the uraeus.

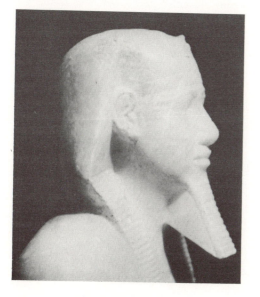

Fig. 148, side view.

Fig. 149, front view.

The hood rises from the lower edge of a *nemes* frontlet; and the ventral column has
individually worked, trapezoid, ventral scales (**Type VIIIA2c: Detailed Ventral Scales; Begins
at Lower Edge of Frontlet**).

Although the body of the cobra is modeled in low relief, it is plump and full bodied; it
winds in six semi-compressed curves, ending with a short tail at the crown of Chephren's head
(**Type VIIIA3e: Slim Bodied; Six Compressed Curves**).

Bibliography: PM III 1981, p. 842.

CATALOG 35

Head and right shoulder
  of royal statue
From Giza,
  Chephren pyramid complex
Attributed to Chephren
Dynasty IV
Gray-brown slate:
  H. .09cm.
Leipzig ÄMKMU 1946
  (Type VIIIA1c,2b,3a)

Fig. 150, front view, Leipzig ÄMKMU 1946.

Found at the pyramid complex of Chephren at Giza, this head of a king wears a uraeus with the rounded nodule of a cobra head remaining (**Type VIIIA1c: Worn or Unfinished Nodule**).

The hood rises from the lower edge of the frontlet; a ventral column is only faintly marked (**Type VIIIA2b: Unmarked Ventral Column; Base at Lower Edge of Frontlet**). Seen in profile, the uraeus body is in high relief as it winds in two open curves (**Type VIIIA3a**), similar in style to the cobra body on the head of Radedef (CAT. 30).

Bibliography: PM III 1974, p. 23.

Fig. 151, side view.

Fig. 152, seated statue,
Cairo CG 39.

CATALOG 36

Seated royal statue
From Mit Rahina
Attributed to Chephren
    or Mycerinus
Dynasty IV
Calcite: H. 65cm.
Cairo CG 39
(Type VIIIA1c,2e,3f)

This uninscribed sculpture most likely represents Chephren.[171] A faintly modeled uraeus is visible on a plain *nemes* with pleated lappets. Its head (**Type VIIIA1c**) and body appear now as faint protuberances or bumps on the King's forehead (**Type VIIIA2e**) and along the top of his head (**Type VIIIA3f: Flattened Nodes on Top of King's Head**).

In iconography, size, and material the statue is similar to the inscribed, seated, alabaster statue of Chephren, also from Mit Rahina (CAT. 34); it is also similar to the gneiss statue of Mycerinus from Mit Rahina (CAT. 45). However, these two statues have clearly delineated uraei, whereas Cairo CG 39 has only the dim suggestion of the cobra on head of the king.[172]

Bibliography: PM 1981, p. 842

Fig. 153, front view.

[171]Vandier 1953, p. 32, pl. VI-1
[172]See n. 223, CAT. 63, *infra*.

CATALOG 37

Fragment of a royal head
From Giza, Chephren
  pyramid complex
Attributed to Chephren
Dynasty IV
Diorite (gneiss):
  H. .165cm.
Leipzig ÄMKMU 1945
(Type VIIIA2e)

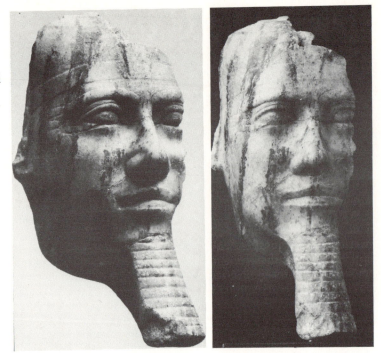

Fig. 154, three-quarter view,   Fig. 155, front view,
Leipzig ÄMKMU 1945.

   Although the fragment of this head was found at the pyramid complex of Chephren and presumably comes from a sculpture of that king, the manner in which the uraeus is modeled is unlike any of those on the inscribed seated statues known to represent Chephren. The faint outline of a broad, flat, and unmarked uraeus hood begins at the lower edge of the king's frontlet (**Type VIIIA2e**). At its base and at its broken off top, the hood is wider than any of those worn by Chephren, except that on the fragment shown in CATALOG 38, also attributed to Chephren.

Bibliography: *PM* III 1974, p. 23.

CATALOG 38

Large fragment of a royal head
From Giza, western cemetery,
 east part
Attributed to Chephren
Dynasty IV
Calcite: H. 20.4cm
Boston MFA 21.351
(Type VIIIA2e, 3f)

 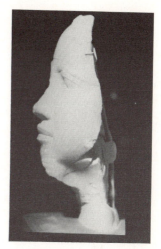

Fig. 156, front view
Boston MFA 21.351.

Fig. 157, side view.

Found by Reisner in the debris of a tomb in the western cemetery at Giza, this alabaster fragment displays the same broad, flat, unmarked style of uraeus hood as that on the gneiss fragment in Leipzig (CAT. 37). Although the king's head is damaged and the uraeus head broken off at the top, much like the fragment in Leipzig, here, the complete uraeus hood is visible (**Type VIIIA2e**). It is modeled in very low relief, rises from the lower edge of the king's headband, and shows the full breadth of the widely expanded hood. A broad uraeus body in low relief can be seen as it begins behind the top of the hood (**Type VIIIA3f**). The remainder of the cobra body and its head are missing.

Bibliography: *PM* III 1974, p. 24.

CATALOG 39

Small royal head fragments
From Giza,
   Chephren pyramid complex
Dynasty IV
Attributed to Chephren
Calcite: H. 13cm. (b.,
   tallest fragment)
a. Leipzig ÄMKMU 1950
       (Type VIIIA2c)
b. Leipzig ÄMKMU 1951
       (Type VIIIA2c)
c. Leipzig ÄMKMU fragment
       (Type VIIIA1b, 2a)
d. W. Berlin ÄM 15048
       (Type VIIIA2c, 3a)

a. Fig. 158, Leipzig ÄMKMU 1950.

Four fragments, attributed to
Chephren, show the remains of uraei
which have features in common with
those on the king's inscribed statues
(CAT. 32-33). One fragment in Leipzig
(c. Fig. 160) seems to retain part
of the head of the snake which would
have jutted out in the round
(**Type VIIIA1b**); the beginning of
its body appears to be in high relief.
The hood rises from the upper edge of
the frontlet and has an unmarked
ventral column (**Type VIIIA2a**). On
the other three fragments (Figs. 158,
159, 161), the hoods begin at the
lower edge of the frontlets with
horizontal lines marking the ventral
scales (**Type VIIIA2c**).

b. Fig. 159, Leipzig ÄMKMU 1951.

c. Fig. 160, Leipzig ÄMKMU fragment, (destroyed).

d. Fig. 161, W. Berlin ÄM 15048.

Bibliography: *PM* III 1974, p. 23; Hölscher 1912, pp. 94-95, figs. 88, 89, 94, 95.

CATALOG 40

Fragment of a statue head
From Giza, western cemetery
Attributed to Chephren
Dynasty IV
Graywacke
Cairo JE 49692
(Type VIIIA2e,3b)

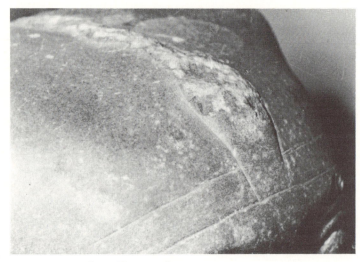

Fig. 162, top view.

When Junker[173] found this
fragment in a tomb of the
western cemetery at Giza,
he attributed the piece to
Chephren, and Smith[174] seems
to agree. The unmarked hood
of the uraeus is modeled in
low relief and springs
from the lower edge of the
frontlet (**Type VIIIA2e**). Although damaged, the winding body of the serpent is similar to
that on the statues of CATALOG 32-33 (**Type VIIIA3b**).

Fig. 163, front view, Cairo JE 49692.

Bibliography: *PM* III 1974, p. 23.

---

[173]1926, p. 105, pl. ix.

[174]1946, p. 34.

a. Fig. 164, Great Sphinx head at Giza.

CATALOG 41

a. Uraeus hood of the Great Sphinx
    Giza
    Attributed to Chephren
    Dynasty IV
    Limestone:
       H. (of hood) 1.80m.
       W. (of hood) 0.90m.
    In situ
    (Type VIIIA2d)
b. Uraeus head
       from the Great Sphinx
    From Giza, found between
       forepaws of Great Sphinx
    Limestone:
       L. .63cm.
       W. .34cm.
    London BM 1204
       (copy in Cairo)
    (Type VIIIA1a)

b. Fig. 165, Great Sphinx uraeus head,
       London BM 1204

a. The date of the colossal limestone sphinx at Giza is uncertain. Located directly north of Chephren's valley temple, the Great Sphinx has been attributed to him by most scholars.[175] The uraeus hood on this colossal sculpture, carved from the limestone bedrock, is proportionately large. It rises from the lower edge of the striped *nemes* frontlet (a. Figs. 166, 167, 169); the ventral column is in rounded relief, higher than the hood, and it is marked with horizontal lines to show the ventral scales (**Type VIIIA2d: Great Sphinx Uraeus Hood; Uniquely Detailed; Base at Lower Edge of Frontlet**). Dorsal scales are shown on the surface of the hood by cross-hatching in a diamond pattern (Figs. 167, 169). The upper two-thirds of the uraeus hood is divided by a wide band which slants diagonally across the hood (Fig. 167, mid-right and Fig. 169). Figure 167, from the Archive Lacau,[176] is a photograph taken from scaffolding in 1926. Since the cross-hatching and other details are barely visible from the ground, Evers[177] must be commended for having noted these detailed markings. Only one other cobra goddess of the

---

[175]Most recently, Wildung 1984, p. 15, speculates that the Great Sphinx probably represents Radedef.

[176]Arch. Lacau C I 5l, 9-1-1926; I am indebted to Mark Lehner for calling my attention to these photographs.

[177]1929 ii, p. 23

Old Kingdom shows similar hood markings - that on the gold encased bed canopy of
Chephren's grandmother, Queen Hetep-heres I (CAT. 27). The uraeus on the plain *nemes* of
the inscribed seated statue of Chephren from Mit Rahina (CAT. 34) has a carefully detailed
ventral column with ventral scales; also, the facial features of this statue are stylistically very
similar to those of the Great Sphinx.

a. Fig. 166, face detail.

a. Fig. 167, uraeus hood detail.

From other photographs of the Archive Lacau, it can be learned that the top of the Sphinx
head is flat; there is a large hole in the center which is now sealed with an iron trap door. A
pronounced bump at the back, to the left, and behind the hole, as well as the rough condition
of the essentially flat surface is shown in Figure 168. The pronounced bump which is shown
in the photogrametry drawing (Fig. 169), may be all that remains of the uraeus body. It is
possible that the hole was made as a fitting for a socket to hold a Double Crown, after the top
of the Sphinx head was leveled off, some time after the Old Kingdom. Several New Kingdom
stelae found by Selim Hassan[178] show the Sphinx wearing a *nemes* with uraeus, surmounted by
a Double Crown. If such a crown was added on top of the *nemes* in the Middle or New
Kingdom, it is possible that the bump is all that remains of the winding body of the Dynasty
IV uraeus which, like the hood, stood out in bold relief.
    Figure 169 shows a photogrametry drawing provided by Mark Lehner, Director, ARCE
Sphinx Project, who has given permission for its prepublication illustration here. Neither the
end of a tail nor a bump are visible from the back of the Sphinx head.[179]

---

[178]1953, fig.66, *passim.*

[179]Lehner 1980, p. 32.

a. Fig. 168, top view of Sphinx head, looking northwest.

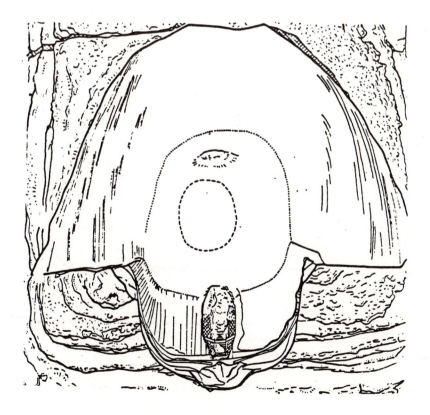

a. Fig. 169, photogrametry drawing of top of Great Sphinx head, looking west.

b. A sizeable fragment of the Great Sphinx uraeus head was found by Captain Caviglia directly below the chin of the Sphinx, between the forepaws, and presented by him to The British Museum in 1817.[180] The drawing of the cobra head (Fig. 170)[181] accurately shows the indented, jagged edges of the broken off mouth (Fig. 171). The head of the cobra, carved in the round, shows an extraordinary number of well observed

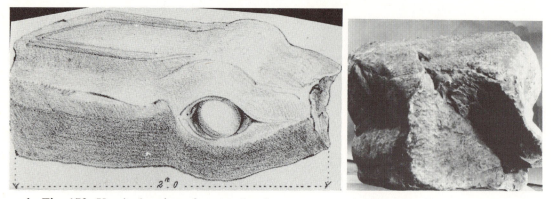

b. Fig. 170, Vyse's drawing of uraeus head.   b. Fig. 171, front view of head.

details: the bone structure of the cranium; rounded eyeballs; sharply edged eyelids; deeply modeled eye socket; a long, indented line marking the closed mouth with full upper jowls (Figs. 171, 172).

On top of the cobra head there is a wide, raised rectangle carved in relief (**Type VIIIA1a: Broken off from Great Sphinx**). Traces of painted gesso remain on the surface - red on the eyes and flecks of white and black elsewhere - undoubtedly due to the post Dynasty IV restorations of the Sphinx. In addition, it should be noted that the underside of the uraeus head is covered with chipped tool marks (Fig. 173).

b. Fig. 172, right side.   b. Fig. 173, underside.

---

[180]Budge 1909, cat. 20.

[181]Vyse 1842, pl. A, fig. 1.

The limestone of the cobra head appears to be the same as that of the Great Sphinx head which is carved from a stratum of bedrock harder than the remainder of the body.[182]

Bibliography: PM III 1974, pp. 35-37; Evers 1929, p. 23.

CATALOG 42

Offering stand
From near Bubastis
Chephren
Dynasty IV
Diorite (gneiss): H. 85cm.
New York MMA 07.288.24
(Type IIA4)

A stone stand for an offering tray, inscribed for Chephren, was found near Bubastis. The form of the cobra goddess in the king's *nebty* title is very similar to those on Hetep-heres I's bed canopy (CAT. 27), although the only detail is a dot for the eye (**Type IIA4**). Deftly incised in the hard stone, the tail slips through the back loop and hangs over the edge of the basket.

Fig. 174, offering stand of Chephren, New York, MMA 07.288.24.

Fig. 175, detail of stand.   Fig. 176, drawing of detail.

Bibliography: Lansing 1907, pp. 180-81; Hayes 1953, p. 64, fig. 4l; Fischer 1977, p. 72, n. 5.

---

[182]Lehner 1980, p. 13.

CATALOG 43

Stamped jar sealing
From Giza, subsidiary
  pyramid of Chephren
Chephren
Dynasty IV
Nile mud
Present location
  not known[183]
(Type IIE1)

Fig. 177, drawing of detail, stamped jar sealing.

Found at Chephren's pyramid complex at Giza and bearing an inscription for Chephren's "eldest son",[184] a mud jar sealing shows two birds - one a falcon - facing each other; the cobra goddess is between them in this, the only example of a Type II variation (**Type II: In Royal Names; E. With Falcon above Horus Name; 1. Between Two Uncrowned Birds**). Wadjet, in front of Horus above the King's Horus title, appears on crudely made seals as early as Cheops and Radedef;[185] however, it is not until the mud sealing of Chephren that a gracefully delineated cobra appears between two birds, according to a drawing from Holscher.[186] The form of her head and upper body is proportionally similar to that on Chephren's stone offering stand (CAT. 42), but on the sealing, as in all representations of the cobra goddess of Type IIE, the body of the snake is not seen, but appears to merge with the falcon's talons. These uraei in front of falcons whose bodies are under or beside the bird's claws are reminiscent of the late Predynastic cobras with elephants (CAT. 1-5) and preclude the argument that the snakes are being trampled upon.[187]

Bibliography: PM III 1974, p. 26; Kaplony 1981, IIA pp.38-39, IIB pl. 14-7.

---

[183]Illustrated in Hölscher 1912, fig. 157.

[184]"A title which should not be taken literally."   O. Goelet, comment to the author, 1983.

[185]Kaplony 1981, A-15, p. 22, B-pl. 9 for Cheops;   A-4, p. 36, B-pl. 13 for Radedef.

[186]912, fig. 157.

[187]*v.s.*, discussion, pp. 40-41.

CATALOG 44

Seated statue of
King Mycerinus,
  c.2515-2487 B.C.
From Giza, valley
  temple of Mycerinus
Dynasty IV
Calcite: H. 1.60m.
Cairo JE 40704
(Type VIIIA2b,3d)

On this inscribed, seated, calcite statue of Mycerinus, the uraeus has lost its head, but is otherwise undamaged. Narrowly expanded, the tall hood only slightly increases in width; it rises from the bottom edge of the *nemes* frontlet. A ventral column is unmarked and centered on the hood in relief (**Type VIIIA2b**); sides of the hood, in lower relief, are slightly concave. Viewed from the top, its wide body in flat relief winds in four semi-open, broad curves. The tail tapers to a short thick point at the crown of the king's head (**Type VIIIA3d**).

Fig. 178, Mycerinus statue, Cairo JE 40704.

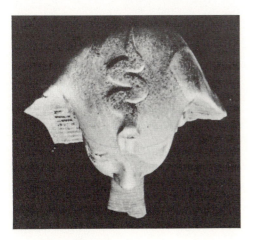

Fig. 179, top view.

Fig. 180, side view.

Bibliography: PM III 1974, p. 29 (quotes Cairo Museum entry erroneously as 40703).

CATALOG 45

Seated statue
From Mit Rahina
Mycerinus
Dynasty IV
Gneiss: H. 55cm.
Cairo CG 42
(Type VIIIA1c,2e,3e)

The uraeus head appears to be
intact on a Memphite statue inscribed
for Mycerinus. If this is the case, it
is either badly worn or summarily
modeled,[188] because the head is only a
small, rounded nodule (**Type
VIIIA1c**). An unmarked hood springs
from the lower edge of the *nemes*
frontlet and is in high relief at its
upper edge (**Type VIIIA2e**).
  Overlooked by Englebach,[189] the
full, rounded body of the cobra is
modeled in low relief in five
compressed curves with a short,

Fig. 181, Mycerinus Memphite statue, Cairo CG 42.

fat tail (**Type VIIIA3e**). The uraeus body type is most like that of the seated calcite statue in
Boston (CAT. 46), except that the Boston statue has a longer tail.

Fig. 182, front view.

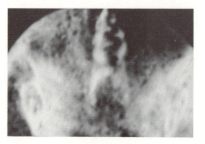

Fig. 183, top view.

Bibliography: PM III 1981, p. 842; Engelbach 1928, p. 20, n.2.; Vandier 1958, p. 26, pl. v-2.

---

[188]See n. 223, CAT. 63, *infra.*

[189]1928, chart, p. 20, n. 2, "The uraeus is represented merely as a small excrescence on the
forehead.".

CATALOG 46

Seated Statue
From Giza,
  valley temple of Mycerinus
Attributed to Mycerinus
Dynasty IV
Calcite: H. 2.35m.
Boston MFA 09.204
(Type VIIIA1b,2c,3d)

A seated calcite statue, also from the
Mycerinus valley temple, is larger but
similar to CATALOG 44. It too was
found by Reisner in fragments.[190] Worn on
a *nemes*, the uraeus is complete except for
its missing head. The tall hood of the
cobra rises from the lower edge of the
frontlet to above the king's forehead,
increasing in the depth of its relief
toward the top. Horizontally incised

Fig. 184, seated statue, Boston MFA 09.204.

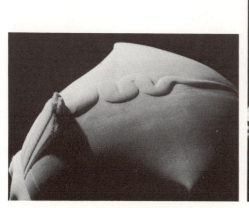

Fig. 185, top view.

Fig. 186, front view.

---

[190]Since heads attributed to Mycerinus (CAT. 46, 47) wear uraei which differ from the two
inscribed statues of Mycerinus (CAT. 44, 45), as well as from one another, the form of the
uraeus on the Boston statue is of no help in deciding whether the disproportionately small
head of the Boston statue represents later recarving as was suggested in an unpublished paper
presented at the third International Congress of Egyptology in Toronto by A. P. Kozloff.

to show the ventral scales, the ventral column is carved in low relief on the hood (**Type VIIIA2c**). The body of the cobra is carved in flat relief and winds in four curves which are more compressed than those in CATALOG 44, and the tail is very slim and long, extending for the first time to a point beyond the crown of the king's head (**Type VIIIA3d**).

Bibliography: *PM* III 1974, p. 32;
   Vandier 1958, pp. 21–22, pl. iv-1.

Fig. 187, side view, Boston MFA 09.204.

CATALOG 47

From Giza,
  Mycerinus valley temple
Attributed to Mycerinus
Dynasty IV
Calcite: H. 34cm.
Cairo JE 40705
(Type VIIIA2c,3c)

Fig. 188, top view, Cairo JE 40705.

On a calcite head, found by Reisner in the valley temple of Mycerinus, the outstanding features are the earliest preserved examples of deep striping on a *nemes* and a fringe of stylized curls under the frontlet extending to the sideburns in front of the ears.

A tall uraeus hood springs from the lower edge of the frontlet to just above the king's forehead. The narrow ventral column, carved in low relief, has fine, horizontal lines marking the ventral scales. The hood is wide and in high relief at its top (**Type VIIIA2c**). Like the uraeus on the seated statue in Boston (CAT. 46), the hood is slightly concave on either side of the spine. The body of the serpent is thin and winds in five open curves with a long, tapered tail which, for the first time, ends at the center back of the royal head, beyond its crown (**Type VIII3c**). None of the cobra head remains.

Fig. 189, front view.

Fig. 190, three-quarter view.

Bibliography: PM III 1974, p. 30 (quotes Cairo Museum entry erroneously as 40704).

CATALOG 48

Inscriptions on throne of statue
From Giza, Mycerinus valley temple
Mycerinus
Dynasty IV
Calcite: H. 98cm., W. 53cm.
Boston MFA 09.202
(Type IID2,E2,E3)

Fig. 191, left side of Mycerinus throne,
Boston MFA 09.202.

One of the seated statues found in
Mycerinus' valley temple no longer has a
torso, but both sides of the throne on which
the king was seated depict representations
of the cobra goddess carved in fine, sunk
relief. A cobra precedes a falcon on top of
the rectangular frames containing the Horus
title of the king. The falcon wears the
White Crown on the right side of the throne
(Fig. 192; **Type II: In Royal Name; E.
With Falcon above Horus Name; 3. With
White Crowned Falcon**) and is uncrowned
on the left (Fig. 191; **Type IIE2. With
Uncrowned Falcon**). Wadjet's long, thin
head is shown in profile; the hood is
frontal with the body under or alongside
the talons of Horus. The uraeus is
formed in much the same way as that
of the cobra with two birds on Chephren's
mud sealing (CAT. 43) and this form is
repeated on a gold cylinder seal of
Mycerinus (CAT. 49).

In its first preserved example, another
type of uraeus appears on the left side of
the throne. Here, Wadjet faces the cobra
and uncrowned falcon above the Horus
name (Fig. 191). She sits on a basket and
offers a *w3s* scepter; her basket is
supported by papyrus; and her name

, 𓆓, appears above her (**Type IID: With
w3s Scepter and *šnw*; 2. Solid Double
Loops with and without Detail; Supported
by Papyrus**). Although the double body
coils are similar to those of Queen Hetep-
heres I's faience inlay, here the O-spaces of
the loops are indicated.

Bibliography: PM III 1974, p. 29;
    Vandier, p. 26, fig. 8.

Fig. 192, right side of Mycerinus throne.

CATALOG 49

Cylinder seal
Provenance not known
Mycerinus
Dynasty IV
Gold: H. 3.2cm.
E. Berlin ÄMP 19999
(Type IIE2)

A tall, slim, cobra goddess in the same style as that on Chephren's mud sealing (CAT. 43) and Mycerinus' throne (CAT. 48) precedes Horus atop rectangles containing the Horus title of Mycerinus on this gold cylinder seal (**Type IIE2**). The text between the repeated titles is, "...merely the 'golden Horus' title."[191]

Fig. 193, one surface of gold seal, E. Berlin ÄMP 19999.

Fig. 194, gold seal impression.

Bibliography: Schäfer 1910, p. 15, no. 7, figs. 1-3; Müller 1938, pp. 33-34, fig. 62; Kaplony 1981, IIA, p. 102, IIB, pl. 33-9.

---

[191]Ogden Goelet, written comment to the author, 1983.

CATALOG 50

Royal head
From Giza,
  Mycerinus valley temple
Attributed to King Shepseskaf,
  c.2487-2480
Dynasty IV
Calcite: H. 28.5cm.
Boston MFA 09.203
(Type VIIIB1a,2a,3a)

Reisner,[192] who found this head from a statue at the valley temple of Mycerinus, attributed it to Shepseskaf, son and successor of Mycerinus. Smith,[193] however, says, "...there is the alternate possibility that it represents...[Mycerinus] at an earlier age than his other portraits.". Whichever king is represented, the head shows the earliest known uraeus lying directly on horizontally striated hair, a wig, or close fitting cap (**Type VIII: On Royal Headdress in Sculpture B. On Short Cap or Wig**). Heretofore all uraei have been on a *nemes* (**Type VIIIA**). A remarkable feature is that the uraeus head is so well preserved, the only one remaining intact and attached from the Old Kingdom. (**Type VIIIB1: Uraeus Head; a. Pointed, Egg-shaped Oval**). Small circles are modeled to indicate the eyes on the tiny cobra head whose oval shape is like that of the king's head.

Fig. 195, three-quarter view of king's head, Boston MFA 09.203.

Starting at the lower edge of the horizontally fluted hair, wig, or striped cap, the hood rises to the top of the king's forehead and is unmarked (**Type VIIIB2: Uraeus Hood; a. Undetailed, Shield Shape; Base at Edge of Horizontally Striated Cap or Wig; Flat Relief**). Its type is like that of uraeus hoods on fragments attributed to Chephren (CAT. 37, 38), but here it is worn on a short fitted cap or wig, instead of the *nemes*.

On top of the king's head, the thick body of the cobra is formed in six semi-compressed curves, modeled in wafer thin relief, the first and only one of this type from the Old Kingdom (**Type VIIIB3: Uraeus Body; a. Full Bodied; Six Semi-compressed Curves**). The slim, tapered tail ends at the highest point on the elongated royal skull, in front of its crown.

---

[192]1931, p. 112.

[193]1960, p. 46.

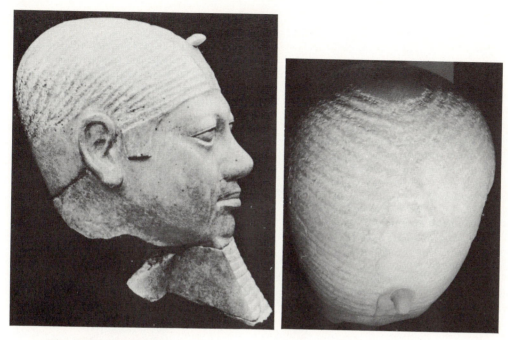

Fig. 196, side view.   Fig. 197, top view.

Bibliography: *PM* III 1974, p. 30.

CATALOG 51

Offering stand of
   Vizier Sethu (*ztw*)
From Saqqara,
   mastaba B.7
Dynasty IV or later
Limestone : H. 1.07m.
Cairo CG 1298
(Type VB)

Fig. 198, offering stand of *ztw*,
Cairo CG 1298.

   Four cobras are carved on top of the straight-sided
hieroglyph, *t3yty*,[194] a vizierial title (**Type V:
Architectural Element; B. In Relief atop Hieroglyph**
t3yty). Two of these offering stands were found by
Mariette in Vizier Sethu's mastaba at Saqqara.
Borchardt[195] hesitently attributes them to Dynasty IV,
but Baer[196] says that the inscriptions of the mastaba are,
"...incompetent....the titles odd....The possibility of a late
attempt at archaism should not be overlooked. Date: ?".
   The hieroglyph, *t3yty*, is translated, "he of the
curtain,[197] "he of the doorway",[198] or "the shrouded
one",[199] a common title of the vizier. The hieroglyph is
composed of cobras on top of a palace or shrine, and, as
Quibell[200] suggests, they seem to represent, in two
dimensions, the series or frieze of cobras first seen
in three dimensions on Zoser's "Cobra Wall" at Saqqara
(CAT. 24).

Fig. 199, detail of offering stand.

Bibliography: PM 1977, p. 491.

---

[194]Gardiner 1957, Sign-list O/16; Faulkner 1976, p. 293; Strudwick 1985, pp. 304-05, 333 for
a full discussion of this title and its forms.

[195]1937, no. 1298, pl. i.

[196]1960, p. 20, no. 417.

[197]Gardiner 1957, Sign-List O/17

[198]Helck 1954, p. 56, n. 9; Strudwick, *op.cit.*

[199]Faulkner 1972, p. 293.

[200]In Firth 1935, p. 111.

111

8 OLD KINGDOM URAEI, DYNASTY V, c.2475-2345 B.C.

CATALOG 52

Colossal royal head
From Saqqara
  Weserkaf pyramid temple
King Weserkaf,
  c.2475-2467 B.C.
Pink granite: H. 75cm.
Cairo JE 52501
(Type VIIIA1b,2b,3g)

In contrast to the low relief of the
hood, a large, fully modeled cobra
head, although damaged, juts out in
the round at the top of the king's
forehead (Figs. 200, 202; **Type
VIIIA1b**), as it does on the much
smaller, calcite head of CATALOG
50. The hood, in very low relief,

Fig. 200, front view, Cairo JE 52501.

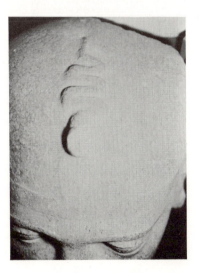

Fig. 201, top view.

Fig. 202, side view.

rises from the lower edge of the frontlet and is only faintly visible. Vertical lines of a narrow ventral column are lightly incised (**Type VIIIA2b**). The body of the uraeus on this granite head from a colossal statue, found at Weserkaf's pyramid temple, is modeled in bold relief. Seen from above, the body of the cobra winds in five semi-open curves with a short, tapered tail ending on the flat crown of the king's head (**Type VIIIA3. Uraeus Body; g. Slim Bodied; Five Semi-Open Curves**).

Bibliography: PM III 1978, pp. 397-98.

CATALOG 53

Relief fragment
From Saqqara,
  Weserkaf pyramid temple
Weserkaf
Dynasty V
Limestone: H. 1.06m.
Cairo JE 56600
(Type IIIB)

Fig. 203, Weserkaf relief,
Cairo JE 56600.

   An example of the royal cobra is preserved on a fragment of Weserkaf relief showing the uraeus winding around a fillet, or diadem, worn on short hair or a valanced wig which is surmounted by a crown consisting of two sets of horns and double plumes (**Type III. On Royal or Divine Headdress in Relief; B. On Diadem**). The forms of crown, diadem, and uraeus are similar to Sneferu's relief from Dahshur CAT. 26), but here the papyrus umbels and knot of the fillet are preserved, while the head of the uraeus is not; in addition, here, the snake is narrower and thinner; and the exceptional quality of the details in flat, crisp relief is even finer than that on Sneferu relief.

Fig. 204, detail of relief.

Bibliography: PM III 1978, p. 398.

CATALOG 54

Dyad sculpture
From Koptos (?)
King Sahura,
    c.2467-2455 B.C.
Dynasty V
Gneiss: H. 63cm.
New York MMA 18.2.4
(Type VIIIA2b,3d)

Fig. 205, Sahura dyad, New York MMA 18.2.4.

"The device which surmounts the *nemes* is the hooded head and serpentine body of the cobra or uraeus, an emblem of the sun god Re', appropriated by his earthly representative, the pharaoh.". Hayes[201] thus describes the prominent uraeus carved on the king's head. Missing is the cobra goddess' head, which would have protruded outward making her even more prominent. The wide hood, marked by a narrow ventral column modeled in low relief, rises from the lower edge of a *nemes* frontlet (**Type VIIIA2b**).

The serpent body winds in four semi-open curves. A long tail ends at the back of the flat crown of the king's head, like that of Weserkaf (CAT. 52), but with two less curves in the body (**Type VIIIA3d**). The uraeus type is similar to that of Mycerinus on his seated calcite statue in Cairo (CAT. 44); but on the head of Sahura the uraeus is in higher relief.

Fig. 206, side view.

Fig. 207, top view.

Bibliography: Hayes 1953, pp. 70-71, fig. 46; Vandier 1958, p. 30, pl. vi-2.

---

[201]1953, p. 71.

CATALOG 55

Large relief panel
From Abusir,
  pyramid complex of Sahura
Dynasty V
Limestone: H. of cobra, 8cm.
Cairo JE 39533
(Type IIIC)

A large relief panel from Sahura's
pyramid temple shows the earliest
occurrence of a single coil uraeus with a
small, enclosed loop (**Type III: On Royal
or Divine Headdress in Relief; C. Coiled
on King's Headdress**). The body winds
under the coil and forms thin, open curves
rising to the top of the king's plain
headcloth. The base of the cobra's
expanded hood, modeled and incised to
show the ventral scales, rests on the
forehead edge of the headcloth. The
uraeus head appears in profile, relatively large, and not tilted upward; cranial
bone structure and a large eye are
indicated (Fig. 209).

Fig. 208, Sahura relief panel, Cairo JE 39533.

Fig. 209, detail of relief.

Bibliography: PM III 1974, p. 331; Stadelmann 1984, pl. 65.

CATALOG 56

Relief fragments
From Abusir,
  Sahura pyramid complex
Dynasty V
Painted limestone
a. Hamburg MKG 1925.63
    (Type IIIB)[202]
b. Bonn ÄSU A 310[203]
    (Type IIIB)
c. Formerly in Breslau[204]
    (Type IIIB)

Fig. 210, Sahura relief,
Hamburg MKG 1925.63.

Several small fragments of painted limestone, elaborately carved in fine low relief, from the pyramid temple of Sahura at Abusir, show the earliest known representation of a king wearing the *atef* crown with its rush-work centerpiece.[205] The crown also has plumes and horns, worn above a diadem entwined with a uraeus (Figs. 210-212; **Type IIIB**). On these fragments the cobra head and hood rise straight up from under the fillet on the king's curled wig; they do not lie back on his forehead. In drawings of fragments, published by Borchardt[206] (Fig. 211), horizontal markings of the ventral shields on the spinal column are visible, as are the upward slanting V-lines which divide the hood. Evers[207] observed the V-division on the "*Vorderflache*" of the Great Sphinx at Giza, but did not mention its occurrence on Old Kingdom reliefs.

The bodies of these uraei wind around the diadem in six - only five are visible - widely spaced curves; on one fragment (Fig. 210), the long tail tapers to a point in open curves, ending at the king's ear level. The diadem is painted gold[208] with small rectangles of red and green and two opposed papyrus umbels at the knot above the streamers. The fillet, with uraeus, appears to represent a jeweled diadem of gold. Evers[209] stated that the model for the uraeus in the Old Kingdom was the living serpent, but that under Sesostris I and in the New

---

[202]Borchardt 1913, pl. 38.

[203]Borchardt *ibid*., pl. 37.

[204]Borchardt, *ibid*., pl. 36.

[205]Abubakr 1937, pp. 7 ff.; *LdÄ* III 1980, "Kronen", p. 814.

[206]1913, pls. 37, 38.

[207]1929, p. 23, par. 149.

[208]Borchardt 1913, p. 50.

[209]1929, p. 22, par. 135.

Kingdom it was taken from metal jewelry. These reliefs show the existence of such jewelry in the Old Kingdom. Indeed, Dunham[210] has demonstrated that diadems of metal did exist in Dynasties IV-V; additionally, a naturalistically accurate cobra, painted gold, is depicted on these gold, red, and green diadems of Sahura. The prototype for the various types of uraei of all periods was undoubtedly the living serpent, interpreted in different styles.

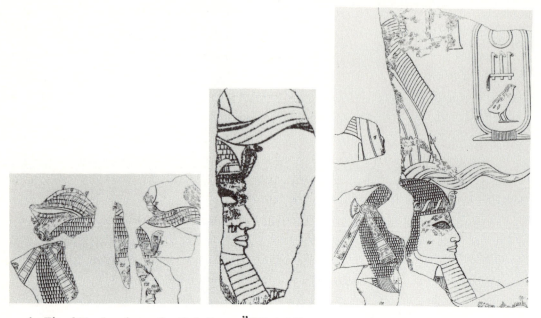

b. Fig. 211, drawings of relief, Bonn ÄSU A 310.

c. Fig. 212, drawing of relief, formerly in Breslau.

Bibliography: *PM* III 1974, p. 332.

---

[210]1946, pp. 24-29, figs. 1-8.

CATALOG 57

Relief fragments
From Abusir,
Sahura pyramid complex
Dynasty V
Limestone
a. Kalingrad, U.S.S.R.(?)
(Type IIIA3)
b. Hamburg, private
     collection[211]
(Type IIIA4)

a. Fig. 213, drawing
    of detail in Kalingrad.

b. Fig. 214, drawing
    of detail in Hamburg.

Carved in fine, low relief, these small limestone fragments depict ceremonial scenes from the pyramid complex of Sahura.   Drawings, taken from Borchardt, show a standard, carried by the king's personified *ka*, and surmounted by a small, royal, bearded head with a uraeus on a plain *nemes* (Fig. 213); the uraeus head and hood are visible only as a projecting protuberance[212] (**Type III: A. On Royal or Divine Headdress in Relief; 3. On Small King's Head Carried on Standard**).

Another small fragment (Fig. 214) shows Sahura's son, Neferirkara, wearing a headdress with uraeus, beard, and strap, all of which were later used in relief of Pepy II (CAT. 105). The clear outline of a uraeus head and expanded hood rise from the frontlet of a plain headdress with beard strap (**Type IIIA4: On Short Cap or Wig of King**). These are the first preserved uraei of a variation of Type III which continues in use in ceremonial relief of Dynasty VI, as well as in royal relief of the Middle Kingdom.

Bibliography: PM III 1974, pp. 326-27, 329, 332.

---

[211]Borchardt 1913, pls. 32, 34, 42, 48.

[212]Sahura reliefs of defeated Libyans, Cairo JE 39531 and E. Berlin 21782, and a relief of Pepy II (*PM* III 1978, p. 427), show Libyan princes wearing head cloths with similar protruberances   which Breasted (1927, p. 32) mistook for uraei; however, Bates (1970, p. 134) corrected this interpretation when he demonstrated that these are not uraei, but simply knots of the Libyans' headcloths.

CATALOG 58

Relief fragments
From Abusir,
  Sahura pyramid complex
Dynasty V
Painted limestone
a. E. Berlin ÄMP 28613[213]
(Type IIA4)
b. E. Berlin ÄMP 28628[214]
(Type IID3)
c. Strassburg, Germany[215]
(Type IID4)
d. Present location not known[216]
(Type IID4)

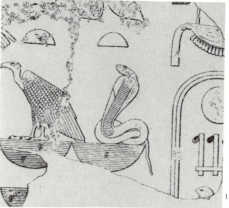

a. Fig. 215, drawing of Sahura relief,
E. Berlin ÄMP 28613.

    a. There are other painted relief fragments
from the Abusir pyramid complex of Sahura which
show his *nbty* title cobra. These fragments depict
naturalistic details and a fully developed form of
the cobra goddess (Fig. 215): the head with large
eye is tilted upward; fine horizontal lines,
indicating ventral scales, are incised on the spinal
column which extends beyond the expanded hood onto
the body of the snake; a V-band divides the hood;
and the body is coiled in a double loop with its tail
slipping through the back loop and falling down beyond
the edge of the basket (**Type II: In Royal Name;
A. On Basket in** *nbty* **Name; 4. Double Loop; Tail
Through Back Loop from Front**). In style, the
limestone carvings of the cobra follow that
executed in gold, representing the *nbty* title of
Sneferu on Queen Hetep-heres I's bed canopy from
a century earlier (CAT. 27).

    b. One of these fragments (Fig. 216), with much
of the color preserved, shows the cobra goddess,
Wadjet, painted gold, offering the *w3s* scepter with
a *šnw* slipped over it (**Type IID: With** *w3s* **Scepter
and** *šnw*; **3. Double Loop; Tail through Back Loop
from Front**). Here, in addition to the V-band dividing
the hood, there are scalloped notches at the upper
edges of the hood, and, like the fragment illustrated above

b. Fig. 216, drawing of relief,
E. Berlin ÄMP 28628.

---

[213]Borchardt 1913, pl. 64.

[214]*ibid.*, pl. 69.

[215]*ibid.*, pl. 70. K-H Priese, Curator, Egyptian Museum of the State Museum, Berlin, DDR in
recent correspondence says that a note in their copy of Borchardt's publication indicates this
relief was, "...nach Strassburg gegeben."

[216]*ibid.*, pl. 70.

(Fig. 215), the fine lines marking the ventral scales extend beyond the base of the serpent hood.

c., d. The royal cobras of Sahura's titulary from the sanctuary of his pyramid temple (Figs. 217-18) are similar in all respects, except that their tails slip through the back loop of the double looped body from behind, rather than from the front (**Type IID4: Double Loop; Tail through Back Loop from Rear**).

c. Fig. 217, drawing of relief.   d. Fig. 218, drawing of relief.

Bibliography: PM III 1974, p. 333.

CATALOG 59
Granite doorway
    inscription
From Abusir,
    Sahura pyramid
    temple
Dynasty V
Red granite
In situ (?)[217]
(Types IID4, IVB2)

Fig. 219, drawing of doorway.

Fig. 220, fragment of Abusir doorway of Sahura.

Two types of representations of the cobra goddess are shown on a doorway and lintel found at Sahura's pyramid temple: Wadjet offering the *w3s* scepter and *šnw* on a lintel fragment (**Type IID4**); and on a standard with an *'nḥ* hanging from the base of her hood at

---

[217]Borchardt 1910, p. 51, fig. 58, pl. 10.

the right edge of the doorway (**Type IV: On Standard; B. Wadjet Standard; 2. Detailed; Entwined on** *w3s* **Scepter in Six Curves;** *'nḥ* **Hangs on Hood**) In a reconstruction from Borchardt,[218] Wadjet with an *'nḥ* is entwined on the *w3s* scepter (Fig. 219); in the photograph (Fig. 220), only a thin cobra head, slim hood, the *'nḥ*, and the front edge of a *w3s* scepter are visible. As drawn, Wadjet's expanded hood, is marked by fine lines indicating ventral scales; she rises up and out at the top of the scepter. This standard showing the entwined uraeus with an *'nḥ* hanging from the base of her hood is the earliest known example of a constantly copied and repeated symbol.[219]

On the left, at the center of the lintel in the drawing (Fig. 219), Wadjet is shown facing a Red Crowned Horus, offering the *w3s* scepter with *šnw*; once again her basket is supported by a papyrus umbel. The cobra is formed in the same way on the painted limestone, raised relief fragment from Sahura's pyramid temple (CAT. 58d), except that, in this case, the V-band dividing the hood and the notched line at its upper edges are not shown. However, the drawings show the work to be finely detailed, as it is on other Sahura fragments.

Bibliography: PM III 1974, pp. 328-29.

---

[218]1910, pl. 10.

[219]Schäfer-Baines 1974, p. 237.

CATALOG 60

Architraves and column
From Abusir,
  Sahura pyramid temple
Dynasty V
Red granite
a. Architrave
    In situ?
b. Column
    W. Berlin ÄM 343/67
(Type IB1, IIA4)

Fig. 221, fragment of Abusir architrave.

Fig. 222, fragment of Abusir architrave.

Fig. 223, column
detail.

The earliest occurrences of a sun disk flanked by uraei were found at the pyramid complex of Sahura on an architrave (Fig. 221) and on a column found near it, now in W. Berlin (Figs. 223-24). On each of these monuments there is a sun disk with two cobras pendent at its sides[220] (**Type I: With Animal or Deity Symbol; B. With Deity Symbol; 1. With Sun Disk**). This decorative element is constantly repeated on temple doorways from the Old Kingdom through the Roman Period.

a. An architrave fragment (Fig. 221) shows a sun disk with two pendent cobras facing two falcons at the center of an inscription. Also displayed (Fig. 222) is a finely detailed *nbty* name cobra formed exactly like the cobra drawn in the reconstruction of Sahura's doorway (Fig. 219).

b. The sun disk with two uraei (**Type IB1**) is also seen at the top of a column, where it is under the sky-sign, *pt*, ⬜ , above the king's Horus title with the Red-Crowned Horus perched on a rectangular frame; *w3s*, ⌇ , scepters hold up the sky and mark the vertical edges of the inscription.[221]

Another *nbty* title cobra appears below the king's Horus title on Sahura's column. Although the back loop is damaged, its upper form is the same as Sahura relief uraei (Figs. 215-19, 222).

Less deeply carved on the column than on the architrave, both examples of uraei (Type IB-1 and Type IIA-4) display heads and expanded hoods which are modeled within the sunk relief; eyes are indicated; fine horizontal lines mark the ventral scales on long ventral columns. Flanking the sun disk, symmetrical bodies hang down and away; and rising heads and hoods are U-shaped forms on each side of the sun's flattened circle.

---

[220]Schäfer-Baines 1974, pp. 236-37

[221]Gardiner 1944, pp. 48 ff. for a discussion of the political and religious significance of these symbols.

Fig. 225, Sahura column detail.

Fig. 224, Sahura column,
W. Berlin ÄM 343/67.

Bibliography: *PM* III 1974, p. 326.

CATALOG 61

Column drum inscriptions
From Abusir,
  Sahura pyramid
Dynasty V
Red granite
Cairo JE 39527, 39529
(Type IIA5, IID2)

Fig. 226, drawing of inscriptions.

Two types of royal cobras used in the titulary of Old Kingdom kings are seen on granite column drums from Sahura's pyramid temple at Abusir. They are the cobra of Sahura's *nbty* title, behind the vulture goddess (**Type IIA5**), and the Wadjet cobra, beneath the hieroglyphs of her name, held aloft on a seven-stem papyrus clump (**Type IID2: Solid Double Loops with and without Detail; Supported by Papyrus**). The latter offers the *w3s* scepter with the *šnw* to the Red Crowned Horus, atop the Horus king's title above a facade (Figs. 226-27).

Fig. 227, titles on Sahura column in Cairo.

Bibliography: *PM* III 1974, p. 328.

Both cobras are carved into red granite in deep sunk relief with simply formed contours, similar in style to those made of faience on Queen Hetep-heres I's curtain box (CAT. 28a, b): hoods lean back and are widely expanded; heads, thrust forward, are tilted slightly upward, just as they are on the examples from Dynasty IV.

Fig. 228, Sahura column in Cairo.

CATALOG 62

Sandstone relief
From Wadi Maghara, Sinai
Sahura
Dynasty V
Red sandstone:
 H. (of cobra) 10.2cm.
 W. (" ") 2.6cm.
Cairo JE 38569
(Type IVA3)

The Wepwawet standard precedes the representation of Sahura wearing the Red Crown on this large rock carving from Sinai. According to Černý,[222] "The design is good, but the execution is poor in comparison with the earlier monuments."

The cobra and canine on the standard are similar to those on the Dynasty III Wepwawet standard of Sa-nekht, also from Wadi Maghara (CAT. 17); but here Wepwawet is slimmer, and the cobra goddess is more fully expanded. The lower part of her hood, at its base, is drawn as one with the *šdšd*. Her head, under that of Wepwawet, is not tilted upward (**Type IVA3: Undetailed Hood in Front View Facing *šdšd***).

Fig. 229, Sahura, Sinai relief, Cairo JE 38569

Fig. 230, detail of Sahura Sinai relief.

Bibliography: PM VII 1951, p. 341.

---

[222]1955, p. 58.

CATALOG 63

Seated statue
From Mit Rahina
King Ne-user-ra, c. 2445-2415 B.C.
Dynasty V
Red granite: H. 0.65cm.
Cairo CG 38
(Type VIIIA1c,2e)

Seen in profile, the rounded nodule of a uraeus head projects out at the top of the king's forehead on this inscribed statue of Ne-user-ra (**Type VIIIA1: Uaeus Head; c. Worn or Unfinished Nodule**). From the front, the outlines of a wide, squat, unmarked hood are only faintly visible. The hood rises from the lower edge of the frontlet to the top of the king's low forehead in very flat relief.[223] The body of the cobra is not indicated on top of the king's head.

Fig. 231, seated statue of Ne-user-ra, Cairo CG 38.

Fig. 232, profile view.

Fig. 233, front view.

Fig. 234, three-quarter view.

Bibliography: Smith 1946, p. 55; Vandier 1958, p. 3l, pl. vi-5; Bothmer 1971, pp. 14-15, pl. ii; Bothmer 1974a, pp. 165 ff., pl. 45.

---

[223]Bothmer 1971, p. 14, n. 23 says, "Bissing calls the uraeus 'nur ein Knups', and concludes the 'the statue is unfinished'." Since then, Mr. Bothmer has studied the problem once more and has come to the conclusion that the uraeus heads are possibly worn off by the touch of numerous hands. This sculpture, like Cairo CG 4l (CAT. 34), CG 39 (CAT. 36), and CG 42 (CAT. 45), was found at Mit Rahina where it was exposed in a sanctuary or shrine, available to the public; unlike most statues remaining from the Old Kingdom, these were not set up in pyramid or valley temples where they would have been inaccessible to the common man.

CATALOG 64

Striding statue (in two parts)
From Karnak
Ne-user-ra
Dynasty V
Red granite: H., torso and head: 31cm.
                          lower portion: 56cm.
Rochester MAG 42.54 (torso and head)
Cairo CG 42003 (lower portion)
(Type VIIIA2e,3f)

B. V. Bothmer discovered that a royal bust in Rochester, New York exactly matches the lower part of a striding statue, in the Cairo Museum, which was found in the cachette at Karnak;

> "There is only the faintest line across the forehead to separate the headcloth from the face, and there is no trace of tabs in front of the ears, nor of the hood of the uraeus, which is lost."[224]

However, there do appear to be traces of the cobra hood **(Type VIIIA2: Uraeus Hood; e. Undetailed; Flat Relief; Base at Lower edge of Frontlet)** and body **(Type VIIIA3: Uraeus Body; f. Flattened Nodes on Top of King's Head)**, in the slight protuberances on the front and upper forehead of the king (Figs. 235-37).

Fig. 235, reconstituted statue, Rochester MAG 42.54 and Cairo CG 42003.

Fig. 236, front view, Rochester MAG 42.54.

Fig. 237, profile view.

Bibliography: Bothmer 1974a, pp. 165-70, pls. 44a,b, 47, 49.

---

[224]Bothmer 1974a, p. 166.

CATALOG 65

Double Statues
Ne-user-ra
Dynasty V
Provenance not known
Calcite: H. 71.8cm, W. 40.8cm
Munich ÄS 6794
(Type VIIIA1c,2e,3g)

According to Wildung,[225] this earliest known double statue of a king represents him as an older man in the statue at its right and as a young man on its left. Inscriptions for Ne-user-ra are found at the feet of each striding statue. Uraei, much better preserved than on other sculptures of Ne-user-ra, rise from the lower edge of frontlets on a plain *nemes* with pleated lappets (Figs. 238-39). On the left figure, shown in the photograph on the right, the remains of the uraeus head exhibit the same, proportionately large, rounded nodule[226] as that of the seated granite statue of the king from Mit Rahina (CAT. 63);

Fig. 238, double statues of Ne-user-ra, Munich ÄS 6794.

Fig. 239, left "older" and right "younger" details.

---

[225]1984, p.78.

[226]*v.s.*, n. 223, Cat. 63.

but on the right statue in the Munich group, at the left in the photograph, the uraeus head is broken off (**Type VIIIA1b**), and the hood (**Type VIIIA2e**) and body (Figs. 239-40) are outlined in low relief. Winding in five curves, the cobra body is similar to that on the head of Weserkaf (CAT. 52), except that its curves are tightly compressed and in low rather than bold relief(**Type VIIIA3g**).

Fig. 240, "older" and "younger" statues, from above.

The uraeus on the "older" figure is not as well preserved, but enough of the uraeus head, hood, and body remain (Figs. 239-40) to indicate that its forms were almost identical to those of the uraeus on the "younger" statue; although the uraeus body worn on the "younger" head seems to be depicted more firmly and tautly than that worn by the "older" king.

Bibliography: Wildung, 1984.

CATALOG 66
Royal busts
Ne-user-ra (?)
Dynasty V
a. From Byblos
    Red granite: H. 0.34cm.
    Beirut MN B.7395
b. Provenance not known
    Red granite: H. 0.34cm.
    Brooklyn 72.58
    (Type VIIIA1c,2e,3f)

a. Fig. 241, profile and front views of Byblos bust, Bierut MN B.7395.

a. The sculpture from Byblos, now in Beirut, is so badly damaged that comparison is difficult, but, "On the headband is the faint trace of the head and shield of the uraeus." (**Type VIIIA2e**), and, "...the only sculpture of which the Beirut bust reminds one is Cairo CG 38....",[227] the red granite seated statue, inscribed for Ne-user-ra (CAT. 63). Since there are also similarities of shape, size, and modeling to the Rochester bust (CAT. 64) and Munich double statues (CAT. 65) whose bases are inscribed, attribution of the Beirut sculpture to Ne-user-ra seems reasonable.

b. Fig. 242, front and top views, Brooklyn 72.58.

b. In front and profile views, the Brooklyn bust is strikingly like the securely dated king's heads in Rochester (CAT. 64) and Munich (CAT. 65). On the head in Brooklyn, the broad, shield-shaped uraeus, rising from the lower edge of the frontlet on a plain *nemes* with pleated lappets, is faintly outlined in low relief and more clearly visible than on the Rochester head. In addition, the Brooklyn bust has the remains of a small, very worn nodule at the top of the forehead. There may be slight indications of a cobra body on top of the king's flat head (**Type VIIIA1c,2e,3f**). Of approximately the same size and material, both the Rochester and Brooklyn heads are flat and broad with the *nemes* shaped in the same fashion. Their naturally modeled eyebrows, rounded eyeballs, wide mouths with full lips, and large ears are also very similar in shape and carving to the inscribed sculptures of Ne-user-ra.

Bibliography: a. Bothmer 1971, pp. 11-16, figs. 1-4. b. *BMA* 14, 1972-73, p. 12; Fazzini 1975, p. 30, cat. 18; Bianchi 1979, p. 22, no. 7; Romano 1983, cat. 12.

---

[227]Bothmer 1971, p. 12.

CATALOG 67

Large panel of wall relief
From Abusir pyramid temple
  of King Ne-user-ra
Dynasty V, 2390-2360 B.C.
Limestone
E. Berlin ÄMP 16100
(Type IIIB, D)

A large fragment of wall relief
shows Ne-user-ra seated, the
canine-headed Anubis before him.
Behind the king, with her arm
around his shoulder, the cobra
goddess is clearly represented in
human female form for the first
time. The epithet, "Wadjet of Pey",
is in hieroglyphs above her head.

Ne-user-ra and Wadjet wear
different types of uraei on their
foreheads. The king's serpent winds
in three or four, widely spaced
curves, entwined on a diadem or
fillet with streamers and papyrus
umbels (**Type III: On Royal or
Divine Headdress in Relief;
B. Entwined on Diadem**).

Fig. 243, large Ne-user-ra relief panel, 16100.
E. Berlin ÄMP 16100.

Fig. 244, detail of Ne-user-ra relief panel.

The puffed out cobra is short and squat, like those on Ne-user-ra's granite statues (CAT. 63, 64); it leans back against the front of the diadem which is worn under the double horned and feathered crown of Horus.[228] In this instance, the king's hair, or wig, is horizontally striated as it is on the head in sculpture attributed to Shepseskaf (CAT. 50).

The uraeus worn by Wadjet (**Type IIID: On Feathered Headdress of Goddess**) swings down from under her feather headdress in a wide U. Here too, the cobra's head and hood are short and squat; they rest against Wadjet's forehead. The relief is low, and the expert workmanship, like that of the Weserkaf and Sahura reliefs (CAT. 53, 56), is elaborately detailed.

Bibliography: PM 1974, p. 337.

CATALOG 68

Relief fragments
From Abu Ghurob,
Ne-user-ra sun temple
Dynasty V
Painted limestone: H. 31cm.
Present location not known[229]
(Type IIIB)

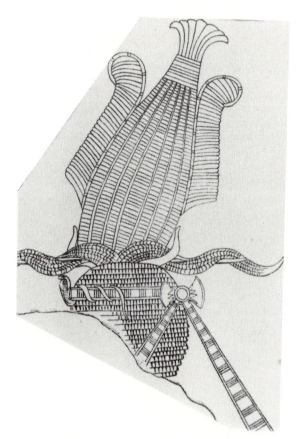

Among relief fragments from Abu Ghurob are those showing Ne-user-ra wearing the *atef* crown consisting of plumes on each side of a tall, basket-like centerpiece which is supported by cow and ram horns.[230] It is worn above a diadem with a papyrus bow (**Type IIIB**) on the short, curled wig already worn by Sneferu (CAT. 26), Weserkaf (CAT. 53), and Sahura (CAT. 56) in their reliefs, and by an unknown king on his sculpture (CAT. 78). Undoubtedly these Abu Ghurob reliefs were painted and, like Sahura's (CAT. 56), represent a diadem and uraeus of gold.

Bibliography: PM 1974, p. 318.

Fig. 245, Ne-user-ra relief fragment.

---

[228]*v.s.* CAT. 26; Fakhry 1961, p. 82.

[229]Bissing 1928 iii, pl.22 no. 352.

[230]Abubakr 1937, pp. 7-24, figs. 1-5, 17.

CATALOG 69

Relief fragments
From Abu Ghurob
  Ne-user-ra sun temple
Dynasty V
Limestone
a. Present location not known
b. Present location not known
(Type IIIA5)

The uraeus and headdress of
Ne-user-ra on these two fragments
are alike. Fragment a. (Fig. 246)
shows the king taking part in a
foundation ceremony; it was found
in the so-called chapel which adjoins
the room with reliefs of the seasons.
The second fragment, b. (Fig. 247),
was found in the Ne-user-ra corridor
surrounding the court.

On both fragments the head and
hood of the uraeus rise high away
from the king's forehead; its body
and tail form two, tightly
compressed curves (**Type III: A. On
Forehead of Plain Headdress; 5.
On** *khat* **Headdress**). A unique
representation of the uraeus, this
type is otherwise not known in the
Old Kingdom. Since, on both
fragments, the headdress worn is
clearly the *khat*,[231] it is possible that
this form of uraeus is particular to
this headcloth.

a. Fig. 246, Ne-user-ra relief fragment.

b. Fig. 247, Ne-user-ra relief fragment.

Bibliography: a. *PM* 1974, p. 316, no. 2; b. *PM* 1974, p. 318, no. 425.

[231]Eaton-Krauss 1977, pp. 21-39.

CATALOG 70

Large Panel Relief fragment
From Abusir, Ne-user-ra valley temple
Dynasty V
Limestone
E. Berlin ÄMP 17911
(Type IIIC [?])

This large fragment of painted relief
shows the lioness-headed goddess, Sekhmet,
suckling the young king who wears a uraeus
on the headband of a headdress which
appears to be similar to that of Sahura in an
almost identical scene (CAT. 55). Here,
however, the king wears no chin strap or
beard. As reconstructed in the drawing, the
uraeus head and hood are separated from
the king's head and rise above his forehead.
The body of the uraeus may form a circular
coil enclosing a small loop, as it does on
the Sahura relief panel (**Type III: C. Coiled
on King's Headdress**). The damaged
condition of the fragment makes it
impossible to determine the type of
headdress worn by the king, or the
form of the cobra rising from the headband.

Bibliography: PM 1974, p. 335.

Fig. 248, Ne-user-ra relief,
E. Berlin ÄMP 17911.

Fig. 249, drawing of relief.

CATALOG 71

Relief fragments
From Abu Ghurob,
  Ne-user-ra sun temple
Dynasty V
Limestone
a. Present location not known
b. Munich Gl 185
c. Munich Gl 183
(Type IIA6)

    These three fragments display a detailed cobra goddess on her basket behind Nekhbet as part of the *nbty* title of Ne-user-ra. Drawings[232] show that a. (Fig. 250) and c. (Fig. 252) are more detailed than b. (Fig. 251). The cobras of a. and c. have fine lines marking the ventral scales of a ventral column which extends down beyond

a. Fig. 250, Ne-user-ra relief fragment.

b. Fig. 251, relief, Munich Gl 185.

c. Fig. 252, relief, Munich Gl 183.

the base of the hood and first curve of the body, as they do in Sahura's *nbty* title cobras (CAT. 58). These cobra goddesses show the V-shaped dividing line on their hoods, and their tails slip through the back loop from behind (**Type II: A. On Basket in *nbty* Name; 6. Double Loop; Tail through Back Loop from Rear**), as do those from Sahura's pyramid temple (CAT. 58c, d).

Bibliography: PM 1974, pp. 315, 318.

---

[232]Bissing 1928, pls. 22, 26, nos. 352, 399, 403.

CATALOG 72

Relief fragment
From Abu Ghurob,
  Ne-user-ra sun temple
Dynasty V
Limestone: H. 31cm.
Göttingen AIU Z.V.I-2t (1912)
(Type IID3)

Fig. 253, Ne-user-ra relief fragment, Göttingen AIU Z.V. I-2t.[233]

Another relief fragment from Abu Ghurob shows Wadjet sitting on her basket, supported by papyrus, and presenting a šnw. She faces Horus, who sits above the Horus name of Ne-user-ra, just as she does on the Mycerinus throne (CAT. 49) and Sahura relief (CAT. 59). Here again, carved on once painted, fine limestone, the body forms double loops; and the tail slips through the back loop from the front, breaking and falling over the edge of the basket (**Type II: D. With *w3s* Scepter and *šnw*; 3. Double Loop; Tail through Back Loop from Front**), as it does on Hetep-heres I's gold encased bed canopy (CAT. 27) from two hundred years earlier. Ne-user-ra's Dynasty V example is, however, less detailed.

Bibliography: PM 1974, p. 318, no. 360.

---

[233]Bissing 1928, pl. 22, no. 360.

CATALOG 73

Column inscriptions
From Abusir,
   Ne-user-ra pyramid
   temple
Dynasty V
Red granite; H. 6m.
Cairo JE 38664
(Type IIA5, IID2)

Papyrus columns from Ne-user-ra's pyramid temple bear inscriptions with the *nbty* title (Fig. 254; **Type IIA5: Solid Loops without Detail**). Also, Wadjet of Pe is on a basket supported by papyrus; she presents the *šnw* to Ne-user-ra's cartouche (**Type IID2: Solid Double Loops with and without Detail; Supported by Papyrus**); her name is carved in hieroglyphs above her (Fig. 256).
The cobras are carved into hard stone in deep sunk relief. Due to the nature of the material and technique employed, there are only simple contours and no interior detail.

Fig. 255, column detail,
   Cairo JE 38664.

Fig. 256, column detail.

Fig. 254, drawing of
   Ne-user-ra column.

Bibliography: PM 1974, pp. 336-37.

CATALOG 74

Rock inscription
From Wadi Maghara, Sinai
Ne-user-ra
Dynasty V
Red sandstone:
  H. (of winged disk) 12.7cm.
  W. (of winged disk) 1.27m.
Cairo JE 38570
(Type IB2, IIA5, IID1)

An inscription, carved
for Ne-user-ra on sandstone
at the entrance to Wadi
Maghara, surmounted the
largest representation there.
It displays three types of
cobra goddess. The first is
at the top where, under a
starred sky, there is a
winged disk flanked by
two uraei (**Type I: With
Animal or Deity Symbol;
B. With Deity Symbol;
2. With Winged Sun Disk**).
This is the first known
example of the winged
disk protected by uraei.
The first disks with
pendent cobras, from
Sahura's pyramid temple,
do not have bird wings (CAT. 60).

Fig. 257, detail of Ne-user-ra Sinai relief, Cairo JE 38570

Fig. 258, detail of Ne-user-ra Sinai relief.

Here, added to the disk in sunk relief, there are long falcon wings in raised relief with feathered detail at their ends. Uraei on each side of the disk are carved in flat, raised relief. One of the cobra heads is damaged, but the other is long and pointed; the eye is indicated, although this detail is not shown in the drawing.[234]   Tall, fully expanded hoods do not swing away from the disk, but lean back against it.

The second type of cobra goddess is part of the *nbty* title, on her basket (**Type IIA-5: Solid Loops without Detail**), behind the vulture goddess and under the winged disk (Figs. 257, 259); the third is below the *nbty* title where Wadjet is seated on a basket behind the hieroglyphs of her name (**Type IID: 1. Solid Double Loops without Detail**). In this instance, Wadjet is behind the papyrus and bread loaf of her name which follow a cartouche containing the name of the king.

---

[234]Also, in the drawing from Gardiner-Peet 1917, pl. vi-10, the damaged head is shown on the right; however, on the relief itself, the damage is on the left.

Fig. 259, drawing of detail from Ne-user-ra Sinai inscription.

Bibliography: *PM* 1951, p. 341.

CATALOG 75

Ḥb-sd relief fragments
From Abu Ghurob,
  Ne-user-ra sun temple
Dynasty V
Limestone
a. Munich Gl 181[235]
b. Cairo JE 57110[236]
c. Cairo JE 57115[237]
d. Göttingen AIU Z.V.I-26 (1912)[238]
(Type IVA3)

a. Fig. 260, Ne-user-ra fragment, Munich Gl 181.

b. Fig. 261, drawing of fragment, Cairo JE 57110.

b. Fig. 262, *ḥb-sd* fragment in Cairo.

The Wepwawet standard is an often repeated element in the *ḥb-sd* representations from the sun temple of Ne-user-ra. In drawings of these fragments, of which only a selection is discussed here, the form of the cobra goddess is always the same, as she rises between the *šdšd* and Wepwawet (**Type IVA: Wepwawet Standard; 3. Undetailed Hood in Front View Facing *šdšd*). The front of her hood touches the *šdšd*; in these relief fragments, her head is never shown rising above it, and is well below that of the canine god.

  a. A row of standard bearers, carrying a series of Wepwawet standards attached to long poles, lead the *ḥb-sd* procession (Fig. 260).

---

[235]Bissing 1923, no. 27.

[236]*ibid*., no. 33b.

[237]*ibid*., no. 44d.

[238]Bissing 1928, pl. 1 no. 102a.

b. The same standard, carried by the personification of the *b3w* spirits of Nekhen, faces the seated king wearing a White Crown and robe. Additionally, the Wepwawet standard precedes the king as he leaves the chapel (Fig. 261) and is also seen behind the figure of the king running (Fig. 262).

c. A White-Crowned king is seated on his throne and carried on a basket sedan chair. The Wepwawet standard is facing the bearers of the king at the lower right (Fig. 263).

d. This fragment displays the standard with bow and arrows, again leading the king from his chapel (Fig. 264).

c. Fig. 263, Ne-user-ra fragment, Cairo JE 57115.   d. Fig. 264, Göttingen AIU Z.V.I-26.

Bibliography: *PM* 1974, pp. 316-17; Kaiser 1971, pp. 87-105.

CATALOG 76

Ḥb-sd relief fragments
From Abu Ghurob,
  Ne-user-ra sun temple[239]
Dynasty V
Limestone
a. Dresden SK A.745
b. E. Berlin ÄMP 20078
c. Present location not known
(Type IVA4)

There are several fragments from Abu Ghurob which show the cobra goddess in front of Wepwawet but without the *šdšd* (**Type IVA5: No** *šdšd*; **Basket-Like Appurtenance Below Uraeus**), also called a Wepwawet standard by Gardiner.[240]

a. Fig. 265, Ne-user-ra relief with drawing, Dresden SK A.745.

a. On a fragment now in Dresden, a sedan chair is brought for the king, and Wepwawet standards lead and follow the procession. There is also a Wepwawet standard with the canine god shown alone.[241]

b. The Wepwawet standard, with uraeus, but without the *šdšd*, appears again behind the

---

[239]Bissing 1923, pls. 15, 16, nos. 38, 39; 1928, pl. 1, no. 103.

[240]1957, Sign-list E/18.

[241]This standard is not listed by Gardiner.

bowman and below or alongside two fan bearers on a fragment in Berlin depicting the robing and coronation of the king.

c. Although the cobra goddess is mostly missing, the Wepwawet standard without the *šdšd* is found in a drawing of another relief fragment of the festival. Here, the standard is also without the small basket-like object under its front edge, visible in its other representations. The headless cobra goddess, with a ventral column indicated, faces a Horus standard under which is seen the top half of a bow.

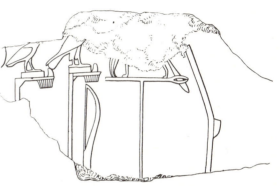

b. Fig. 266, Ne-user-ra relief,
    E. Berlin, ÄMP 20078.

c. Fig. 267, drawing of Ne-user-ra
    relief.

Bibliography: PM 1974, pp. 316-17.

CATALOG 77
Cylinder seals
Ne–user–ra
Dynasty V
a. Provenance not known
     Limestone: H. 7.5cm.
     Brooklyn 44.123.30
b. Provenance not known
     Blue frit: H. 3.9cm.
     Brooklyn 44.123.31
c. Provenance not known
     Limestone
     London UCL 11103[242]
(Type IIA1, IIE2, IIE4)
    a. A cylinder seal, oval
in diameter, shows the cobra
goddess preceding an un-
crowned Horus on top of

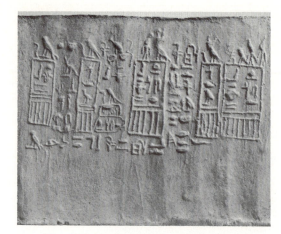

a. Fig. 268, Neferirkara and Ne–user–ra
    seal impression, Brooklyn 44.123.30.

a rectangle containing the Horus titles of Kings Neferirka–ra and Ne–user–ra (**Type II: E. Uraeus With Falcon above Horus Name; 2. With Uncrowned Falcon**). The uraeus also precedes Horus wearing the Red Crown above the Horus title of Ne–user–ra (**Type IIE4: With Red Crowned Falcon**); and the cobra goddess is seen again, formed in a simple line drawing above her basket in the *nbty* title of the king (**Type IIA1: Hieroglyphic *d* Cobra Goddess; Head and Hood in Profile**).

    b. Carved on a cylinder of blue frit, this seal shows the cobra goddess preceding an uncrowned Horus atop a rectangle containing Ne–user–ra's Horus title above a facade (**Type IIE2**).

    c. A third cylinder seal of limestone again displays the cobra goddess preced-ing an uncrowned Horus above the king's Horus title (**Type IIE2**).

b. Fig. 269, Ne–user–ra seal
      impression, Brooklyn 44.123.31.

c. Fig. 270, Ne–user–ra seal impression,
      London UCL 11103.

Bibliography: a. James 1974, no. 35, pp. 12-13, pls. iii, xix.   b. James 1974, no. 43, p. 16, pl. xxi; c. Petrie 1917, pl. ix 5.8.l; Kaplony 1981, A, pp. 235-36, B, pl. 70-1.

---

[242]Petrie 1917, pl. ix 5.6.1.

CATALOG 78

Royal head
Provenance not known
Unknown king,
Dynasty V?
Limestone: H. 13cm.
E. Berlin ÄMP 14396
   (Type VIIIC2a)

A smooth diadem or headband encircles a short, curled wig of a royal head.
At the front, the hood of a uraeus rises
in low relief from the lower edge of the
headband or diadem. Two faint, vertical
lines indicate the ventral column on the
cobra hood. The uraeus head is lost; its
body is not indicated on the rounded top
of the royal head, nor is it shown wound
around the diadem, as it is on Old
Kingdom relief[243] (Type VIII: **On Royal
Headdress in Sculpture; C. On Diadem
1. Uraeus Hood; a. Undetailed Ventral
Column, Faintly Modeled**). Since this is
the only uraeus worn on a diadem in
royal sculpture from the Old Kingdom,
its position is unique, and Schäfer's[244]
attribution to Dynasty IV or V is based
on no precedent. The head's facial
features most resemble late Dynasty V
and early Dynasty VI private sculpture.
The low, wide, shield shape of the
uraeus hood, modeled in low relief, is a
type used by Ne-user-ra on a *nemes*.
Rounded eyeballs, long plastic eyebrows,
and a wide mouth are also features of
Ne-user-ra sculpture. Shown here in
in more fully developed form, this head

Fig. 271, front view of royal head,
E. Berlin ÄMP 14396.

Fig. 272, profile view.

probably belongs to one of the later kings or princes of Dynasty V or early Dynasty VI for
whom inscribed statues have only recently been found.[245]

Bibliography: Schäfer 1904, pp. 62-65.

---

[243]See CAT. 67, 68.

[244]1904, p. 63.

[245]See recently discovered and published statues of Raneferef, Verner 1985.

CATALOG 79

Royal bust
Provenance not known
Unknown king
Late Dynasty V
  or early Dynasty VI (?)
Calcite: H. 32.5cm.
Athens NAM L.120 (4039 Rostovitz coll.)
(Type VIIID1)

The hole at the center front of the *nemes* frontlet on this bust was undoubtedly made to provide attachment for a uraeus which is now missing (**Type VIIID: Cavity; Uraeus Missing; Form Undetermined; 1. On** *nemes*).[246] Similar holes occur on sculpture of Pepy I (CAT. 90, 91). Bothmer[247] attributes this bust to early Dynasty VI, because, "The holes under the chin and above the forehead indicate that beard and uraeus were once attached....The head, however,

Fig. 273, front view of unknown king, Athens NAM 4039

is earlier than Pepy I and II whose *nemes* are always fully pleated.". Although there are no sculptures of Ne-user-ra with these holes, his three inscribed statues (CAT. 63-65) do show many of the same features, such as: long plastic eyebrows; convex eyes with modeled upper eyelids; wide, straight mouths with full lips; plain *nemes* headdresses with straight frontlets, triangular wings, and pleated or striped lappets. The torso modeling is almost identical to that on statues of Ne-user-ra. This bust, with its well preserved modeling on soft stone, seems to belong to late Dynasty V or early Dynasty VI developments in royal sculpture.

Bibliography: Bothmer 1978, pp. 51-53, pl. vi.

─────────────────────────────

[246]Not published until late 1985, a statue head recently found at the Raneferef pyramid by the Czechoslovak Institute of Egyptology excavations at Abusir also has cavities made to hold a missing uraeus; others have remains of uraei on top of the king's heads; see Verner 1985, pp. 271-73, pls. xlv-xlviii, p. 276, pls. lii-liii, p. 277, pl. liv, lv. Unfortunately, these statues were not published in time to be included in this study.

[247]1978, pl. vi.

CATALOG 80

Rock relief
Wadi Maghara, Sinai
King Isesy (Zedkara),
   c.2405-2365 B.C.
Dynasty V
Sandstone: H. 50cm. W. 68cm.
Now destroyed[248]
(Type IIIA1)

Fig. 274, Isesy Sinai relief.[249]

   The drawing reproduced here was taken from a squeeze made early in this century. It shows the much damaged, rock representation of Isesy in Wadi Maghara, Sinai. Enough remained to show the king wearing a uraeus which rises high above his head (**Type III: On Royal or Divine Headdress in Relief; A. On Forehead of Plain Headdress; 1. Hood in Profile High above Royal Head**). The cobra's form is similar to that on the forehead of Dynasty I's King Den (CAT. 10) on his small, ivory, "Smiting Plaque" from five hundred years earlier, and to that on the head of Dynasty III's King Zoser on his Sinai relief, three hundred years earlier (CAT. 19).

Bibliography: PM 1951, p. 341.

---

[248]Cerný 1955, p. 61.

[249]Gardiner-Peet 1917, pl. viii-14.

CATALOG 81

Relief fragment
From Saqqara,
 pyramid temple of Isesy,
Isesy (Zedkara)
Dynasty V
Limestone
Present location not known[250]
(Type IIID)

Wadjet appears on this limestone fragment from Isesy's pyramid temple at Saqqara in human form below her name and epithet. Her far hand is on the king's shoulder, her near hand at his elbow. She wears a uraeus on a feathered headdress which rises above and away from her forehead **(Type IIID: On Feathered Headdress of Goddess)**.

Bibliography: PM 1978, p. 424.

Fig. 275, Isesy relief from Saqqara.

[250]Illustrated in Goyon 1969, pl. xxix.

CATALOG 82

Inscriptions of Isesy (Zedkara)
Dynasty V
a. Doorjamb
   From Abusir,
      pyramid temple of Isesy
   Red granite
   E. Berlin ÄMP 17933
b. Relief fragment
   From Abusir, south field
   Calcite
   Brooklyn 64.148.2
(Type IIA3)

a. A door-jamb from Ne-user-ra's pyramid temple at Abusir was reused by Isesy, and the inscription reworked accordingly. The double loop form of the cobra goddess in the *nbty* title of the king (**Type IIA3: Double Loop; Hood Front View**) is similar to that used on red granite columns of Sahura (CAT. 61) and Ne-user-ra (CAT. 73) also from Abusir.

b. An almost identical *nbty* name cobra with the cartouche of Isesy is found on a relief fragment from the mastaba of the noble lady, Nebty, now in Brooklyn. In each of these examples the uraeus on a basket is carved in sunk relief with a sharply pointed head, widely flared hood, and solid double loops with a long tail hanging over the basket's edge.[251]

a. Fig. 276, Isesy door-jamb, E. Berlin ÄMP 17933.

---

[251]According to Verner 1982, p. 73, this relief fragment "...represents very probably the right upper part of the false-door of Khekerentnebty....".

b. Fig. 277, Nebty relief fragment.

Bibliography: a. PM 1974, p. 336. b. Duke U. 1965, no.4; Scott 1968, p. 17; James 1974, p.20, no. 52; Verner 1978, p. 158; Verner 1982, pp. 72-75, fig.3.

CATALOG 83

Relief fragment
Saqqara, Unas causeway[252]
King Unas, c.2365-2345 B.C.
Dynasty V
Limestone
Present location not known
(Type IIIA4)

Fig. 278, Unas relief.

This hitherto unpublished relief was photographed in the early 1960's at the Unas causeway where it is no longer visible. It shows Unas, his cartouche before him, wearing a close fitting, plain cap or wig, with a uraeus rising straight up from its forehead edge (**Type IIIA4: On Short Cap or Wig of King**). The uraeus head and hood are slightly separated from the royal cap. Faintly visible, the body of the serpent may twist back upon itself in tightly compressed double curves in the same style as that of a Ne-user-ra relief fragment (CAT. 69b) where he wears a pig-tailed headcloth or *khat*, rather than the short cap; or, possibly, the body forms a circular loop as it does on the head of Sahura's relief (CAT. 55). Davies[253] shows later caps with uraei as possible precursors of the Blue Crown. The Unas fragment may be an even earlier example.

At the left edge of the limestone block, not visible in Figure 278, a damaged cobra goddess is seen on her basket, supported by papyrus, and facing Horus atop the rectangle containing the king's Horus title above a facade. Unfortunately, its damaged condition prevents further analysis of the cobra's form.

Bibliography: None.

---

[252]Photograph courtesy of The Brooklyn Museum.

[253]1982, pp. 70-75.

CATALOG 84

Relief fragment
Saqqara, Unas Causeway[254]
Unas?
Limestone
Present location not known
(Type IID3)

Fig. 279, Unas causeway relief.

On this fragment, photographed at the Unas causeway causeway in 1977, but no longer visible there, Wadjet sits on her basket, supported by a detailed papyrus umbel. The hieroglyphs of her name are carved above her. She faces Horus, presenting the *w3s* scepter and *šnw* (**Type IID3: Double Loop; Tail through or across Back Loop from Front**). The form of the cobra goddess in low, crisp, raised relief is similar in its details to that on a Sahura limestone relief from Abusir (CAT. 58a) of about one hundred-fifty years earlier. However, in this example, a long tail curves up, crosses in front of the back loop, and falls over the edge of the basket. Since the names of the king are destroyed, it is impossible to be certain that the block was made for Unas, but its location and the quality of its modeling point to an attribution to his reign.

Bibliography: None.

---

[254]Photograph courtesy The Brooklyn Museum.

CATALOG 85

Palm column inscriptions
From Saqqara,
Unas pyramid temple[255]
Red Granite
Cairo JE 35131
(Type IIA5, IID2)

Four, red granite,
palm columns inscribed
for Unas were found at
his pyramid temple at
Saqqara. They are now
in Cairo (JE 35131), New
York (MMA 07. 229.2),
the Louvre (E 19959),
and the British Museum
(1385). Inscriptions
are carved in shallow
sunk relief and clearly
visible on the column
in Cairo. Two cobra
goddesses are repre-
sented; one is behind

Fig. 280, Unas column
detail, Cairo JE 35131.

Fig. 281, Unas column
detail.

Nekhbet in the *nbty* title of the king (**Type IIA5: Solid Loops without Detail**); the other is
Wadjet, supported by papyrus. She presents a lightly incised *šnw* to the cartouche of Unas
(**Type IID2: Solid Double Loops with and without Detail; Supported by Papyrus**). Both
cobras have very small heads and widely expanded hoods, bodies formed in solid double loops,
and long, thin tails hanging over the edge of their baskets.

Bibliography: PM 1978, p. 420.

---

[255]Labrousse, Lauer, Leclant 1977, p. 25, fig. 18; also see Moussa 1985, pp. 9-10, pls. 1-2 for
a granite column with similar inscriptions *in situ*, valley temple of Unas at Saqqara.

CATALOG 86

Hieroglyphic names of uraei
  in Pyramid Texts
From Saqqara, antechamber and
  sarcophagus chamber of Unas pyramid
Dynasty V
Limestone

In situ
  a. *ỉ'rwt* [Iarwet], (Utterance 249),
      Spell 265d[256]
  (Type IIF1)
  b. *nbty* [Nebty], (Utterances 44, 248),
      Spells 34, 263b[257]
  (Type IIF3)
  c. *3ḫt* [Akhet], (Utterance 256),
      Spell 302a[258]
  (Type IIF2)
  d. *ỉ'rwt* [Iarwet], (Utterances 273,
      318) Spells 396b, 511a[259]
  (Type IIF3)
  e. *sbỉ* [Sebi], (Utterance 273),
  (Type IIF4)
  f. *rnnwtt* [Rennewetet],
      (Utterances 256),
      Spells 302b, 454c[260]
  (Type IIF5)
  g. *nsrt* [Nesret],
      (Utterances 220, 221),
      Spells 194, 196[261]
  (Type IIF5)
  h. *ỉḫt–wtt* [Ikhet-Wetet],
      (Utterance 221), Spell 198[262]
  (Type IIF5)

a. Fig. 282, Iarwet, Spell 265d.

b. Fig. 283, Nebty, Spell 263.

c. Fig. 284, Akhet, Spell 302a.

---

[256]Piankoff 1968, p. 29, pl. 12.

[257]*ibid.*, pp. 29, 79, pls. 12, 61.

[258]*ibid.*, p. 34, pl.17.

[259]*ibid.*, pp. 18, 45, pls. 2, 28.

[260]*ibid.*, pp. 34, 54, pls. 19, 35.

[261]*ibid.*

[262]*ibid.*, p. 69, pl.51.

At least seven different designations for the
uraei of Unas can be found written in hieroglyphs
on the walls of his pyramid. Although each of
these representations of the cobra goddesses is
formed in a slightly different style, all have the
same small head and widely expanded hood as the
uraei on monuments of Unas from the same site
(CAT. 83-85).

a. On the west gable, center wall of the
pyramid's antechamber, "Unas... who watches over
the Uraei [Iarwet] on that night of the great flood."
Here three cobras on baskets indicate the plural.
Their bodies bend back upon themselves in two
curves with tails hanging over the edge of baskets.

b. In the two columns preceding the above,
"Unas has come to his throne which is over the
Two Goddesses {Nebty}....", Wadjet and Nekhbet
are shown sitting on their baskets in the traditional
manner; the cobra body is formed in circular
double loops.

c. On the lower, west wall of the antechamber,
"The heat of the fire of his Uraeus {Akhet}....".
Here, the tail of the cobra goddess slips through the
back loop from the front, and hangs over the edge
of the basket.

d. A different method of writing the plural of
uraeus, Iarwet, is found on the right of the east
gable in the antechamber, "...his Uraei {Iarwet}
are on his head." Here the plural is indicated
by three vertical marks under the cobra basket.
At the entrance to the antechamber, on the east
wall, "[Unas is the Nau-snake, the leading bull]
who has swallowed his seven uraei {Iarwet}, and so
his seven neck vertebrae came into being,....";
in this spell there are seven vertical marks under
the uraeus basket.   Each of these cobras making
up the plural, Iarwet, shows the serpent body in
double circular loops, as in Nebty (b).

e. In the next column on the same wall,
"The guide-serpent {Sebi} of Unas is on his
brow, ...". This is the earliest known instance
of a cobra goddess in relief that is shown without a
basket and whose body forms three curves behind
the base of her widely expanded hood, detailed
with a ventral column. The action of guiding the
king would seem to be the reason that she is not
shown coiled or looped on a basket.

f. Spell 454, on the upper east wall of the
antechamber, "The Renenutet-snake shall love
thee." The cobra goddess body is here composed of
circular, double loops; its tail makes a horizontal
line across the back coil, then breaks and falls
below the basket.

d. Fig. 285, Iarwet, Spells 396b, 511a.

e. Fig. 286, Sebi, Spell 396c.

f. Fig. 287, Rennewetet, Spells, 302b, 454c.

g. Fig. 288, Nesert, Spells 194, 196.

h. Fig. 289, Ikhet-Wetet, Spell 198.

g. In the sarcophagus chamber on the lower, east wall, "He has come to thee, Net (crown of Lower Egypt), he has come to thee, Nesert (Uraeus),...."; and again, one column over, on the upper east wall, "O Great of Magic, O Nesert (Uraeus)! Inspire fear before Unas as fear before thee...." Both cobra goddesses sit on baskets and have solid double loop bodies with tails breaking and falling over the basket edge.

h. On the upper east wall of the sarcophagus chamber, "The Great Ikhet [has given thee birth], Ikhet Utet has adorned thee, the Ikhet-Utet has given birth, the Great Ikhet [has adorned thee], for thou art indeed Horus who fought to protect his eye.". Here, again, the tall cobra goddess has a small head, widely expanded hood tapering to a narrow base, and a double loop body with the tail slipping through the back loop from the front.

Fig. 290, Unas pyramid antechamber.

Bibliography: Piankoff 1968, pp. 18, 28, 29, 34, 45, 54, 68, 69, 79, 99; pls. 12, 17, 19, 28, 35, 49, 50, 51, 61.

CATALOG 87

Relief obelisk of
   Vizier Ptah-hotep (pth-ḥtp)
From Saqqara, private tomb
Dynasty V
Limestone: H. 68cm.
Cairo CG 1308
(Type VB)

A limestone obelisk found
in a private tomb at Saqqara
has on it the engraved vizierial title, *t3yty*, and the
name, *pth-ḥtp*.[264] Six cobras
shown on top of a rectangle
in the hieroglyph, *t3yty*,
(**Type V: Architectural
Element on a Wall or in
Relief; B. In Relief atop
Hieroglyph** *t3yty*) are incised,
wiggling lines in a photograph of the obelisk, but are
five fully developed cobras
in the drawing. Attributed
to Dynasty V by Borchardt,
the relief is included here
with Dynasty V representa
tions of cobra goddesses.

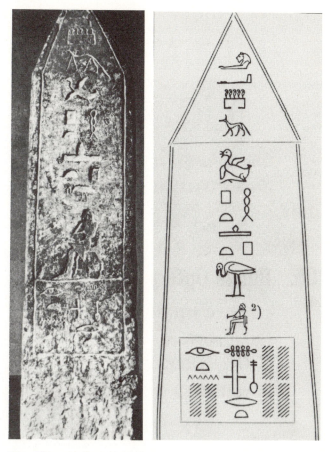

Fig. 291, obelisk of Ptah-hotep with drawing,
Cairo CG 1308.

Bibliography: Borchardt 1937 i, p.6; ii, no. 1308, pl. ii.

---

[264] Borchardt 1937 ii, no. 1308, pl. ii; Strudwick 1984, pp. 85-88 for several Dynasty V, VI
tombs of Ptah-hoteps.

9 OLD KINGDOM URAEI, DYNASTY VI, c.2345-2195 B.C.

CATALOG 88

Votive sistrum
Provenance not known
King Tety, c.2345-2323 B.C.
Dynasty VI
Calcite: H. 26.5cm.
New York MMA 26.7.1450
(Type VIIB, IIA2)

A small cobra goddess is carved fully in the round at the top of this votive sistrum (**Type VII: On Sculpture; B. Stone**). She rises in front of Horus, the falcon. The god and goddess, in their animal forms, sit on the shrine-shaped rectangle of the sistrum whose handle is in the form of a papyrus umbel and stem, a symbol for Lower Egypt and the

w3ḏ, ⚱ , of Wadjet's name.[265]

The concept and symbolism of the snake and bird are the same as those of Horus and Wadjet when they appear atop a rectangle with the Horus title of kings above a facade.[266] Seen from the front (Fig. 293), the cobra's expanded hood, under her tilted, raised head, is twice as wide as it is at its base; ventral scales are indicated

Fig. 292, side view of Tety's sistrum, New York MMA 26.7.1450.

---

[265]Hayes 1953, pp. 125-26 says the sistrum was always closely associated with the goddess Hathor. However, there is no representation or mention of the cow goddess on this sistrum, and the papyrus handle and representation of the cobra goddess would seem to indicate that, in this case, the association applies to Iaret or Wadjet rather than to Hathor who is always closely associated with the cobra goddess.

[266]cf., CAT. 48, 77,.

by small, overlapping rectangles or trapezoids; the upper hood is marked by a notched circle; and there are small, bow-like marks which suggest the Neith, (*nt*), sign[267] incised on the second ventral shield. All of these details are rather crudely worked.

Wadjet is also incised on her basket in the *nbty* title of Tety, found at the upper left on one side of the shrine (Fig. 292). Her form is the same, single loop outline (**Type IIA: On Basket in *nbty* Name; 2. Single Coil; Hood in Profile**) as that seen on Dynasty I stone vases (CAT. 13).

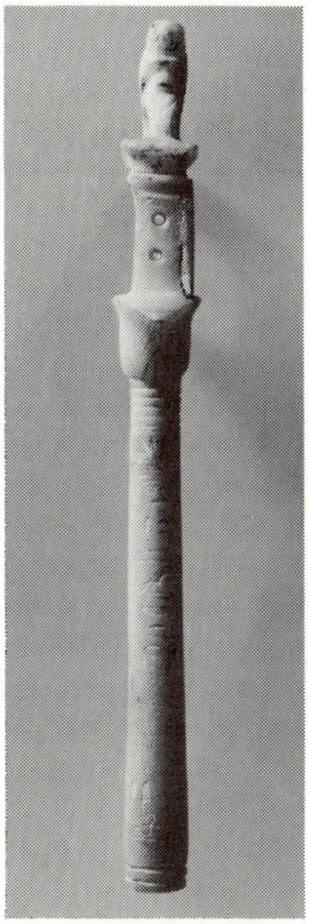

Fig. 293, front view
of Tety sistrum.

Bibliography: Hayes 1953, pp. 125-26, fig. 76.

---

[267]Gardiner 1957, Sign-list R/24.

CATALOG 89

Relief fragments
From Saqqara,
  pyramid temple of Tety
a. Limestone: H. 50cm.
   Saqqara magazine[268]
(Type IIID)
b. Painted limestone: H. 1.45m.
   In situ[269]
(Type IID3)

a. This fragment was once undoubtedly part of a *ḥb-sd* scene at Tety's
pyramid temple. Wadjet, the cobra
goddess in human form, is pictured at
the lower right wearing a feathered
headdress with a uraeus whose small head
is not tilted upward (**Type IIID: On
Feathered Headdress of Goddess**). Its
tall, slim hood is separated from the
goddess' forehead.

b. At the left, on a large fragment
from the tympanum of Tety's pyramid
temple, the familiar cobra goddess sits
on her basket supported by a clump of
papyrus. Again, she offers the *w3s*
scepter and presumably the *šnw* which is
broken off (**Type IID: With *w3s* Scepter
and *šnw*; 3. Double Loop; Tail across
or through Back Loop from Front**).
The cobra's wide hood is marked by
vertical lines of a narrow spinal column.
In the drawing of the fragment, a narrow
ring band is indicated, just below the
head, and the V mark, dividing the hood,
appears near its base. The long, slim
tail seems to cross behind the loops of
the body and falls over the basket's
edge to below its base.[270]

a. Fig. 294, Tety relief fragment.

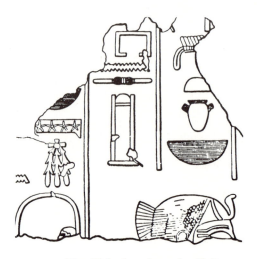

a. Fig. 295, drawing of relief.

---

[268]Lauer-Leclant 1972, pl. xxiv, fig. 23, bloc 9; Leclant, 1986 correspondence with author, says this relief is now in the Department of Antiquities magazine at Saqqara.

[269]*ibid.*, pl. xxiii A, fig. l5 b, bloc 1; Leclant, 1986 correspondence, places this block *in situ*.

[270]The goddess Nekhbet is shown in human form to the right of Wadjet on her basket; but since the top of the vulture goddess' head is missing, it is impossible to determine whether she wears a vulture or cobra head on her headdress.

b. Fig. 296, drawing of Tety relief fragment.

Bibliography: *PM* 1978, p. 394.

CATALOG 90
Kneeling statuette
Provenance not known
King Pepy I, c.2323-2283 B.C.
Dynasty VI
Green schist: H. 15.2cm.
Brooklyn 39.121
(Type VIIID1)

An inscribed statuette of Pepy I shows him
kneeling, holding a *nw* pot in each hand. This
attitude occurs in relief of Ne-user-ra who is
shown kneeling and offering *nw* pots at his
foundation deposit at Abu Ghurob (CAT. 69a).
Although, here, the king wears the *nemes* rather
than the *khat* or pig-tailed headcloth; and there is
no trace of a cobra body on the king's *nemes* (**Type
VIIID: Cavity; Uraeus Missing; Form Undetermined; 1. On Nemes**); it is obvious that a uraeus
was once fitted into the large hole at the center of
Pepy I's forehead, and also secured on top of the
head where there is a smaller hole. As Aldred[271]
suggests, the uraeus for Pepy I's head was probably
made of gold.[272]

Fig. 297, Pepy I statuette, Brooklyn 39.121.

Bibliography: BMB 1947 (March), pp. 4-5; Cooney 1949, pp. 74-76; Aldred 1949, p. 38,
pls. 60-61; Aldred 1952, no. 20; Wolf 1957, p. 174, fig. 245; Vandier 1958, pp. 36-37, pl.
viii-3; James 1974, p. 25, no. 62; Aldred 1980, pp. 94-95; Bothmer 1982, p. 37, fig. 25.

---

[271]1968, p. 38, pls. 60-61.

[272]If the body of the presumed gold uraeus formed two compressed curves, as it does on the
khat headdress in Ne-user-ra relief (CAT. 69a, b), it would resemble the later, Dynasty XII,
jewelled uraeus of Sesostris II found at Lahun (Cairo CG 52702); also, Christie's 1984, p. 44,
no. 176 illustrates a small steatite royal sphinx, holding two *nw* pots, inscribed for Mernera,
and wearing a prominent uraeus with a body which appears to wind in two open curves. The
Royal Museum of Scotland, Edinburgh, is now the owner of the sphinx, no. 1984.405.

CATALOG 91

Copper striding statue of
  King Pepy I or Prince
  Mernera
From Hierakonpolis
Dynasty VI
Copper: H. 70cm.
  H. of head 11 cm.
Cairo JE 33035
(Type VIIID2)

Fig. 298, 3/4 view.

Fig. 299, top view.

This statue is the smaller of two royal, copper statues found at Hierakonpolis. The accompanying, much larger statue carries the name of Pepy I on its base, but since it is missing a crown or headcloth and uraeus, the life-size, copper statue is not illustrated here.

There is a hole at the center front, upper edge of the small statue's headband on a plain, close fitting cap or wig. The large hole again suggests that a uraeus was once attached (**Type VIIID2**). Rough, raised relief protuberances of copper at the top of the head (Figs. 298-99) can be seen to extend to the center back of the head. These bumps of copper possibly indicate the corroded remains of the body of a uraeus similar to those on a small sphinx inscribed for Mernera, now in the Royal Museum of Scotland (1984.405)[273] or on the head of young Pepy II (CAT. 96-97).

The small copper statue is uninscribed, and Vandier[274] favors identification as a youthful Pepy I for this statue which was found with the inscribed, striding statue of Pepy I where the king is much larger and appears to be much older.

Evers,[275] Smith,[276] and Aldred[277] say the smaller statue is probably Pepy I's son, Mernera, and Smith[278] adds, "This group may commemorate a co-regency of the two kings."

Fig. 300, copper statue of Pepy I
or Mernera, Cairo JE 33035.

Bibliography: PM 1939, p. 193; Smith 1946, pp. 82-83, 1958, p. 80, pl. 53 b; Vandier 1958, pp. 34-35, pl. vii-2,3; Aldred 1968, p. 40, pl. 69, 1980, p. 94, fig. 52.

---

[273]Christie 1984, p. 44, no. 176; see n. 272.

[274]1958, p. 34.

[275]1929, p. 27.

[276]1946, p. 83.

[277]1968, p. 40, pl. 69.

[278]1946, p. 80.

CATALOG 92

Gateway fragment
From Tell Basta
Pepy I
Dynasty VI
Limestone
Cairo JE 72132
(Type IB2, IIA3,
IIIF)

Fig. 301, Pepy I gateway fragment, Cairo JE 72132.

Three types of repre-
sentation of the cobra
goddess are seen on this
limestone relief. Uraei
flanking a widely
stretched, winged sun
disk are at the top
center edge of this
large block of stone
(Type I: With Animal
or Deity Symbols;
B. With Deity Symbol;
2. With Winged Sun
Disk). Cobra heads and
expanded hoods are close
to the sides of the sun
disk, their bodies
pendent from it. The
uraeus on the right of
the disk in Figs. 301-02
lifts her head slightly,
and hangs a bit lower
than the serpent on the left.

Fig. 302, drawing of Pepy I gateway fragment.

The earliest known uraeus worn by Hathor, represented in human form, is another type
found on this gateway (Type III: On Royal or Divine Headdress in Relief; F. Pendent From
Sun Disk above Deity). The goddess, who is always closely associated with Wadjet, stands
behind the king. A cobra hangs from a double contoured disk, under the forward horn of
Hathor's headdress. It it the first known example of a uraeus which swings down and forward
in a wide arc with its head tilted slightly downward. Neither Pepy I nor Bastet, who faces
him, wears a uraeus on their crowns.

A third type of cobra goddess is found in the king's *nbty* title, at the lower right, where she
sits on her basket (Type II: In Royal Name; A. On Basket in *nbty* Name; 3. Double Loop;
Hood Front View). Her head is tilted up above an expanded hood; the unmarked body is
formed of double loops with a long tail breaking at the basket's edge.

Bibliography: Habachi 1957, pp. 14-18, fig. 2, pl. ii.

CATALOG 93

Rock inscription
Wadi Maghara, Sinai
Pepy I
Dynasty VI
Sandstone
Now destroyed[279]
(Type IB2, IIA2)

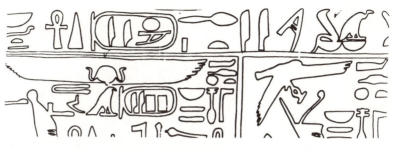

Fig. 303, drawing of Pepy I Sinai inscription.[280]

Above the familiar smiting scene in which Pepy I wears the White Crown, without uraeus, there is a winged sun disk with two uraei **(Type IB2)**, "...representing the Horus 'of Behdet'.".[281] The forms of the cobras, swinging down on each side of the sun disk, resemble those in sunk relief on the granite architrave of Sahura at Abusir (CAT. 60a); they are slim and widely separated from the sun disk, unlike the uraei on the winged disk of Ne-user-ra's Sinai inscription (CAT. 74) or Pepy I's winged disk from Tell Basta (CAT. 92).

Also seen on this drawing of Pepy I's Sinai inscription is the cobra goddess of his *nbty* title at the upper right. The cobra has the simple, single loop form of Early Dynastic vases **(Type IIA2: Single Coil Body; Head and Hood in Profile)**, inscribed with the titles of Dynasty I kings (CAT. 13). It is seen again on Tety's votive sistrum (CAT. 88) and appears on an alabaster vase of Pepy I in Brooklyn (37.70E)[282] and in inscriptions at Pepy I's pyramid.[283]

Bibliography: PM 1951, p. 342.

---

[279]Černý 1955, p. 62.

[280]Gardiner-Peet 1917, pl. viii-16.

[281]*ibid*., p. 63.

[282]James 1974, pp. 24-25, no. 61, pl. xxivB.

[283]Leclant 1970, pl. xxv 33; 1972, pl. xiii 10.

CATALOG 94

Relief fragment
From Lisht
Pepy I?
Dynasty VI
Limestone: H. 29cm., W. 28cm.
Montreal MFA 964.B.6[284]
(Type IID3)

Fig. 304, relief of Pepy I (?),
Montreal MFA 964.B.6.

A name used by both Pepy I and Pepy II, Sa-Pepy-Ra, occurs in a cartouche on this limestone relief fragment found reused at the Dynasty XII pyramid complex of Amenemhat I at Lisht.[285] Wadjet, in cobra form, is facing the king's cartouche and presenting the *w3s* scepter with the *šnw* hanging on it. She is on her basket supported by papyrus (**Type IID: With *w3s* Scepter and *šnw*; 3. Double Loop; Tail through, across, or under Back Loop from Front**). Her tall, relatively slim, but expanded hood is marked with three, V-shaped dividing lines and a narrow ventral column. The lower body is formed in double loops; its tail not visible, but it seems to cross under the back loop in the same style as that of Wadjet on a Tety fragment from Saqqara (CAT. 89b). On the Pepy I fragment the *w3s* scepter is held at a low angle, and the *šnw* is proportionately large. The form of the double coils and tail is similar to the *nbty* name cobra in the titulary of Pepy I on the right of his gateway fragment from Tell Basta (CAT. 92). Although the *nbty* cobra is not supported by papyrus, the umbels, worn on the head of the Nile god on the left in the Tell Basta fragment, are formed like the papyrus umbels supporting the cobra in this block found reused at Lisht. For these reasons, and because this fragment is also modeled in flat relief with the *w3s* scepter attached at the base of the cobra hood,[286] Hayes' attribution to Pepy I, seems at least as well founded as does Goedicke's to Pepy II.

Bibliography: Hayes 1953, p. 127, n. 2; Goedicke 1971, pp. 27-28, pl. 9.

---

[284]Formerly New York, MMA 09.180.27.

[285]Hayes 1953, p. 127, n. 2; Goedicke 1971, pp. 27-28 where he says the fragment is, "Part of the titulary of Pepy II (?)", but adds that, "...the cartouche itself gives no decisive evidence.".

[286]*ibid*., p. 28; see, also, Habachi 1957, p. 30, fig. 12, a drawing of a similarly formed cobra and scepter on a damaged fragment from the Pepy I gateway at Tell Basta.

CATALOG 95

Cylinder seal
Provenance not known
Pepy I
Dynasty VI
Steatite: H. 7.1cm.
Brooklyn 44.123.32
(Type IIE5)

On this cylinder seal of
Pepy I, Horus, the falcon,
wears "...a double feathered
crown with horns."[287] He is
preceded by a short cobra
goddess whose head and hood

Fig. 305, Pepy I cylinder seal impression and drawing,
Brooklyn 44.123.32.

are raised; both surmount a rectangle containing the hieroglyphs of the king's Horus title
above a facade (**Type II: In Royal Name;   E. With Falcon above Horus Name;   5. With
Feather and Horn Crowned Falcon**) Wadjet appears with Horus in a similar composition on
the mud sealing of King Chephren (CAT. 43), Mycerinus' throne and cylinder seal (CAT. 48,
49), and on the cylinder seals of Ne-user-ra (CAT. 77); but here the uraeus precedes a falcon
whose double feather crown is indicated. Horus wears the double feathered crown with horns,
but is unaccompanied by the cobra goddess in early Dynasty IV on the gold-cased bed canopy
of Queen Hetep-heres I (CAT. 27).

Bibliography: James 1974, no. 64, p. 26.

---

[287]James 1974, no. 64, p. 26.

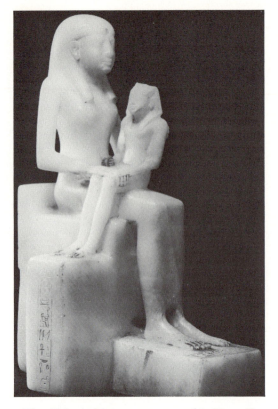

CATALOG 96

Seated statue of
  Queen Ankhnes-mery-ra
  and King Pepy II, c.2276-2193 B.C.
Provenance not known
Dynasty VI
Pepy II
Calcite: H. 39.2cm.
Brooklyn 39.119
(Type VIIIA2f, 3h)

Although his comparative size is
that of a child, Pepy II is in the
proportions and dress of an adult.
He sits on his mother's lap and
wears a *nemes* with pleated lappets.
The uraeus rises from the upper
edge of the frontlet. Narrow at its
base, the hood expands widely and
stands out in high relief at the top
of the boy-king's forehead (Figs.
306, 307; **Type VIII: On Royal
Headdress in Sculpture; A. On
Nemes; 2. Uraeus Hood;
f. Apparently Undetailed,
Badly Damaged; Base at Upper**

Fig. 306, Ankhnes-mery-ra with Pepy II,
Brooklyn 39.119.

Edge of Frontlet). Seen from the top (Fig.308), the body of the cobra winds in eight
compressed curves, ending with a very short tail (**Type VIIIA3. Uraeus Body; h. Slim
Bodied, Eight Semi-Compressed Curves**).

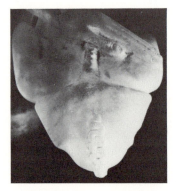

Fig. 307, front view.   Fig. 308, top view.   Fig. 309, profile view.

It has been assumed that the hole at the center of Queen Ankhnes-mery-ra's feathered
headdress held a "...vulture's head...once made of a different material and set into the mother's
forehead."[288] It is possible that a cobra head was inserted here, since there is, in relief,

another representation of a queen (CAT. 104) and several of the goddess, Wadjet (CAT. 67, 81, 89, 100b, 102), which show a serpent's head worn on the vulture headdress; however, since vulture talons are indicated in relief on top of the Queen's head, it is probable that the hole once held a separately worked vulture head.

Bibliography: Smith 1958, p. 80, pl. 56 A; Vandier 1958, pp. 38 ff., pl. viii-4; Bothmer 1974 b, pp. 30-31; Fazzini 1975, p. 31, cat. 19; Vandersleyen 1976, p. 41, no. 17; Bianchi 1979, p. 26, no. 9; Romano 1983.

---

[288]Bianchi 1979, p. 26.

CATALOG 97

Squatting statuette
From Saqqara, pyramid temple of
  Pepy II
Dynasty VI
Calcite: H. l6cm.
Cairo JE 50616
(Type VIIIB2b,3b)

An inscribed statuette of Pepy II was
found at his pyramid temple. The young
king is naked, but wears a plain, close-
fitting cap without frontlet. A large
uraeus hood rises from the edge of the
cap, at the center of the child-king's
forehead (**Type VIIIB: On Short Cap or
Wig; 2. Uraeus Hood on Short Cap or
Wig; b. Badly Damaged, Tall, Shield
Shape; Base at Edge of Plain Cap or
Wig; High Relief**); it is almost as wide
at its base as at its top (Fig. 310). The
cobra head is missing. Winding right and
left, its body forms seven curves (Fig.
311) which are less compressed than
those of the cobra on the Brooklyn Pepy
II (CAT. 96). There is a long, tapering
tail reaching to well below the crown of
the young king's head.[289]

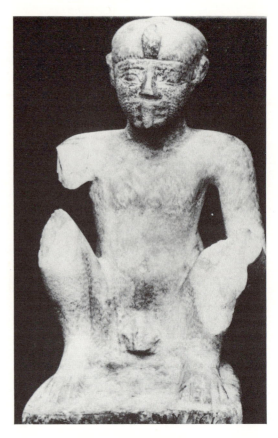

Fig. 310, Pepy II statuette, Cairo JE 50616.

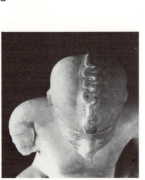

Fig. 311, top detail.

Fig. 312, 3/4 view detail.

Bibliography: PM 1978, p. 429.

---

[289]Two small alabaster bust fragments, one in Marseille at the Musée Borely no. 433, the other
in the Köfler-Truniger collection, Lucern, have uraei and facial expressions much like this
statuette in Cairo. The bust in Lucern has been attributed to Pepy II by M. Müller 1978, pp.
53-54, cat. 173a-c;   however, since this author prefers a First Intermediate Period date for
both busts, they are not cataloged in this volume.

CATALOG 98

Relief fragment
From Saqqara pyramid temple of
  Pepy II
Dynasty VI
Limestone
Present location not known
(Type IIIC)

A fragment from Pepy II's pyramid
temple shows his head with pleated
nemes and striated lappets. The uraeus
hood and head rise from just above the
forehead edge of what appears to be a
narrow frontlet. The cobra does not lean
back on the king's forehead, but is
separated from it, rising to the height of
the top of Pepy II's head. Forming a
pressed, small loop within a circular coil,
the slender body of the serpent then
curves in an undulating line to just
beyond the crown of the king's head
**(Type III: On Royal or Divine
Headdress in Relief; C. Coiled on
King's Headdress)**, similar to Sahura's
uraeus in CATALOG 55.

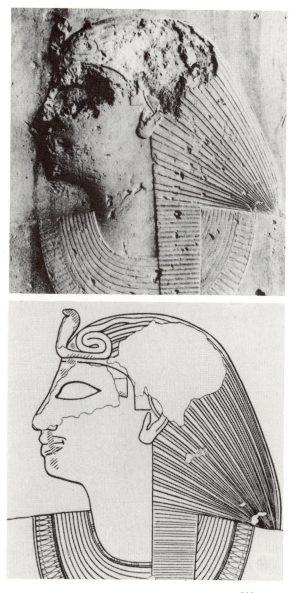

Fig. 313, Pepy II relief and drawing.[290]

Bibliography: PM 1978, p. 428.

---

[290]Jéquier 1938, pl. 63.

CATALOG 99

Relief fragments
From Saqqara pyramid temple
  and valley temple of
  Pepy II
Dynasty VI
Limestone
a. Present location not known[291]
(Type IIIC, IIIF)
b. Present location not known[292]
(Type IIIF)

a. Fig. 314, Pepy II pyramid
   temple fragments.[293]

a. In a reconstructed scene,[294] using fragments (Fig. 314) from Pepy II's pyramid temple, Hathor embraces the king who wears a uraeus on a striated headdress (**Type IIIC**). A narrow ventral column is indicated on the hood of the cobra. The thin body of the serpent forms a circular coil enclosing a loop and continues in open curves, presumably to the top of the king's head, in much the same style as an aforementioned fragment of Pepy II (CAT. 98).

Hathor wears a horned sun disk with pendant uraeus (**Type IIIF**), as she does on Pepy I's relief from Tell Basta (CAT. 92); but here the base of the uraeus hood touches Hathor's forehead; and the cobra head and hood rise close to the cow horn. An eye and ventral column are indicated.

b. Fig. 315, reconstructed scene from Pepy II valley temple.[295]

b. Three fragments from the valley temple of Pepy II have been reconstructed in a drawing to show Hathor in a procession of deities. Again, she wears the horned sun disk with pendent uraeus which touches her forehead (Fig. 315; **Type IIIF**).

Bibliography: PM 1978, pp. 426-27.

---

[291]Jéquier 1938, pls. 8, 10.

[292]*ibid.*, pl. 21.

[293]*ibid.*, pl. 10.

[294]*ibid.*, pl. 8.

[295]*ibid.*, pl. 21.

CATALOG 100

Tablets of wood with
  plaster inlay
From Saqqara
Pepy II
Dynasty VI
a. Painted and gilded plaster
      on wood:[296] H. approx. 10cm.
    Cairo JE 62950
    (Type IIIF, VI)
b. Gilded plaster
      on wood: H. 10cm.
    Cairo CG 53836
    (Type IIID)

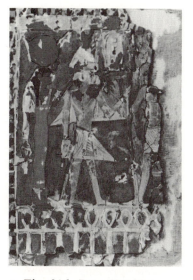

a. Fig. 316, Pepy II tablet,
   Cairo JE 62950.

   a. Two types of uraei are represented on this
small tablet found by Jequier in a private tomb
near the pyramid of the king.[297] The first
hangs down from Hathor's horned sun disk
touching her forehead (**Type IIIF**) in the same
form as the Hathor uraeus on the Pepy II
relief of CATALOG 99. Faint traces of gilt
remain on the inlaid surface of the plaster
serpent.
   The second type of cobra goddess is seen
at the lower edges of Pepy II's blue sash,
where two cobras rise up, one on each side,
at the lower edge of the sash panel (**Type
VI: On Royal Clothing**). Uraei may have
been worn on royal clothing earlier than
Dynasty VI, but these tiny representations
are the first preserved example of a type of
uraeus cobra which is frequently used in the
Middle and New Kingdom.
   b. Another small tablet of wood in the
Cairo Museum is covered with gilded plaster. It was found early in this century in
debris near Tety's pyramid.[298] Pepy II's
name, Nefer-ka-ra, is in a cartouche at the
top of the plaque opposite the hieroglyphs
of Wadjet's name. The cobra goddess, in
human form, stands before the king holding
his hand and raising an 'nḥ to his nose.

b. Fig. 317, Pepy II tablet, Cairo CG 53836.

---

[296]Jéquier 1934, p. 78, pl. 1; Smith 1946, p. 205.

[297]Jéquier,*ibid.*.

[298]Quibell 1907, pl. v.

On her head she wears the plumage of a vulture with a proportionately large cobra hood and head rising from her forehead (**Type IIID: On Feathered Headdress of Goddess**).

Bibliography: a. Jéquier 1934, p. 78, pl. i; Jéquier 1940, frontispiece; Smith 1946, p. 205.
    b. *PM* 1978, p. 395.

CATALOG 101

Quartzite relief fragment
From Saqqara pyramid temple of Pepy II
Dynasty VI
Quartzite
In situ?[299]
(Type IIIF)

In the court of Pepy II's pyramid temple, a fragmentary pillar or door-jamb was found, on which the king and Horus, with a falcon's head and human body, are carved in sunk relief. Above the falcon god, there is a sun disk and - barely visible on the badly pitted stone - what appears to be the first example of a pendant uraeus above the beak of the god Horus represented with a man's body (**Type IIIF; Pendent From Sun Disk above Deity**).

The uraeus hangs in a wide arc, like that on Hathor's horned sun disk in the relief from Pepy I's temple at Tell Basta (CAT. 92).

Fig. 318, Pepy II quartzite relief.

Bibliography: PM 1978, p. 427.

---

[299]Jéquier 1927, p. 56, pl. iii; Jéquier 1940, fig. 9, pl. 45, pp. 23-24.

CATALOG 102

From Saqqara pyramid temple of
  Pepy II
Dynasty VI
Limestone
a. Present location not known[300]
b. Present location not known[301]
(Type IIID)

Two fragments from Pepy II's
pyramid temple show Wadjet as a
woman who wears a uraeus rising
from the forehead of her vulture
headdress (**Type IIID; On Feathered
Headdress of Goddess**).
    a. On a fragment which is part of
this reconstructed scene, only the
head and upper hood of a uraeus
remain beneath the name and
epithet of Wadjet. Presumably
they rise from Wadjet's head where
only the top portion remains. She
wears the feathered headdress.
    b. This fragment shows the bird's
feathering clearly marked and, although the
uraeus hood is damaged at its base, it is
clear that a cobra head and hood rise above
the goddess' head.

a. Fig. 319, reconstructed relief.

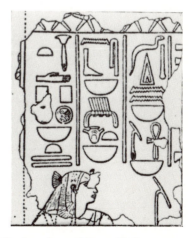

b. Fig. 320, drawing of Pepy II fragment.

Bibliography: PM 1978, p. 427.

---

[300]Jéquier 1938, pl. 36.

[301]*ibid.*, pl. 36.

CATALOG 103

Rock inscription
Wadi Maghara, Sinai
Pepy II
Dynasty VI
Sandstone
Formerly *in situ*[302]
(Type IIIA2)

Fig. 321, detail of Pepy II Sinai inscription.[304]

Fortunately preserved in British Museum squeezes and drawings, this inscription which is said to have now been destroyed, shows "...only [one] pictorial representation..., the small figure of the Queen-Mother 'Ankhnesmeryre'."[303]   The queen is shown holding a papyrus umbel in one hand and an *'nḫ*-sign in the other.   The uraeus rises from her forehead in the same, simple form (**Type III: On Royal or Divine Headdress in Relief; A. On Forehead of Plain Headdress; 2. On Short Cap or Wig of Queen Mother**) as that on the foreheads of Zoser and Isesy in their inscriptions in Sinai (CAT. 19, 80).

Ankhnesmeryra, like the goddess, Wadjet, in Pepy II relief (CAT. 100a, b; 102a), wears the uraeus and is depicted with an *'nḫ*; here the queen also holds a papyrus to her nose and her name, rather than Wadjet's, appears above the figure's head.   This representation of Queen Ankhnes-mery-ra in the Sinai is the first record of a queen wearing the uraeus and carrying an *'nḫ* and papyrus.

Bibliography: PM 1951, p. 342.

---

[302]Now destroyed, according to Černý 1955, p. 64.

[303]Černý, *op. cit.*, p. 64.

[304]Gardiner-Peet 1917, pl. ix 17.

CATALOG 104

Relief fragment
Saqqara, pyramid
  of Neith
Queen Neith,
  Wife of Pepy II
Dynasty VI
Limestone
Present location
  not known[305]
(Type IIIE)

A fragment from
the entrance hall
of Neith's pyramid
temple depicts
the daughter of
Pepy I, half-
sister and wife
of Pepy II.[306]
This is the
earliest known

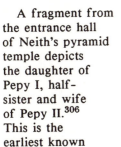

Fig. 322, relief fragment and drawing of Neith.

representation of a queen wearing the feather headdress with uraeus head and hood (**Type III: On Royal or Divine Headdress in Relief; E. On Feathered Headdress of Queen**). The cobra is widely separated from the queen's forehead.

Bibliography: *PM* 1978, p. 431.

---

[305]Jéquier 1933, pls. iv, v.

[306]Hayes 1953, p. 129.

CATALOG 105

Relief fragments
From Saqqara pyramid
Pepy II
Dynasty VI
Limestone
a. Present location not known[307]
    (Type IIIA3)
b. Present location not known.
    (Type IIIA4)

These small fragments from Pepy II's
pyramid show small, royal heads similar
to those on fragments which represent
Sahura's coronation scenes from Abusir
(CAT. 57).

a. The head carried on a standard wears
a headdress which falls behind the king's
shoulders with a proportionately large
uraeus rising from under the headcloth on
the king's forehead (**Type IIIA; On
Forehead of Plain Headdress; 3. On
King's Head Carried on Standard**).

b. Another small head wears a beard
strapped onto or under a plain cap or wig
with lappets similar to that worn by
Sahura's son (CAT. 57b). However, here,
the uraeus rises high above and away from
the prince's head, and the body of the cobra
is visible on the forehead portion of the
of the headdress (**Type IIIA4; On Short
Cap or Wig of King**).

Bibliography: PM 1978, p. 426-27.

a. Fig. 323, Pepy II fragment.

b. Fig. 324, Pepy II fragment.

---

[307]Jéquier 1938, pls. 9, 42.

CATALOG 106

Relief fragments
From Saqqara pyramid
Pepy II
Dynasty VI
a. Limestone
     Present location not known[308]
     (Type IIA6, D4)
b. Limestone
     Present location not known[309]
     (Type IID4)

Each of these scenes,
reconstructed from fragments
found at Pepy II's pyramid,
shows Wadjet, the cobra
goddess, her basket supported
by a papyrus clump, opposite
Horus on a rectangle
containing the Horus name
and a facade. Wadjet offers
Horus the *w3s* scepter with a
šnw hanging on it. In each
fragment the tail of the cobra
goddess slips through the
back loop of her body from
behind, (**Type IID4; Double
Loop; Tail through Back
Loop from Rear**).

a. Behind the Horus
name, on the left, there are
fragments showing the lower
portion of a *nbty* name cobra
whose tail also appears to slip
through the back loop from
the rear (Type IIA-6). The
cobra supported by papyrus,
offering the scepter and *šnw*,
has an enlarged ventral scale
marked with a *nt*-sign (?) at
mid-point on the ventral
column. There are also
scalloped double lines
outlining the interior

a. Fig. 325, Pepy II fragments and drawing.[310]

---

[308]Jéquier 1938, pls. 50, 81, 83, 84.

[309]*ibib.*, pl. 50.

of a wide hood, and a large eye is indicated on the comparatively large, pointed head. These
fragments also depict a very long *w3s* scepter with a small *šnw* sign hanging from it, quite
different in their forms from those offered by Wadjet on the Pepy I (?) block from Lisht
(CAT. 94).

b. A scene reconstructed from
two fragments represents Wadjet on
a papyrus clump of three umbels,
flanked by two upright buds and
two bent buds on the outside. A
small fragment clearly shows her
body curved in double loops with
the tail slipping through the back
loop from behind; as it does on
Sahura fragments (CAT. 58c, d).

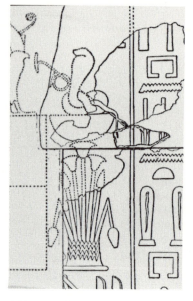

b. Fig. 326, drawing of Pepy II fragments.[311]

Bibliography: PM 1978, p. 428.

---

[310]*ibid.*, pls. 83, 84.

[311]*ibid.*, pl. 50.

CATALOG 107

Relief fragment
From Saqqara pyramid temple
Pepy II
Limestone
Present location not known[312]
(Type IVA3)

Fig. 327, drawing of Pepy II fragment.[313]

A fragment from the vestibule of Pepy II's pyramid temple shows the cobra goddess between the *šdšd* and the canine god on a Wepwawet standard (**Type IV: On Standard; A. Wepwawet Standard; 3. Undetailed Hood in Front View Facing *šdšd***). The front of the cobra's widely expanded hood touches the *šdšd*, and her back is against Wepwawet's upper leg in a somewhat crowded composition. Her oval head shows the cranial bump, and it is marked with a large eye.

Bibliography: PM 1978, p. 427.

---

[312]Jéquier 1940, pl. 40.

[313]*ibid.*

CATALOG 108

Relief fragments
From Saqqara pyramid
Pepy II
Dynasty VI
Limestone
Present location not known[314]
(Type IVB3)

Fig. 328, drawing of Pepy II fragments.

These small fragments, from the vestibule to the court of Pepy II's pyramid temple, show a Wadjet standard with the cobra goddess entwined around a pole or stem (**Type IVB: Wadjet Standard; 3. With** *w3s* **Scepter on Papyrus ?**) and to the right, the tops of a bow and staff with bird feathers behind them (Fig. 328).

In the drawing of a recon- tructed scene, the bow and staff are carried by the king wearing the White Crown without uraeus (Fig. 329). Although the cobra goddess, wound around the pole, is reminiscent of Sahura's Wadjet standard in sunk relief on a red granite doorway from Abusir, the form of the serpent is here quite different from that shown in the doorway reconstruction (CAT. 59a). The Pepy II fragment depicts Wadjet's lower body arching back from the base base of the hood to form a wide loop; it then swings forward

Fig. 329, drawing of Pepy II fragments
in reconstructed scene.

and winds around the standard in two open curves. The tail is not visible, nor are the ends of the standard. A *w3s* scepter projects out at the top of the cobra goddess' hood. It is impossible to tell, from what remains, whether Wadjet is entwined on a *w3s* scepter or a papyrus stem.

Dating from more than a century later, there are three large, limestone blocks at the Metropolitan Museum of Art in New York showing similar Wadjet standards with bent papyrus umbels at the top end of the staffs. The first is from Deir el Bahari and belonged to the reign of Dynasty XI's King Mentuhotep II, c.2065-2014.[315] Two painted blocks are from

---

[314]*ibid.*, pls 31, 30.

Fig. 330, relief of Amenemhet I,
New York, MMA 09.180.113

Fig. 331, relief of Amenemhet I,
New York, MMA 08.200.10[316]

the Dynasty XII pyramid of Amenemhat I, c.1994-1964 B.C., at Lisht (Figs. 330-31).

In later periods, Wadjet is also shown entwined on the lily of Upper Egypt and the papyrus of Lower Egypt, wearing the *atef* or White and Red Crowns. Wadjet standards continue to be shown in Egyptian relief through Roman times.[317] These standards were probably the prototypes for the concept, symbolism, and design of Moses' brazen serpent on a pole with which he led the Israelites from Egypt and for the caduceus of modern medicine,[318] although these emblems use different snakes.

Bibliography: *PM* 1978, p. 426; Hayes 1953, pp. 172-73, fig. 104.

---

[315]MMA 08.200.6.

[316]Hayes 1953, pp. 172-73, fig. 104.

[317]*e.g.*, door-jambs of the Temple of Dendur, now at The Metropolitan Museum of Art; *BMMA* 36 (1978), p. 52, fig. 37.

[318]*v.s.*, p. 3; Minton and Minton 1969, p. 154, 160

CATALOG 109

Relief fragments
From Saqqara pyramid temple
Pepy II
Dynasty VI
Limestone
Present location not known[319]
(Type VB)

a. Fig. 332, Pepy II fragments.

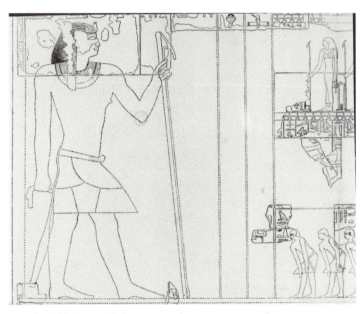

b. Fig. 333 Pepy II fragments in reconstructed scene.

a. At the lower right of these fragments (Fig. 332) there are six cobras with hoods raised, heads facing left (**Type V: Architectural Element; B. In Relief atop Hieroglyph,** *t3yty*). The series of cobras undoubtedly form the top of the hieroglyph, *t3yty*, as they do on the Dynasty IV?, offering stands of Vizier Sethu (CAT. 51), on the Dynasty V incised obelisk of Vizier Ptah-hotep (CAT. 87), and the Dynasty VI, obelisk of Prince Tety (CAT. 111).

b. It is the vizier of Pepy II who leads the bowing officials in the bottom register of the reconstructed scene (Fig. 333).

Bibliography: PM 1978, p. 428.

---

[319]Jéquier 1938, pls. 50, 51.

CATALOG 110

Cylinder seal
Provenance not known
Pepy II
Dynasty VI
Steatite: H. 12.5mm.
London BM 25422
(Type IIE5)

A falcon and cobra appear together
again on this finely executed seal of
Pepy II. The cobra goddess precedes
Horus who wears a crown of double
feathers and curving horns (**Type II:
In Royal Name; E. With Falcon above
Horus Name; 5. With Feather and Horn
Crowned Falcon**). The composition of
Horus name, with Wadjet and a feather
and horn crowned Horus on top of a
rectangle above the Horus name and
facade, is similar to that on a
cylinder seal of Pepy I (CAT. 95),
but Pepy II's seal is more carefully
modeled. H. Müller[320]says of these
seals, which show Horus with a
feathered headdress, "Die bildlichen
Darstellungen des Horus mit dem

Fig. 334, cylinder seal impression,
London BM 25422.[321]

Federnpaar sind ebenso haufig - der goldene Falkenkopf aus Hierakonpolis, der Titel auf
unserem Siegel hier u. a. m. -, wie ihre schriftliche Erwahnung in den Texten aller Zeiten."

Bibliography: Hall 1913, no. 2602; Müller 1938, pp. 33-35, fig. 65; Petrie 1917, pl. x-4;
    Kaplony 1981, A-p. 376, B-pl. 102.

---

[320]1938, p. 34.

[321]Petrie 1917, pl. x-4.

CATALOG 111

Obelisk of Vizier Tety (*tti*)
From Saqqara
Late Dynasty VI
Limestone
Cairo JE 63404
(Type VB)

This small obelisk is one of two found by Jéquier[322] flanking the doorway to the tomb of Tety at Saqqara. Both display the hieroglyph, *t3yty*, in sunk relief. Titles and the name of the vizier are given but his lineage is not mentioned; Jequier, attributes the tomb to late Dynasty VI or slightly later; Baer[323] and Strudwick[324] to the end of Pepy II's reign.

Hieroglyphs are deeply carved and competently done on the obelisk.

Fig. 335, obelisk with *t3yty* detail, Cairo JE 63404.

Heads and expanded hoods of six cobras are on top of the sign for palace or shrine to which a ledge has been added, possibly to indicate a roof line or the uppermost course of a wall[325] **(Type VB: In Relief atop Hieroglyph, *t3yty*).**   All six cobras lean back, and their heads are carefully modeled. It is interesting that a frieze of cobras shown in a *t3yty*-sign attributed to Dynasty IV (CAT. 51) has four cobras; while another, attributed to Dynasty V (CAT. 87) has six; and this obelisk, attributed to Dynasty VI, has six cobras in the hieroglyphic vizieral title. The number of cobras cannot, of course, be used as a dating criteria;[326] however, a ledge or projection added to the hieroglyph *t3yty* does not occur until very late in the Old Kingdom.

Bibliography: Jéquier 1934, pp. 76-78, pl. i.

---

[322]1934, pp. 76-78, pl. i.

[323]1960, p. 152.

[324]1985, p. 158.

[325]Strudwick, *ibid.*, pp. 304-305 for a different explanation of this ledge.

[326]*ibid.*, where Strudwick also suggests that omission of the *t3yty* hieroglyph in a vizier's tomb is "...doubtles to avoid the presence of potentially hostile creatures in the burial chamber....". This can hardly be true, since so many cobra goddesses are preserved in other tombs, both royal and private of all periods, and although other "potentially hostile" animals have been rendered harmless, cobra goddesses are left undisturbed.

CATALOG 112

Uraeus worn on diadem
  of gold-headed falcon
From Hierakonpolis
Late Old Kingdom (?)
Gold: H. of uraeus,
      approx. 7.5cm.
Cairo CG 52701
(Type VIIC)

Attached to a diadem
surmounted by open-work
plumes, this is the first
preserved uraeus of gold
(**Type VII: Sculpture; C.
Gold**). It is worn on the
hammered gold head of a
falcon, and was found in a,

"...small brick temple,
which appears to be of
the XIIth dynasty,...in
the middle of the central
chamber, a square brick-
lined pit, in which was
placed a figure of the
mummified hawk which
was the god of Hier-
akonpolis ...; the body
was of bronze plates
over-laid on wood....we
may say that as the
great falcon head with
uraeus and diadem, copper
group of Pepy and his
son [CAT. 91] was likewise
buried beneath this temple,
it seems probable that the
hawk may be of the same age.".[327]

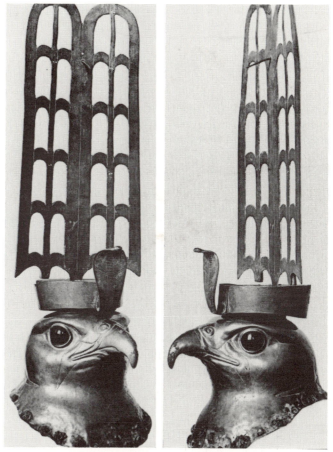

Fig. 336, falcon head with uraeus and diadem
3/4 and profile view, Cairo CG 52701.

---

[327]Quibell - Green 1900, p. ll; B. Adams 1974, endpiece maps show the findspot of the
falcon, but her supplement to the publications of Petrie, Quibell, and Green sheds no further
light on its date.

Although this attribution has been questioned by Hostens-Deleu,[328] Rössler-Kohler,[329] and Eaton-Krauss,[330] it has been generally attributed to Dynasty VI by W. S. Smith,[331] Vandier,[332] and most other scholars.

There are ample Old Kingdom precedents for the concept, design, and workmanship of this monument,[333] and, "When we find the piece associated with another complicated copper work of Dyn. VI, it is reasonable to assume that the hawk is of the same date.".[334] The diadem and uraeus of the

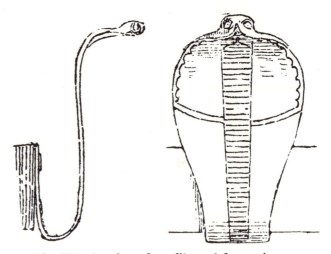

Fig. 337, drawing of profile and front view.

gold falcon head are also cataloged here with Dynasty VI uraei. Beginning with Dynasty IV's first king, Sneferu, c.2570-2545 B.C., Old Kingdom relief shows kings, who were the earthly counterparts of Horus, wearing diadems with uraei below double feathered and horned headdresses (CAT. 26, 53, 56, 67, 68); an Old Kingdom limestone head of an unknown king wears a uraeus on a diadem (CAT. 78); and the falcon, Horus, wears the two feathers as early as Hetep-heres I, on her gold-cased bed canopy (CAT. 27; Fig. 129a, b), as well as on Dynasty VI cylinder seals (CAT. 95, 110).

The proportions of the small uraeus head and wide, flaring hood which tapers to its base, only one-half as wide (Figs. 336-37, 339), are common in late Old Kingdom uraei in relief and sculpture. The hood is marked by chasing in a manner also seen in early Old Kingdom relief; the earliest known are details hammered and chased in gold on Hetep-heres I's bed canopy to form cobra goddesses as a part of Sneferu's *nbty* titles (CAT. 27).

The three-dimensional, solid gold uraeus on this diadem also has markings indicating ventral scales; a broad, V-shaped band dividing the upper one-third of the hood; and a scalloped, tooth-like line at its upper edges. Small eyes, as well as a long triangular mouth and jaw are skillfully modeled and chased. Seen in three-quarter, profile, and front view (Figs. 336-37), the carefully modeled, small head appears to tilt very slightly upward.

In the simplicity and nobility of its style, the uraeus of the gold falcon of Hierakonpolis is more in keeping with the sculptural canons of the Old Kingdom than with those of the Middle or New Kingdoms. Comparison of the uraeus from Hierakonpolis with that of the gold and

---

[328]1971, p. 20.

[329]1978, pp. 117 ff.

[330]1981, pp. 15-18.

[331]1946, p. 83.

[332]1948, pp. 35-36.

[333]Aldred 1971, p. 88, *passim*.

[334]Smith 1946, p. 83.

jeweled diadem from Lahun (Figs. 338-39) or the uraeus without diadem from the same location,[335] or a uraeus of Tutankhamun[336] show that the cast gold cobra goddess from Hierakonpolis has a much smaller head and a considerably wider hood; it is also of simpler and more naturalistic design.

Fig. 338, detail of Lahun diadem, Dynasty XII, Cairo CG 52641.[337]

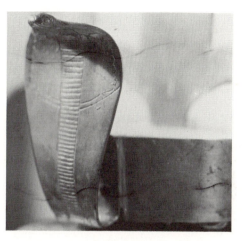

Fig. 339, detail of Hierakonpolis gold uraeus, Cairo CG 52701.

Bibliography: PM 1962, p. 191; Smith 1946, pp. 83-84; Dunham 1946, fig. 9; Hayes 1947, pp. 3-ll; 1953, p. 347; Vandier 1948, pp. 35-36, pl. viii-5; Hostens-Deleu 1971, p. 20; Adams 1974, endpiece maps; Rössler-Köhler 1978, pp. 117 ff.; Eaton-Krauss 1981, pp. 15-18.

---

[335]Cairo CG 52702.

[336]Cairo T 256, 4-0

[337]Cairo CG 52641.

10   CONCLUSIONS AND SUMMARY OF TYPES

CONCLUSIONS

From the beginning of kingship and a state religion, c. 3000 B.C., Egyptian kings and priests continued to give expression to the already well established belief in the cobra as a powerful, divine spirit or goddess. Their artisans represented the cobra as a protecting, royal-divine symbol of life and order bestowed by the creator god, carried out and maintained by his son, Horus the king, who united Upper and Lower Egypt. Presence of the vulture (Nekhbet) and cobra (Wadjet) goddesses combined (Nebty) with Horus or the king of Upper and Lower Egypt signified the legitimacy of the crown as well as protection of it; alone, a cobra goddess could insure continued power and vitality (Aket, Seby, Nesret), as well as prosperity and order (Rennewtet, Maat); and worn on the forehead of kings, queens, gods, and goddesses she signified all of these advantageous qualities. The cobra symbol - *i'rt* [Iaret], "The Rising One", in ancient Egyptian, *ouraios* in Greek, or uraeus in Latin and English, acquired many different names through the millennia of ancient Egyptian mythological - religious - political history. Wadjet in human form is often represented as the attractive female companion of the king - Horus in human form; and a cobra became the determinative hieroglyph for the written names of all female goddesses: as mythological mother, wife, or sister, a cobra goddess could be all three in one (CHAP. I, pp. 5-11). A prehistoric goddess and symbol of the fertile delta of Lower Egypt, she became the quintessential sign for the king's sovereignty over that region, as well as a symbol for protection, power, and beneficence. The cobra is subtly present in the iconography of royal ancient Egyptian art from its beginnings, c.3200 B.C., until its end, c.30 B.C..

Probably totemic in origin, the earliest known cobras in Egyptian art are very small, naturalistically accurate, and well executed. It is likely that the first of these is represented in an abstract Z form on an Amratian, rhomboid, slate palette, c.4000 B.C. (Fig. 61); however, since the abstract Z cannot be proved to be a cobra, CATALOG entries begin with late Predynastic handles, c.3200-3000 B.C., whose serpents are clearly cobras with raised heads and hoods shown in profile. Also represented preceding elephants, these late Predynastic cobras lead processions of animals on handles of knives, a comb, and a mace (CAT. 1-5). Thereafter, a simple, hieroglyphic _d_ cobra with a vulture, both on baskets as "The Two Mistresses", form the first king's *nbty* name (CAT. 6) with religious - political significance. Since every king who ruled Upper and Lower Egypt used this name, the cobra goddess of Lower Egypt on her basket is a constant part of royal iconography. Her characteristic form of small, profiled head, wide frontal hood, and double looped body above a basket, first seen at the end of Dynasty II (CAT. 14-15), also occurs in the Pyramid Texts of Dynasties V (CAT. 86) and VI.

The most carefully detailed and executed cobras of any type are *nbty* name uraei of early Dynasty IV (CAT. 27). They become the basic prototype for representation of the cobra symbol, with minor variations, for the remainder of ancient Egyptian art history. Basic forms and details for the cobra symbol were devised in Dynasty III and early Dynasty IV in a naturalistically elegant style that was never to be improved.

Wadjet, goddess of Lower Egypt, identified by her name in hieroglyphs behind her, first appears in the form of a cobra on a basket, as she offers a *šnw* and *w3s* scepter to the cartouche of Sneferu (CAT. 28). On a throne of Mycerinus (CAT. 48) Wadjet's basket is supported by papyrus, her name written above her; she offers the *w3s* scepter to another cobra (divine queen) preceding a falcon (divine Horus, the king) atop the Horus name of Mycerinus, a form of royal titulary often seen thereafter.

The earliest known theanthropic depiction of a goddess is that of Wadjet on a large relief panel of Ne-user-ra with her name written above her human form (CAT. 67). The first preserved representation of a queen wearing a feathered headdress with uraeus much like Wadjet's belongs to Queen Neith, wife (?) of Pepy II (CAT. 104). The earliest known representation of the goddess Hathor as a human figure with horned disk and uraeus occurs in the reign of Pepy I (CAT. 92).

Kings, pictured in relief, beginning with Den in Dynasty I, wear the uraeus on a variety of headdresses including a plain *nemes* (CAT. 10, 19, 55, 70, 80), a striped *nemes* (CAT. 98, 99), a plain cap or wig (CAT. 57, 83, 105), a *khat* (CAT. 69), a diadem worn below a double horned and plumed crown (CAT. 26, 53, 56, 67, 68).

The earliest known uraeus on sculpture occurs on quartzite heads attributed to Radedef, third king of Dynasty IV (CAT. 30-31). These uraei and most of those on sculpture of the Old Kingdom are worn on a plain *nemes* with pleated lappets. Found at Mycerinus' pyramid complex, there is a head wearing a striped *nemes* with uraeus (CAT. 47), as also occurs on the Great Sphinx (CAT. 41). Another head with striated hair or wig wears a cobra placed directly upon it (CAT. 50). Also belonging to the Old Kingdom period is an unknown king's head with short, curled hair or wig wearing a diadem with uraeus hood (CAT. 78), but no trace of the snake's body.[338] No White or Red Crown of the Early Dynastic or Old Kingdom periods is shown with a uraeus in sculpture or relief. There are also no preserved sculptures of gods as human figures nor of kings as gods wearing the uraeus from these periods; however, on a badly damaged quartzite relief there is, from late Dynasty VI, representation of a falcon-headed, man-god with a disk and possibly pendent uraeus above his head (CAT. 101).

No queen is pictured wearing a uraeus until the Dynasty VI Sinai relief of Pepy II where his mother, Ankhnesmeryra, is shown with a cobra rising from a close fitting cap (CAT. 103). Neith, wife (?) of Pepy II, is the first queen to be shown wearing the vulture headdress with uraeus (CAT. 104), although the goddess Wadjet, in human form is represented wearing the elaborately feathered head covering as early as the reign of Ne-user-ra (CAT. 67). Beginning in the reign of Pepy I, Hathor is also shown in human form wearing a uraeus pendent from her horned disk crown (CAT. 92). There are no preserved statues of queens nor of human figured goddesses who wear uraei from the Early Dynastic or Old Kingdom periods.

In general, styles of uraei worn by individual kings as depicted in relief and on their statues seem to be related. Thus, the tall, prominent uraeus worn by Sahura on his dyad statue (CAT. 54) is also seen rising high and away from the king's forehead in his relief (CAT. 55, 56). Uraei worn by Ne-user-ra in his relief are relatively short; their heads and hoods lie back close to the king's forehead (CAT. 67-70); and on Ne-user-ra statues and fragments of statues uraei are also short and not at all prominent (CAT. 65-66).

Although style is difficult to define verbally, careful visual scrutiny reveals that each king for whom we have inscribed monuments had his own style of uraei on his statues and in relief. Usually, this style is related to that of the preceding monarch, but each king's uraeus forms seem to have their own distinctive characteristics. For example on statue heads: thin uraei bodies winding in four open curves with tall, plain, or marked hoods in low relief probably belong to Chephren (CAT. 32, 33, 39c,d, 40), while a uraeus body of eight curves with a large prominent hood in high relief are no doubt of much later date and most likely

---

[338]See notes 245-46, *supra*, for reference to recently excavated and published Dynasty V royal sculpture at Abusir wearing uraei.

belong to Pepy II (CAT. 96, 97). In relief: Zoser's elegantly simple *nbty* name cobras on baskets (CAT. 20-21) differ markedly from the beautifully detailed cobras of Sahura's titles (CAT. 58-59). In such manner, careful analysis of uraeus style can be used to help with the attribution and dating of uninscribed monuments (CAT. 112).

Representations of cobras from Predynastic times until the end of the Old Kingdom make use of uraei as divine-royal symbols in essentially eight different ways, classified in this study as Types I-VIII. Monuments displaying uraei are illustrated and presented chronologically in **PART 2: HISTORY OF THE URAEUS, CHAPTERS 5-9** (Catalog 1-112), where each uraeus is discussed and given a type.

CHRONOLOGICAL SUMMARY OF TYPES

The following brief chronological summmary can be followed visually by reference to the drawings in **CHAPTER 11: URAEUS CHRONOLOGY CHART.**

EARLY PREDYNASTIC, c.4000 B.C.
An abstract Z cobra (?) precedes an elephant decorated with triangular forms of the Amratian Period and is probably the earliest preserved example of the uraeus or rising cobra (Fig. 61, Type IA2).

LATE PREDYNASTIC, c.3200-3000 B.C.
Interlaced and single cobras with elephants are the only preserved examples of uraei from the late Prehistoric Period in Egypt (CAT. 1-5; Type IA1,2). These depictions, whether totemic or mythological, show cobras clearly cooperating with elephants and in a position of protection, power, and leadership. The elephants are *not* "trampling on" or fighting off the cobras; also, since cobras are the only serpents which can raise their hoods to as much as one-third their body length, these serpents are certainly cobras and *not* pythons or boas, snakes not found in Egypt.

EARLY DYNASTIC, c.3000-2670 B.C.
DYNASTY I, c.3000-2820 B.C.
A *nbty* name cobra in hieroglyphic $\underline{d}$ form is first used at the beginning of Dynasty I on an ivory tablet of HOR AHA (MENES) (CAT. 6; Type IIA1). Also from Dynasty I, a cobra in profile view is shown with a single loop to its body in *nbty* names of SEMERKHET and QAY-A (CAT. 12, 13; Type IIA2). An elaboration of the hieroglyphic $\underline{d}$ cobra occurs in several early examples of the name of ZET (WADJI) above a facade (CAT. 8, 9; Type IIB). On an ivory plaque from the reign of DEN (WEDYMU), there is development of style to a two looped cobra body with tilted up head and hood in profile above the signs for "gold" and "infinity" or "enclosure" (CAT. 11; Type IIC). The first uraeus worn on a royal headdress and the first Wepwawet Standard with a canine and cobra occur on another ivory tablet of Den (CAT. 10; Types IIIA1, IVA1). A serpent head of ivory, from the tomb of ZER, third king of Dynasty I, is detailed with head plates and dorsal scale markings; carved in the round, it is the first preserved, three-dimensional cobra (CAT. 7; Type VIIA).

DYNASTY II, c.2820-2670 B.C.
Rudimentary *nbty* name cobras on seals or sealings are the only uraei found in Dynasty II until its close when KHASEKHEMUWY's *nbty* name uraei are the first to show an expanded cobra hood in front view with its body formed in double loops (CAT. 14-15; Type IIA3).

There is also an example of a three-dimensional cobra at the top of an ivory pin from a tomb dated to Dynasty II (CAT. 16; Type VIIA).

Thus, even before the beginning of the Old Kingdom, five major types (I, II, III, IV, and VII) of uraeus representation had been introduced. Basic forms, styles, or subdivisions of these types were developed in Early Dynastic times and used for approximately three-thousand years, until the end of ancient Egyptian art history.

OLD KINGDOM, c.2670-2195 B.C.
DYNASTY III, c.2670-2600 B.C.

Profiled, undetailed uraei are shown on the Wepwawet standard of SA-NEKHT (CAT. 17; Type IVA1), and on the forehead of ZOSER (CAT. 19; Type IIIA1) in their Sinai inscriptions. In contrast, the *nbty* name (CAT. 20-21; Type IIA4) and Wepwawet standard cobras (CAT. 23; Type IVA2) on Zoser's Saqqara reliefs are beautifully executed in finely modeled and detailed, low raised relief. A series or frieze of uraei, used architecturally at the top of a wall, occurs at Zoser's pyramid complex, Saqqara (CAT. 24; Type VA). This is a new use of the cobra goddess and its only preserved occurrence in the Old Kingdom.

DYNASTY IV, c.2600-2475 B.C.

SNEFERU relief displays the first preserved example of the uraeus entwined around a diadem, worn by the king beneath a feathered and horned crown (CAT. 26; Type IIIB). An expanded and detailed cobra hood leans forward, away from Sneferu's forehead. His *nbty* name cobra follows the Zoser style (CAT. 25; Type IIA4). The gold-encased bed canopy of Sneferu's Queen, Heterp-heres I, shows the most beautifully detailed cobra goddess of the Old Kingdom (CAT. 27; Type IIA4). Found with her furniture, a wooden curtain box inlaid with faience hieroglyphs displays the first preserved example of Wadjet offering the *w3s* scepter and *snw* to the names of Sneferu (CAT. 28a,b; Type IID1); the box also shows the earliest known Wadjet standard (CAT. 28c; Type IVB1).

CHEOPS relief fragments from three different locations display *nbty* name cobras which follow earlier styles (CAT. 29a,b,c; Types IIA4). They are the only uraei preserved from his reign.

The first uraei worn on the heads of sculpture in the round are those of RADEDEF, carved on quartzite statue heads. This important new use of the cobra goddess is the only type introduced in Dynasty IV. These uraei are worn on a plain *nemes* headdress as are most of their type in the Old Kingdom (CAT. 30, 31; Type VIIIA1b,2a,3a).

CHEPHREN has more preserved statuary inscribed for or attributed to him than any other king of the Old Kingdom. All of these sculptures or fragments of statues show a uraeus worn on a plain *nemes*. Their uraei display a variety of forms in the manner in which the cobra heads, hoods and bodies are modeled (CAT. 32-41; Types VIIIA1a-c,2a-e,3a,b,e,f). Chephren reliefs show a *nbty* name cobra in the style of Hetepheres (CAT. 42; Type IIA4) and, in a mud sealing, the first preserved, well executed uraeus preceding one bird and facing another atop a rectangle which was meant to contain two Horus names above palace facades (CAT. 43; Type IIE1).

Heads of MYCERINUS statues also wear the uraeus carved in a variety of styles (CAT. 44-47; Types VIIIA1b,2b,c,e,3c-d); three statue heads, attributed to Mycerinus, show a thicker cobra body than heretofore (CAT. 44-46; Type VIIIA3d); another depicts a slim body winding on the first preserved, striped *nemes* headdress. Mycerinus sunk relief on a calcite throne and on a gold cylinder seal shows elegantly carved uraei in three variations of titulary style: offering a *w3s* scepter to the king's Horus name (CAT. 48; Type IID2); preceding an uncrowned falcon (CAT. 48, 49; Type IIE2); and preceding a White Crowned falcon (CAT. 48; Type IIE3) atop his Horus name. From the valley temple of Mycerinus, a statue head is attributed to SHEPSESKAF. The king wears a short, horizontally striated cap or wig; placed on it is a thick, six curve uraeus with a plain hood and the only totally preserved uraeus head on stone sculpture from the Old Kingdom (CAT. 50; Type VIIIB1a,2a,3a).

An offering stand inscribed for Vizier Sethu (*ztw*), dated to Dynasty IV or later, shows the hieroglyph *t3yty* with a frieze of four profiled cobras on the top wall of the sign for "palace" or "shrine", an early example of the use of a uraei frieze as an architectural element in relief (CAT. 51; Type VB).

DYNASTY V, c.2475-2345 B.C.

WESERKAF'S colossal granite head wears a uraeus of five curves in medium high relief; the cobra hood is barely visisble in flat relief (CAT. 52; Type VIIIA1b,2b,3g). There is very little relief preserved from the reign of this king, but one finely executed, large fragment shows the king wearing a cobra entwined on a papyrus bow diadem or fillet (CAT. 53; Type IIIB).

Painted relief fragments of SAHURA show the king wearing this same diadem with entwined uraeus. The cobra hood, unlike the first example from Sneferu relief, is close to the kings wigged forehead (CAT. 56a, b, c; Type IIIB). A dyad sculpture of Sahura depicts a uraeus of four curves worn on his *nemes* (CAT. 54; Type VIIIA2b,3d). One of several Sahura reliefs from Abusir shows the first example of a cobra body in an oval coil on a plain headdress (CAT. 55; Type IIIC1). Two other relief fragments show the king's small head carried on a pole and wearing a miniscule uraeus; and a representation of Neferirkara with a small uraeus on the forehead of his short, close fitting cap are from the same wall (CAT. 57a, b; Type IIIA3, 4). Uraei flanking a sun disk, symbol of the deity Ra, appear in their first preserved examples on granite fragments from Sahura's pyramid temple (CAT. 60a, b; Type IB1). Titles of the king from this site displays cobras with tall, expanded hoods which are naturalistically detailed on raised limestone relief and unmarked in sunk granite relief. These uraei include those of Sahura's *nbty* name (CAT. 58a, 60a,b, 61; Types IIA4,5) as well as representations of Wadjet, supported by papyrus clumps, and offering the *w3s* scepter and *šnw* to the Horus name of the king (CAT. 58b,c,d, 59, 61; Types IID3,4,5). His Sinai inscription, in raised sandstone relief, shows an undetailed Wepwawet standard (CAT. 62; Type IVA3); while a granite fragment from Abusir displays a detailed Wadjet standard with the cobra goddess entwined on a *w3s* scepter, an *'nh* hanging from the base of her hood (CAT. 59; Type IVB2).

Inscribed double statues of NE-USER-RA show the king wearing a uraeus with five compressed curves (CAT. 65; Types VIIIA1c,2e,3g). Two other inscribed statues (CAT. 63; Types VIIIA1c,2e; CAT. 64; Types VIIIA2e,3f) and two attributed to Ne-user-ra (CAT. 66a, b; Types VIIIA2e,3f) have uraei which are either unfinished or badly worn and barely visible. Ne-user-ra reliefs are not as plentiful as Sahura's and they are usually not as naturalistically detailed. One exception is a large panel carved in fine detail which shows the seated king with Wadjet behind him in human form. The king wears a uraeus, entwined on a diadem, close to the forehead of his horizontally striated wig. Wadjet wears the first preserved feather headdress with uraeus emerging from under the feathers (CAT. 67; Types IIIB, D). Two fragments of relief from Abu Ghurob show the first preserved examples of the king wearing *khat* headcloths with uraei formed in two compressed curves with a long, undulating tail (CAT. 69; Type IIIA5). The earliest known sun disk with wings and flanked by uraei occurs on the Sinai inscription of Ne-user-ra (CAT. 74; Type IB2). The only new type of uraei preserved from Ne-user-ra's reign is in his titulary on a seal showing a crudely drawn Red Crowned falcon preceded by a cobra above his Horus name (CAT. 77a; Type IIE4); his *nbty* name cobras (CAT. 71, 73, 74, 77; Types IIA1,5,6) and those on papyrus offering the *w3s* scepter (CAT. 72, 73; Types IID2,3) follow basic forms of earlier styles. Wepwawet standards with cobras used in *hb-sd* reliefs also follow earlier forms (CAT. 75, 76; Types IVA3, 4).

There is only one statue head from the Old Kingdom shown with a stylized, curled, short wig on which is worn a diadem and uraeus hood. It belongs to an UNKNOWN KING, probably of Dynasty V. The cobra head is missing, and there is no trace of a cobra body on the diadem or on the wig (CAT. 78; Type   VIIIC2a). A calcite bust of another UNKNOWN KING probably also belongs to one of the kings who follow Ne-user-ra. One of three examples from the Old Kingdom and the first preserved occurrence,[339] this head has a hole at the center front of a plain *nemes* frontlet where a separately worked uraeus was once undoubtedly attached (CAT. 79; Type VIIID-1)

A drawing of the Sinai inscription of ISESY (ZEDKARA) shows the king wearing the same type of uraeus as that of Dynasty I's Den (CAT. 80; Type IIIA1). Isesy reliefs depict Wadjet with the king; she is wearing the feathered headdress displaying a similarly prominent uraeus (CAT. 81; Type IIID) and tall *nbty* name cobras with wide hoods and small heads (CAT. 82a,b; Type IIA3).

UNAS, on a limestone block of relief, is also shown with a tall, wide, small-headed uraeus worn on a close fitting cap (CAT. 83; Type IIIA4); and cobras of his titles are formed in a similar manner (CAT. 84, 85; Type IIA5, D2, 3). The earliest preserved Pyramid Texts are found in his pyramid at Saqqara, and contain at least seven different hieroglyphic names for the uraeus (Iarwet, Nebty, Akhet, Sebi, Rennewtet, Nesert, Ikhet-wetet). Cobra determinatives for these names all have small heads, tall, wide hoods, and double looped, or coiled bodies, formed in different ways (CAT. 86; Types IIF1,2,3,4,5). One of these, a determinative for the name Sebi, "guide serpent" is unique in the Old Kingdom. It shows the cobra without a basket or other support, its body in three, profiled, undulating curves behind the base of a widely expanded hood (CAT. 86e; Type IIF4).

A cobra frieze on the hieroglyph *t3yty* is incised on an obelisk in relief, inscribed for Vizier Ptah-hotep and dated to Dynasty V (CAT. 87; Type VB2).

There are no new basic types of uraei introduced during Dynasty V; however, several variations of Types I-V and VIII, listed above, do have their first occurrences in Dynasty V.

DYNASTY VI, c.2345-2195 B.C.

A calcite votive sistrum, inscribed for TETY, displays the earliest known, three dimensional, stone cobra goddess (CAT. 88; Type VIIB). Tety's *nbty* name on the side of the sistrum shows a simple, single loop cobra like those of Dynasty I (CAT. 88; Type IIA2). Relief from Tety's Saqqara pyramid depicts Wadjet with feathered headdress and a tall uraeus (CAT. 89a; Type IIID) and a cobra on papyrus offering a *w3s* scepter (CAT. 89b; Type IID3)

The only statue inscribed for PEPY I is an example of the type which shows holes at center front and on top of the head where a uraeus was once attached (CAT. 90; Type VIIID1). Yet another of this type occurs on the copper statue of the boy Pepy I or Mernera where the hole is in the center front of the headband of a close fitting cap; corroded nodes on its top surface may indicate remains of a cobra body (CAT. 91; Type VIIID2). A Pepy I door lintel from Tell Basta displays a finely executed, winged sun disk flanked by uraei (CAT. 92; Type IB2); the first preserved representation of Hathor with horned disk and pendant uraeus (Type IIIF); and a *nbty* name cobra (Type IIA3). His Sinai inscription also shows a winged sun disk with uraei (CAT. 93; Type IB), as well as a single loop *nbty* name cobra (Type IIA2). A relief fragment, reused at Lisht, which probably belongs to Pepy I's reign, shows a more developed and detailed cobra on papyrus offering a *w3s* scepter and *šnw* (CAT. 94; Type IID3). The first preserved example of a uraeus preceding a feather and horn crowned Horus above the *serekh* of the Horus name occurs on a cylinder seal of Pepy I (CAT. 95; Type IIE5).

Two statues of a young PEPY II depict him wearing uraei with eight curves. Seated on the lap of his mother, Ankhnes-mery-ra, he wears a *nemes* headdress with eight, tightly compressed cobra curves on its top surface (CAT. 96; Type VIIIA2f,3h); his squatting statue wears a close fitting cap with eight cobra curves more widely spaced on top of the cap (CAT. 97; Type VIIIB2b,3b). Reliefs from Saqqara show Pepy II with uraei fashioned in styles similar to those of Sahura: an oval, coiled uraeus on a striped *nemes* headdress (CAT. 98,

---

[339]A recently found head broken off from a statue attributed to Raneferef should now be added to these; *v.s.*, n. 246, p. 146.

99a; Type IIIC1); a small head carried on a pole (CAT. 105a; Type IIIA3); and a head of his son with a uraeus on a close fitting cap (with lappets?) (CAT. 105b; Type IIIA4). Wadjet wears a feathered headdress with uraeus in gilded plaster inlay on a wooden tablet of Pepy II (CAT. 100b; Type IIID) and on fragments of relief (CAT. 102a, b; Type IIID). His mother, Ankhnes-mery-ra, holds a papyrus umbel and wears a uraeus, projecting vertically from her close fitting cap, in a drawing of Pepy II's Sinai inscription; his wife, NEITH, is the first queen who wears a feathered headdress with uraeus shown on relief from her pyramid (CAT. 104; Type IIIE). Hathor wears the horned disk with pendant uraeus on Pepy II relief fragments (CAT. 99a, b; Type IIIF), and in painted plaster inlay on a wooden tablet (CAT. 100a; Type IIIF). Dim outlines of a uraeus pendant on a sun disk above the head of a falcon-headed deity are barely visible on a badly damaged, quartzite pillar of Pepy II (CAT. 101; Type IIIF). Also damaged, the remains of a *nbty* name cobra (CAT. 106a; Type IIA6) and Wadjet on papyrus, offering a *w3s* scepter and *snw* (CAT. 106a, b; Type IID4), occur on Pepy II relief fragments; and a well executed cobra precedes a feather and horn crowned falcon atop his Horus name on a cylinder seal (CAT. 110; Type IIE5). Damaged examples of the cobra goddess on Wepwawet and Wadjet standards occur on relief fragments of Pepy II (CAT. 107, 108; Types IVA3, B3). The first preserved uraei on royal clothing are seen in painted plaster inlay on the small blue sash of Pepy II on a wooden plaque (CAT. 100a; Type VIA). A frieze of six, well executed cobras are shown on top of the hieroglyph *t3yty* on another damaged relief fragment from Pepy II's pyramid temple (CAT. 109; Type VB). Another frieze of six, well modeled uraei occur on an obelisk from the late Dynasty VI mastaba of Vizier Tety (*tti*) in the *t3yty* hieroglyph (CAT. 111; Type VB).

Dated here to the late Old Kingdom, the cast gold uraeus on the diadem of the golden falcon from Hierakonpolis is the first known example of a three dimensional cobra of gold. Its small, modeled head and wide, detailed hood fit Old Kingdom canons for representation of the cobra goddess (CAT. 112; Type VIIC).

All eight uses of uraeus representation (Types I-VIII) occur in Dynasty VI. Their forms and styles are precursors and prototypes for cobra goddess representation in Middle Kingdom Egypt.

STYLISTIC SUMMARY OF TYPES

NOTE: The following summary describes in detail the stylistic development of various types of uraei and is intended primarily for reference purposes. It should be used with the illustrations provided in **CHAPTER 12: URAEUS TYPE CHART.**

TYPE I. WITH ANIMAL OR DEITY SYMBOLS
  A. With Elephant.
  1. Two Interlaced Uraei (CAT. 1-3) Late PREDYNASTIC knife handles and a mace handle show two interlaced cobras with elephants leading processions of animals. The cobras are not trampled upon by the elephants.
  2. Single Uraeus (CAT.4-5). The earliest depiction of a cobra is probably the Z-shape preceding an elephant on a rhomboid, slate palette of Amratian date, c.4000-3500 B.C. (Fig. 61). Since the abstract, Z form of this early palette cannot be said with certainty to be a cobra, Catalog entries begin with late PREDYNASTIC handles, c.3200- 3000 B.C., depicting serpents that can be proved to be cobras; two ivory handles (CAT. 4-5) show a single cobra with an elephant leading processions of animals.
  B. With Deity Symbol
  1. With Sun Disk. A Dynasty V monument of SAHURA depicts the first preserved example of two uraei with a deity; they are shown flanking a sun disk, symbol for the sun god, Ra (CAT. 60).

2. With Winged Sun Disk. NE-USER-RA's Dynasty V Sinai inscription shows the first preserved representation of uraei flanking a sun disk with wings (CAT. 74). Two more representations of pendent cobras flanking a winged disk are found on Dynasty VI monuments of PEPY I (CAT. 92, 93).

TYPE II. IN ROYAL NAMES

Close association of the cobra goddess with royal names and titles has long been recognized; from Dynasty I through Dynasty VI, there are five subdivisions, Types IIA-E, of this second type of uraeus, forming a part of pharaonic names. Under these five subdivisions, further subdivisions occur as the forms of the cobra change and develop different styles.

A. On Basket in *nbty* Name

1. Hieroglyphic _d_. The first preserved example of this type is incised on an ivory tablet from Nagada (CAT. 6), inscribed for the first king of Dynasty I, HOR AHA (MENES). Profiled in the simple, curved line of a hieroglyphic _d_, the cobra symbol is incised above a basket, the hieroglyph *nb*. This same, simple hieroglyphic _d_ form of the cobra is also found in inscriptions for the last king of Dynasty I, QAY-A (CAT. 13b) and on a seal of the sixth king of Dynasty V, NE-USER-RA (CAT. 77a).

2. Single coil; Hood in Profile. Inscriptions for SEMERKHET and QAY-A, the last kings of Dynasty I, show their *nbty* name cobras also in profile but with the development of single loop bodies sitting on baskets (CAT. 12a, b, 13a). A single coil form of the uraeus is seen again in early Dynasty VI when it is used in inscriptions of TETY (CAT. 88) and PEPY I (CAT. 93).

3. Double Loop; Hood Front View. An important development in form is seen in the *nbty* name uraeus of the last king of Dynasty II, KHASEKHEMUWY, when the cobra hood is shown frontally with a double loop body (CAT. 14a, b, 15). Dynasty VI *nbty* cobras of PEPY I are in the same form (CAT. 92).

4. Double Loop; Hood Front View; Tail through or across Back Loop from Front; Eye, Ventral Column, and/or Other Details. At the beginning of the Old Kingdom, during Dynasties III and IV, further elaboration and detail occurs in representations of the uraeus in fine, low, raised relief inscriptions. Dynasty III monuments of ZOSER are the first to show naturalistically developed and detailed *nbty* name cobra goddesses whose bodies end by crossing in front of double loops (CAT. 20, 21, 22). SNEFERU and CHEOPS, the first two kings of Dynasty IV, continue using this form with added details of modeled eye sockets, mouths, and bodies ending with thin tails (CAT. 25; CAT. 29a, b). These *nbty* name cobras set the standards for representation of the type throughout the Old Kingdom, although details and body forms vary. The most beautifully detailed *nbty* cobra is found on a gold-encased bed canopy which belonged to Sneferu's wife, Queen HETEP-HERES I (CAT. 27). Her son, CHEOPS, and grandson, CHEPHREN, have similarly formed uraei, without detail, in inscriptions carved for them (CAT. 29c, 42).   In Dynasty V, SAHURA's *nbty* uraeus takes the same form, shown with many of the same details as Hetep-heres I's gold cobra, and with a thin, undulating tail hanging over the basket's edge (CAT. 58a); while the same form of cobra, with ventral column details only, is carved in the hard granite of a Sahura architrave (CAT. 60a).

5. Solid loops, without Detail. On granite columns of SAHURA (CAT. 61) and NE-USER-RA (CAT. 73) the uraei are carved in sunk relief without interior markings; however, the cobra hood and back loop of the bodies do show interior modeling, indicating fullness; the thin tails hang down from the back edge of the baskets; although this modeling is not shown in the drawings of the columns, it can be seen in photographs. The softer sandstone of NE-USER-RA's Sinai inscription shows this type of cobra in low raised relief without modeling or detail (CAT. 74).   Inscriptions of ISESY (CAT. 82a,b) and UNAS (CAT. 85), at the close of Dynasty V, also show Type IIA5 in sunk relief without interior modeling or detail of any kind, but with the same small, pointed cobra head as that seen in Isesy's relief.

6. Double Loop; Tail through Back Loop from Rear. Although this style first appears in Dynasty V on relief of SAHURA (CAT. 58c, d), which has been classified under Type IID4, it is on Ne-user-ra raised relief fragments that the first example of the form occurs in a *nbty* name inscription (CAT. 71a-c). A fragment of late Dynasty VI PEPY II relief also depicts the detailed form of a cobra symbol of this type (CAT. 106a).

B. Detailed, Hieroglyphic *ḏ* above *Serekh*. The first great monument in Egyptian art is from the early Dynasty I reign of ZET (WADJI); his limestone stela represents an early version of the Horus name with a beautifully carved and detailed, hieroglyphic *ḏ* cobra above a *serekh*, enclosed in a rectangle with a great Horus falcon perched on top (CAT. 8). Because it is unique, this detailed, hieroglyphic *ḏ* cobra is classified separately.

C. Detailed, Double Loop above *nbw* and *šnw*. Another unique representation of the uraeus cobra is incised on an ivory tablet inscribed with the name DEN (WEDYMU), fifth king of Dynasty I (CAT. 11). Incised on ivory with a detailed head, tilted upward, a profiled hood marked horizontally with multiple ventral scales, this tall cobra symbol is an important part of an essentially vertical, elegant composition; the goddess' double loop body with long, thin tail is marked with cross-hatched dorsal scales. Since the cobra is placed above the signs for "gold" and "dominion" or "enclosure" and she faces a falcon above a rectangle containing the name Den, this is undoubtedly the first representation of the cobra symbol associated with a king's "Golden Horus" name.

D. With *w3s* Scepter and/or *šnw* and the Name, Wadjet. Invariably associated with and facing the Horus name of kings, this type of uraeus representation always sits on a basket, which is usually supported by papyrus, and has the hieroglyphic word, *wḏt*, Wadjet, above, behind, or beside her. Almost invariably a *w3s*, "dominion", scepter and/or *šnw*, "enclosure" or "infinity", are attached to the front of her hood. Formation of the bodies of the cobras usually corresponds to the style found in the same king's *nbty* name uraei.

1. Solid Double Loops without Detail. The earliest preserved cobra body representations with solid double loops are fashioned on the early Dynasty IV Queen HETEP-HERES I wooden curtain box in colored faience inlay. Two examples, one on each side of the box, show the goddess behind the cartouche of Sneferu with the *šnw* attached to the front loop of her body. On top of the box, where she faces the king's cartouche, both a *w3s* scepter and *snw* are attached to the front loop of the cobra. None of these examples is supported by papyrus. Wadjet, the goddess' name, is inlaid in hieroglyphs behind the cobras (CAT. 28a, b). NE-USER-RA's Dynasty V inscription from Sinai has a similar cobra goddess in raised relief on sandstone without scepter or cartouche. The name, Wadjet, precedes the cobra who is behind the cartouche of the king (CAT. 74).

2. Solid Double Loops or Coils with and without Detail; Supported by Papyrus. A three-umbel clump of papyrus supporting the basket upon which the cobra Wadjet sits, her me above her, is beautifully carved on a calcite throne of MYCERINUS in the first preserved example of this form. Papyrus clump, basket, and cobra goddess with an angled *w3s* scepter face the Horus name of the king. The cobra hood is delicately modeled within the sunk relief; the body's double loops are represented by oval spaces and an undulating tail breaks at the basket's back edge (CAT. 48). Dynasty V granite columns of SAHURA, NE-USER-RA, and UNAS also show this type of uraeus on a basket supported by papyrus. Sahura's columns show the cobra goddess offering a *w3s* scepter with *šnw* over it; "Wadjet of Depp" or "Depy" is in hieroglyphs above the cobra whose basket is supported by a seven-stem papyrus clump (CAT. 61). On a column of Ne-user-ra, Wadjet's name is above the cobra; a *šnw*, without scepter, is placed just above the base of her hood; and the basket is supported by a three-stem clump of papyrus (CAT. 73). Unas columns show a similarly formed cobra goddess, but without scepter or cartouche; here also, the basket is supported by a simple, three-umbel papyrus (CAT. 85b).

3. Double Loop; Tail through, across, or under Back Loop from Front. Drawings of painted relief fragments of Dynasty V's SAHURA show an elaborately detailed cobra goddess with *w3s* scepter and *šnw* placed above the base of her hood; the front loop of the body curves forward over the ventral shields and slips through the back loop (CAT. 58b). A NE-USER-RA fragment depicts a less detailed cobra of the same type offering the šnw only (CAT. 72). At UNAS' causeway, a block of limestone relief, heretofore unpublished, shows the same type of cobra, but with a scepter and much smaller šnw placed midway between the base and top of the expanded hood (CAT. 84). A damaged, early Dynasty VI relief fragment of TETY shows the same type of uraeus supported by a five-stem clump of papyrus (CAT. 89b). Found reused at Lisht and attributed to Pepy II, a low raised relief fragment displays a cobra without head and with a large šnw and w3s scepter placed at a low angle on the base of the hood. The style of cobra symbol is unlike any other Pepy II cobra; and the five-stem papyrus clump supporting the cobra goddess' basket is formed exactly like that on the heads of fecundity figures on the Pepy I lintel from Tell Basta (CAT. 92). For these reasons the fragment is probably from the reign of PEPY I (CAT. 94).

4. Double Loop; Tail through Back Loop from Rear. Formed like the cobra bodies of Type IIA6, the first preserved examples of tails emerging through back loops from behind cobras supported by papyrus occur on painted limestone, raised relief and on granite, sunk relief fragments of SAHURA in early Dynasty V. Drawings show these goddesses carefully detailed with scepter and šnw placed above the base of the cobra hood (CAT. 58c, d, 59). Fragmentary reliefs of PEPY II, late Dynasty VI, also show this uraeus (CAT. 106a, b).

E. With Falcon above Horus Name. Cobra goddesses of this type precede falcon-atop-Horus name rectangles containing the royal name in hieroglyphs above a palace facade .

1. Between Two Uncrowned Birds. Although the cobra precedes Horus on crudely made seals of CHEOPS and RADEDEF, the earliest, naturalistically drawn cobra goddess of this type appears on a drawing of CHEPHREN's mud sealing between two birds who probably symbolize father and son (CAT. 43).

2. With Uncrowned Falcon. A beautifully carved cobra precedes a single, uncrowned falcon on what would have been the north side of the calcite throne of MYCERINUS (CAT. 48) and on a small, gold cylinder seal (CAT. 49). More crudely executed are the uraei preceding uncrowned falcons on Dynasty V seals of NEFERIRKARA and NE-USER-RA (CAT. 77a-c).

3. With White Crowned Falcon. A variation of Type IIE is seen on the south side of the MYCERINUS throne where the falcon behind the cobra and above the king's Horus name wears the White crown of Upper Egypt (CAT. 48).

4. With Red Crowned Falcon. The limestone cylinder seal of NEFERIRKARA and NE-USER-RA depicts one of the Horus names surmounted by a crudely drawn, hieroglyphic d cobra preceding a falcon wearing the Red Crown of Lower Egypt (CAT. 77a). Atop other Horus names on this seal, there are figures wearing White Crowns, but they are not accompanied by the cobra goddess.

5. With Feather and Horn Crowned Falcon. Above the early Dynasty VI Horus name of PEPY I, on a steatite cylinder seal, there is a small cobra in profile preceding a falcon wearing a feather and horn crown (CAT. 95). A steatite cylinder seal of PEPY II shows a more detailed and better executed representation of the same style and type (CAT. 110). The cobra goddess here has a modeled, expanded hood, shown frontally. Behind her, the falcon is well drawn wearing a crown with angled horns and two, tall feather plumes.[340] Other, finely executed, Old Kingdom representations of Horus wearing the feather and horn crown are not accompanied by the cobra goddess.[341]

F. Determinative in Names of Cobra Goddess. Cobras in deep sunk relief are carved on the walls of the pyramid of UNAS in the earliest preserved *Pyramid Texts* (*PT*). There are many earlier examples of the "Two Mistresses" cobra in royal *nbty* names and, beginning in Dynasty

---

[340] *cf.* the Gold Falcon of Hierakonpolis (CAT. 112).

[341] *i.e.*, on Queen Hetep-heres I's gold encased bed canopy (CAT. 27).

IV, of the cobra named Wadjet on a basket supported by papyrus; however, it is in these *Pyramid Texts* that at least six additional names or epithets for the uraeus are written in their first preserved examples. Cobras are carved as determinatives for these names in essentially the same form as on other monuments of Unas. Their fully expanded hoods with narrow waists or bases rise up tall with small heads in profile. Cobra bodies are formed in four distinctly different ways:

1. **Body in Two Curves on Basket in Iarwet, "Rising Ones" or "Uraei"** (CAT. 86a). The cobra body curves back upon itself, its hood fully expanded.

2. **Double Loop Body on Basket with Tail through Back Loop from Front in Akhet, "Great One" or "Uraeus", Rennewtet, "Harvest Goddess", Nesret, "Uraeus" or "Royal Serpent", Iket-wetet, "Uraeus-Begetter"** (CAT. 86c,f,g,h). A form of representation most commonly used when representing uraei on baskets is here seen in the Unas *PT* as determinative at the end of four different names for the cobra goddess.

3. **Body of Double Coils or Solid Loops on Basket; Tail behind Rear Coil in Iawret "Rising Ones" or "Seven Uraei"** (CAT. 86d). Two circular coils of the body are similar to the Wadjet cobra on Mycerinus' throne (CAT. 48).

4. **Without Basket; Body in Three Curves behind Base of Hood in Sebi, "Guide Serpent" or "Uraeus"** (CAT. 86e). This is the earliest preserved cobra symbol represented without a basket, standard, or other means of support due, perhaps, to the action implied by her name.

TYPE III. ON ROYAL OR DIVINE HEADDRESS IN RELIEF. Worn on the foreheads of kings and divinities Type III, on relief, and Type VIII, on statues, are the cobra goddesses usually meant when the term "uraeus" is used. Although the cobra does not occur on the head of a royal statue until early Dynasty IV's King Radedef, c.2550-2540 B.C., the first preserved occurrence in relief is worn by a king of Dynasty I, approximately four hundred years earlier; Wadjet, identified by her name and epithet, is appropriately the earliest known human female figure to wear a uraeus on a Dynasty V relief of Ne-user-ra; Queen Ankhnes-mery-ra, Dynasty VI, is the first queen depicted wearing the uraeus on Pepy II relief. Subdivided according to the kind of headdress upon which cobras are worn, Type IIIA through F is further subdivided as to style or form of the uraeus.

A. On Forehead of Plain Headdress. Uraei classified under this subdivision occur on plain or undetailed headdresses of several types.

1. **Hood in Profile High above Royal Head.** The earliest preserved uraeus worn on the forehead of a king's headdress is incised on an ivory tablet of DEN, Dynasty I, where a thick cobra hood and head rise from the forehead of a plain, *nemes*-like head covering (CAT. 10). Next seen in this form on the Sinai inscription of ZOSER, Dynasty III, the uraeus projects horizontally forward from the king's forehead (CAT. 19). A similar type of uraeus is recorded from the Sinai inscription of ISESY (ZEDKARA), Dynasty V. Here, the cobra rises vertically from the forehead of the king's headdress (CAT. 80).

2. **On Short Cap or Wig of Queen Mother.** On a PEPY II, Dynasty VI, Sinai inscription the name ANKHNES-MERY-RA is written in hieroglyphs above the figure of the queen mother who wears a close fitting cap or wig with uraeus rising vertically at her forehead. This earliest example of a queen wearing the uraeus no longer exists, but is fortunately preserved in a drawing (CAT. 103).

3. **On King's Head Carried on Standard.** Relief fragments of SAHURA, Dynasty V (CAT. 57a) and of PEPY II, Dynasty VI (CAT. 105a), show small heads of kings, who wear tiny uraei on a *nemes*, atop standards carried by human figures representing the kings' *k3*, translated, "soul", "spirit", "essence".[342]

---

[342]Faulkner 1962, p. 283.

4. On Short Cap or Wig of King. Fragments of SAHURA and PEPY II from the same locations also show the kings' sons wearing uraei on close fitting caps or wigs (CAT. 57b; CAT. 105b). There is also a relief fragment of UNAS showing the king wearing a cap or wig with uraeus, published here for the first time (CAT. 83).

5. On *khat* Headdress. Shown in the Old Kingdom in two examples, a two curve form of the uraeus appears on relief fragments of NE-USER-RA, Dynasty V, worn on the *khat* headdress (CAT. 69).

B. Entwined On Diadem. The uraeus is also depicted wound around a diadem worn on short, curled hair or a close fitting wig of kings beneath a double horned and feathered crown. There are Dynasty IV and V examples of this type, but none, thus far, from Dynasty VI. SNEFERU, early Dynasty IV, relief fragments show the cobra goddess, head in profile, detailed hood in front view, and body entwined around a diadem in six curves (CAT. 26). A cobra wound on a diadem is not preserved again until the reign of WESERKAF, Dynasty V, on a beautifully carved example from his pyramid temple (CAT. 53). There are painted relief fragments of SAHURA which also portray this type of uraeus (CAT. 56a, b, c). A large relief panel and a small painted relief fragment of NE-USER-RA again show this type of cobra goddess entwined on a diadem (CAT. 67, 68). Colored fragments of Sneferu, Sahura, and Ne-user-ra depict the diadem as gold, red, and green, and the cobra is painted yellow or gold, indicating that the kings wore jeweled diadems with cobras fashioned from gold and represented in relief.

C. Coiled on King's Headdress. A form of uraeus frequently seen on statues and in relief from the Middle Kingdom onward, Type IIIC occurs in its first preserved example on a large relief panel of SAHURA, early Dynasty V (CAT. 55); here, for the first time, a uraeus at the forehead edge of the king's plain headcovering shows a body which curves back upon itself to form an oval loop, then under the coil in widely spaced, undulating curves to the top of the king's head. Although too badly damaged to determine its form, it is probably this type of uraeus which appears on a fragment of NE-USER-RA (CAT. 70). The same coiled uraeus is clearly seen on PEPY II relief showing the uraeus worn on striped headcoverings (CAT. 98, 99a).

D. On Feathered Headdress of Goddess Wadjet. The first known uraeus on the head of a deity occurs on a feathered headdress worn by the goddess Wadjet who is represented in human form on a large relief panel of NE-USER-RA, Dynasty V (CAT. 67). Wadjet is seen again wearing the feathered headdress with uraeus on a relief fragment of ISESY (ZEDKARA), Dynasty V (CAT. 81). In Dynasty VI Wadjet is seen with feathered headdress and uraeus in reliefs of TETY (CAT. 89) and PEPY II (CAT. 100b,   102).

E. On Feathered Headdress of Queen. A relief fragment from the late Dynasty VI pyramid of Queen NEITH, Wife of PEPY II, is the first to show a queen wearing the feathered headdress with uraeus (CAT. 104).

F. Pendent from Sun Disk above Deity. In Dynasty VI this form of uraeus appears for the first time, hanging from the horned disk worn by Hathor on reliefs of PEPY I (CAT. 92) and PEPY II (CAT. 99, 100). A large, very badly damaged quartzite pillar from PEPY II's pyramid temple seems to show a uraeus hanging from a plain sun disk above the head of a falcon-headed deity (CAT. 101).

TYPE IV. ON STANDARD. Uraei are seen on two kinds of standards from Early Dynastic through Old Kingdom periods, Type IVA-B; these are further subdivided according to the form of uraeus.

A. Wepwawet Standard. Invariably accompanying or leading the king and occuring as a part of smiting scenes or *ḥb-sd* festival processions, these standards depict the cobra goddess on a standard, behind the bag-like *šdšd*, 𓊪 , and preceding the canine god, Wepwawet.

1. Uraeus Head and Hood in Profile Facing *šdšd*. The first preserved Wepwawet standard is incised on an ivory tablet of DEN (WEDYMU), Dynasty I (CAT. 10). It is next

seen on the Sinai inscription of SA-NEKHT, Dynasty III (CAT. 17) and on a relief fragment
which probably also belongs to his reign (CAT. 18). In each of these examples, the uraeus
head and hood are without detail and thickly profiled; the body of the serpent is not shown.

2. Detailed Hood in Front View Facing *šdšd*; Body Between Legs of Canine. On finely
executed reliefs of Dynasty III's NETERKHET (ZOSER) the uraeus hood is shown frontally,
detailed with a modeled ventral column and horizontal scales; the profiled head is modeled to
show eye and socket; the body stretches out in a straight, tapered line between the front paws
of Wepwawet (CAT. 23).

3. Undetailed Hood in Front View Facing *šdšd*. After Dynasty III, there are no
preserved examples of Type IVA until a Dynasty V, Sinai inscription of SAHURA, (CAT. 62).
Ḥb-sd festival reliefs of NE-USER-RA depict multiple Wepwawet standards in undetailed
form (CAT. 75a-d). A relief fragment of PEPY II also shows this standard with the cobra
head and an eye indicated (CAT. 107).

4. No *šdšd*; with and without Basket-like Appurtenance Below Standard. At least three
ḥb-sd festival relief fragments of NE-USER-RA, show a Wepwawet standard without the
bag-like *šdšd*. The undetailed cobra goddess preceding the canine god is shown with a
basket-like object beneath the base of her hood (CAT. 76a-c).   A drawing of one of these
fragments (CAT. 76c) shows the base of the cobra hood with a ventral column; the standard is
drawn without a *šdšd* or a basket-like appurtenance.

B. Wadjet Standard. The cobra goddess seen alone is entwined on a papyrus stem and on a
w3s scepter.

1. Undetailed; Three Solid Loops (Six Curves) Entwined on Papyrus Stem. This type of
standard is first preserved in faience inlay on the wooden curtain box of Queen HETEP-
HERES I, Dynasty IV; the name of Wadjet is written above the standard placed behind the
Horus name of Sneferu and facing the seated figure of the king (CAT. 28c). A papyrus umbel
with its stem looped at the base of the cobra hood indicates a papyrus stem supporting the
goddess.

2. Detailed; Entwined on *w3s* Scepter in Six Curves; *'nḫ* Hangs on Hood. Next seen in
Dynasty V relief of SAHURA, Wadjet is entwined on a *w3s* scepter with an *'nḫ* hanging from
the base of her hood whose ventral column is marked by horizontal scales extending beyond
the base of the hood onto its body (CAT. 59).

3. With *w3s* Scepter on Papyrus. Drawings of relief fragments from the pyramid of
PEPY II, Dynasty VI, show the base of a cobra hood, a wide loop of the body at the bent top
of a standard, and three curves of the cobra body entwined on a pole (CAT. 108a). The
remainder of the cobra and standard are missing. As reconstructed in a drawing (CAT. 108b),
the top end of a *w3s* scepter is attached to the upper hood of the cobra. Since reliefs of
MENTUHOTEP II and AMENEMHAT I, approximately a century later, show a similarly
formed cobra goddess with *w3s* scepter attached to her hood and body entwined on papyrus, it
is likely that these Pepy II fragments once depicted a papyrus standard also.

TYPE V. ARCHITECTURAL ELEMENT. A series or frieze of cobra goddess heads and
hoods is carved as architectural decoration on the top course of building walls.
Representations of these walls are also found in two-dimensional Egyptian relief in the
hieroglyph *t3yty* (Type VA-B).

A. On Wall. The first and only preserved example of this type from the Old Kingdom is at
Saqqara on top of the south tomb chapel wall of NETERKHET (ZOSER), Dynasty III.
Projecting cobra heads and hoods with modeled ventral columns and scales are carved almost
three-dimensionally in the limestone blocks of the top course of the wall (CAT. 24).

B. In Relief atop Hieroglyph, *t3yty*. In the Old Kingdom, probably from DYNASTY IV,
an offering stand inscribed for Vizier Sethu (*ztw*) shows a frieze of four cobra heads and
hoods in the hieroglyph *t3yty*, meaning "he of the curtain", "he of the doorway", or "the
shrouded one" which is a vizerial title (CAT. 51). From DYNASTY V, an obelisk is carved in
relief and inscribed for Vizier Ptah-hotep (*ptḥ-ḥtp*); the hieroglyph *t3yty* with five or six

cobra heads and hoods is incised near its pointed top (CAT. 87). In Dynasty VI, a drawing of
PEPY II relief fragments depicts a series of six detailed cobra heads and expanded hoods
below hieroglyph determinatives meaning "pyramid city", and in front of a courtier with
bowed head. This frieze of cobras is undoubtedly the top part of the hieroglyph *t3yty*,
although its shrine or palace segment is missing (CAT. 109). Similarily formed cobras are seen
on a well carved obelisk inscribed for the Vizier Prince Tety (*tti*), dated to DYNASTY VI or
later. Here, six cobras are above a palace or shrine to which a ledge has been added, a later
variation of the hieroglyph *t3yty* (CAT. 111).

TYPE VI. ON ROYAL CLOTHING. The only preserved example of this type before the end
of the Old Kingdom occurs in gilded and painted plaster inlay on a small wooden tablet of
PEPY II, Dynasty VI, where two cobras rise up at the bottom edges of the king's blue sash
(CAT. 100).

TYPE VII. SCULPTURE. Three dimensional examples of the cobra goddess are carved from
ivory and stone, and cast in gold.
   A. Ivory. A fragmentay ivory serpent head, carved in the round, from the tomb of ZER,
Dynasty I, has the horizontal ventral scales, large head plates, and cross-hatched dorsal scales
of a cobra (CAT. 7). An ivory pin from a DYNASTY II tomb is decorated at its top with the
risen hood and head of a cobra carved in the round in profile (CAT. 16).
   B. Stone. The first known example of a single uraeus carved three-dimensionally in stone
is on top of a votive sistrum of TETY, Dynasty VI. Preceding the Horus falcon, the back of
the cobra goddess' projecting head touches the bird's breast; the cobra's expanded and
detailed hood leans back from its base attached to the top of the sistrum; its head projects
forward; the cobra body merges with the falcon's talons (CAT. 88).
   C. Gold. Cast in solid gold, the three-dimensional, heavy uraeus attached to the diadem
worn by the gold-headed falcon from Hierakonpolis is dated here to DYNASTY VI or earlier.
Its small, modeled head and widely flared, detailed hood correspond to forms of the uraeus
found in the late Old Kingdom, and there is ample precedent from the period for its
workmanship (CAT. 112).

TYPE VIII. ON ROYAL HEADDRESS IN SCULPTURE. Uraei worn on heads of kings are
seen in their first preserved examples in Dynasties I and III relief (CAT. 10, 19). Beginning
with RADEDEF in Dynasty IV, the uraeus is worn on kings' sculpture on the head of every
king for whom we have preserved statue heads. Uraei on royal statue heads are subdivided to
indicate the kind of headdress on which they are worn, Type VIIIA-C; one subdivision, Type
VIIID, classifies a type which shows only a cavity at the center front of kings' headdresses,
where a separately worked uraeus, now missing, was once attached. These uraei worn on
statue heads are further subdivided to classify a great variety of head (1), hood (2), and (3)
body forms.
   A. On Nemes.
      1. Uraeus Head
         a. Broken off from Great Sphinx. Attributed to CHEPHREN, Dynasty IV, the
uraeus head from the Great Sphinx, although broken off and now separately located, appears
to be carved from the same limestone as the Sphinx head; the careful modeling of eye
sockets, cranial and jaw bones of the Sphinx's uraeus head is similar to that of the Great
Sphinx head itself (CAT. 41b).
         b. Remains of Damaged Head. At least five royal heads from Old Kingdom statues
have enough of the cobra head remaining to determine that it would have projected forward,
tilted slightly upward. The first preserved uraeus on a king's statue - RADEDEF, Dynasty
IV, - has this type of missing cobra head (CAT. 30). Other examples are: CHEPHREN
(CAT. 34, 39c,d); MYCERINUS (CAT. 46); WESERKAF (CAT. 52); NE-USER-RA (CAT.
65).

c. Worn or Unfinished Nodule. A small statue head fragment found at Giza and attributed to CHEPHREN, Dynasty IV, displays a round, somewhat flattened cobra head which appears unfinished or worn (CAT. 35). Three statues whose uraei heads are smoothly rounded nodes were found at Mit Rahina where they would have been accessible to the touch of human hands, a possible cause of the worn appearance of these uraeus heads on the statues of: CHEPHREN OR MYCERINUS ?, Dynasty IV (CAT. 36); MYCERINUS, Dynasty IV (CAT. 45); NE-USER-RA, Dynasty V (CAT. 63).[343]

2. Uraeus Hood

a. Unmarked ventral Column; Base at Upper Edge of Frontlet. Shown on kings' heads in Dynasty IV and V, this form depicts the cobra's expanded hood with a deeply incised ventral column centered on its surface. The ventral scales are not indicated. These hoods are preserved on statue heads of RADEDEF, Dynasty IV (CAT. 30-31) and CHEPHREN, Dynasty IV (CAT. 32).

b. Unmarked Ventral Column; Base at Lower Edge of Frontlet Examples of this form show a ventral column modeled in slightly raised relief on the surface of the cobra hood. A small statue head attributed to CHEPHREN has a cobra hood whose ventral column is barely visible (CAT. 35); while a seated statue of MYCERINUS wears a cobra whose ventral column is clearly visible in rounded, raised relief (CAT. 44). The Dynasty V statue head of WESERKAF again shows only a faintly visible column on its cobra hood (CAT. 52); while that of SAHURA is more readily seen in higher relief (CAT. 54).

c. Detailed Ventral Scales; Base at Lower Edge of Frontlet. Five statue heads or fragments which display ventral scales on their hoods are carved from calcite, a soft stone which may account for these details. The seated statue of CHEPHREN from Mit Rahina shows fourteen or more very carefully carved, tiny, rhomboidal, ventral scales in low raised relief on the hood of its uraeus (CAT. 34). Two fragments of statue heads found at Giza and attributed to CHEPHREN display the same details (CAT. 39b, d). Well known statue heads attributed to MYCERINUS also have these details (CAT. 46, 47).

d. Great Sphinx Uraeus Hood; Uniquely Detailed; Base at Lower Edge of Frontlet. Cross-hatched dorsal scales and slanted, V-shaped band dividing the hood are details on the cobra hood of the Great Sphinx which do not appear on any other king's statue from the old kingdom (CAT. 41a)[344].

e. Undetailed; Flat Relief; Base at Lower Edge of Frontlet. Varying from tall and slim to short and squat, at least eleven statue heads or fragments of heads from sculpture of Old Kingdom kings have uraei with hoods in this form. Modeled in very flat relief, most of these cobra hoods are scarcely visible. Five of the examples are worn on the headdresses of statues inscribed for or attributed to CHEPHREN (CAT. 33, 36, 37, 38, 40); one is on a statue of MYCERINUS (CAT. 45); three are on statues inscribed for NE-USER-RA, Dynasty V (CAT. 63, 64, 65); two, on statues attributed to Ne-user-ra (CAT. 66a, b).

f. Apparently Undetailed, Badly Damaged; Base at Upper Edge of Frontlet. PEPY II, Dynasty VI, shown as a small, boy-king who sits on his mother's lap, wears a *nemes* on which a large and protruding uraeus hood is prominent. Since its surface is missing, it is impossible to determine whether it was ever detailed (CAT. 96).

3. Uraeus Body.

a. Full Bodied; Three Open Curves. The first preserved cobra body on the top of a *nemes* headdress is on a large quartzite head from the pyramid of RADEDEF, Dynasty IV. Carved in bold relief, it winds to the crown of the king's head in three widely spaced curves (CAT. 30). A small statue head from Giza, attributed to CHEPHREN, shows a similar cobra

---

[343]*v.s.*, n. 223, p. 126.

[344] These details do, however, occur in relief in early Dynasty IV on the gold-encased bed canopy of Queen Hetep-heres I (CAT. 27).

body in lower relief (CAT. 35).

b. **Slim Bodied; Four Open Curves.** Two, hard stone statues of CHEPHREN, from his pyramid temple, have uraei whose thin bodies wind in four open curves, carved in flat relief on top of a plain *nemes* with striped lappets (CAT. 32-33).

c. **Slim Bodied; Five Open Curves.** Attributed to Chephren's son, MYCERINUS, a calcite head shows the same slim uraeus with five widely spaced curves winding on top of a striped *nemes* (CAT. 47).

d. **Full Bodied; Four Semi-open Curves.** Seated calcite statues of MYCERINUS display a very different style of uraeus body on plain *nemes* headdresses with striped lappets; carved in low relief, a wide cobra body winds in four closely spaced curves (CAT. 44, 46). SAHURA sculpture, from Dynasty V, shows a similar style uraeus body, carved in higher relief (CAT. 54).

e. **Full Bodied; Six Semi-compressed Curves.** Two, seated statues, one of calcite inscribed for CHEPHREN (CAT. 34), the other of gneiss inscribed for MYCERINUS (CAT. 45) show plump cobra bodies in moderately high relief winding in six narrow, compressed curves on top of a plain *nemes* with striped lappets.

f. **Flattened Nodes on Top of King's Head.** Whether unfinished, or damaged and worn down by the elements, human hands, and time, there are at least three sculptures from the Old Kingdom which faintly show only worn bumps of cobra bodies on top of the *nemes* headdress. One is attributed to CHEPHREN (CAT. 38), another to CHEPHREN OR MYCERINUS (CAT. 36), and another is inscribed for NE-USER-RA, Dynasty V (CAT. 64).

g. **Full Bodied; Five Semi-compressed Curves.** A colossal statue head of WESERKAF, first king of Dynasty V (CAT. 52) and double statues of NE-USER-RA (CAT. 65) depict uraei bodies on top of a plain *nemes* with striped lappets which wind in five wide, semi-compressed curves.

h. **Slim Bodied; Eight Semi-compressed Curves.** In Dynasty VI, on the small, calcite head of the boy-king PEPY II, there are eight compressed uraeus body curves (CAT. 96).

B. On Short Cap or Wig. Two examples of uraei on sculpture are worn on short, close fitting wigs or caps in the Old Kingdom; one, attributed to SHEPSESKAF, is from the end of Dynasty IV; the other, inscribed for PEPY II, is from the end of Dynasty VI.

1. Uraeus Head.

a. **Pointed, Egg-shaped Oval.** The only completely preserved uraeus head on a statue in the Old Kingdom occurs on a calcite head, found at Mycerinus' valley temple but attributed to SHEPSESKAF, late Dynasty IV, c.2487-2480. It is undetailed, tilted upward, and projects out at the top of the king's forehead (CAT. 50).

2. Uraeus Hood.

a. **Undetailed, Shield Shape; Base at Edge of Horizontally Striated Cap or Wig; Flat Relief.** In contrast to the striations of the cap or wig worn by SHEPSESKAF (?), the surface of the wide uraeus hood is modeled in plain, flat relief (CAT. 50).

b. **Apparently Undetailed, Badly Damaged Surface; Base at Edge of Plain Cap or Wig.** On the small, squatting, calcite statue of PEPY II, Dynasty VI, the young king wears a plain, close fitting cap or wig with a very large cobra hood, prominently modeled in high relief. It is too damaged to determine whether its surface was originally plain or detailed (CAT. 97).

3. Uraeus Body.

a. **Full Bodied; Six Semi-compressed Curves.** The wide cobra body on the head attributed to SHEPSESKAF winds on the striated cap or wig in six closely spaced curves (CAT. 50).

b. **Slim Bodied; Eight Semi-open Curves.** On the plain short cap or wig of PEPY II's squatting statue, the uraeus winds in eight evenly spaced curves (CAT. 97).

C. On Diadem. There is only one statue head, of an UNKNOWN KING, from the Old Kingdom showing the uraeus worn on a diadem over a short, curled wig.

2. Uraeus Hood.

    a. Undetailed Ventral Column Faintly Modeled. Dated, here, to late Dynasty V or early Dynasty VI, the uraeus on this diadem shows only a small, shield-shaped hood modeled in flat relief with its ventral column in somewhat higher relief. The uraeus head is missing, and there is no trace of a cobra body on the curled wig of the unknown king (CAT. 78).

D. Cavity; Uraeus Missing; Form Undetermined. At least three statue heads of the late Old Kingdom show a cavity where the uraeus was once attached.[345] Centered on a *nemes* headdress frontlet in two instances and on a short cap in the other, these holes once held cobras which were probably fashioned of a different material than the statue.

1. On Nemes. A calcite bust of an UNKNOWN KING has a large hole at the center of the frontlet on its plain *nemes* with striped lappets. The bust is here dated to late Dynasty V or early Dynasty VI (CAT. 79). The kneeling, schist statue inscribed for PEPY I, Dynasty VI, c.2323-2283 B.C. also has a very large hole which extends above the narrow frontlet of his widely striped *nemes* (CAT. 90); a smaller cavity on top of the statuette head probably once helped to secure the separately worked uraeus.

2. On Short Cap; Corroded Nodes May Indicate Uraeus Body. Representing either PEPY I or his son Prince MERNERA, Dynasty VI, a copper statue of a boy also has a large hole at the center of the headband on his close fitting, short cap. There are corroded nodes of copper on top of his cap which may be the remains of the cobra body (CAT. 91).

---

[345]The recently discovered head of Raneferef makes the fourth of this type preserved from the Old Kingdom; *v.s.*, n. 246.

PART 3

CHARTS OF PREDYNASTIC, EARLY DYNASTIC, AND OLD KINGDOM URAEI

11   URAEUS CHRONOLOGY CHART

PREDYNASTIC URAEUS (?), c. 4000 B.C.

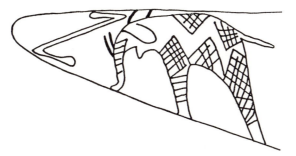

Fig. 340, AMRATIAN uraeus (?) on palette, Fig. 61 (Type IA2)

LATE PREDYNASTIC URAEI, c.3200-3000 B.C.

Fig. 341, Cat. 1 (Type IA1)   Fig. 342, Cat. 2 (Type IA1)   Fig. 343, Cat. 3 (Type IA1)

Fig. 344, Cat. 4 (Type IA2)   GERZEAN uraei on handles   Fig. 345, Cat. 5 (Type IA2)

EARLY DYNASTIC URAEI, c.3000-2670 B.C.

DYNASTY I, c.3000-2820 B.C.

Fig. 346, HOR AHA, Cat. 6 (IIA1)   Fig. 347, ZER, Cat. 7 (VIIA)

Fig. 348, Cat. 9a,b (IIB)   ZET (WADJI)   Fig. 349, Cat. 8 (IIB)

Fig. 350, Cat. 10 (IIIA1)   Fig. 352, Cat. 10 (IVA1)

Fig. 351, DEN (WEDYMU), Cat. 11 (IIC)

Fig. 353, SEMERKHET, Cat. 12a (IIA2)

Fig. 354, Cat. 12b (IIA2)   Fig. 355, Cat. 13a (IIA2)   Fig. 356, Cat. 1b (IIA1)
QAY-A

DYNASTY II, c.2820-2670 B.C.

Fig. 357, SEMTI-IRYNETJER, Cat. 13c (IIA1)   Fig. 358, PERIBSEN, Cat. 13d (IIA2)

Fig. 359, Cat. 14a (IIA3)   KHASEKHEMUWY   Fig. 360, Cat. 14b (IIA3)

Fig. 361, Attributed to KHASEKHEMUWY, Cat. 15 (IIA3)

Fig. 362, Ivory pin attributed to Dynasty II, Cat. 16 (VIIA)

OLD KINGDOM URAEI, c.2670-2195 B.C.

DYNASTY III, c.2670-2600 B.C.

Fig. 363, SA-NEKHT, Cat. 17 (IVA1)   Fig. 364, SA-NEKHT or ZOSER?, Cat. 18 (IVA1)

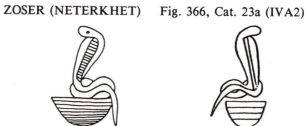

Fig. 365, Cat. 19(IIIA1)   ZOSER (NETERKHET)   Fig. 366, Cat. 23a (IVA2)

Fig. 367, Cat. 20 (IIA4)   Fig. 368, Cat. 21 (IIA4)   Fig. 369, Cat. 22 (IIA4)

Fig. 370, ZOSER, Cat. 24 (VA)

DYNASTY IV, c.2600-2475 B.C.

Fig. 371, Cat. 25 (IIA4)   SNEFERU   Fig. 372, Cat. 26 (IIIB)

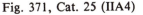

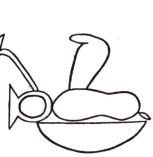

Fig. 373, Cat. 27 (IIA4)   Fig. 374, Cat. 28a,b (IID1)   Fig. 375, Cat. 28c (IVB1)

HETEP-HERES I, Wife of SNEFERU

Fig. 376, Cat. 29a (IIA4)   Fig. 377, Cat. 29b (IIA4)   Fig. 378, Cat. 29c (IIA4)

CHEOPS (KHUFU)

Fig. 379, Cat. 30 (VIIIA1b,2a,3a)   RADEDEF   Fig. 380, Cat. 31 (VIIIA2a,3a)

Fig. 381, Cat. 32
(VIIIA2a,3b)

Fig. 382, Cat. 33 (VIIIA2e,3b)
CHEPHREN

Fig. 383, Cat. 34
(VIIIA1b,2c,3e)

Fig. 384, Cat. 35
(VIIIA1c,2b,3a)

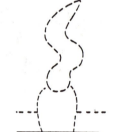

Fig. 385, Cat. 36 (VIIIA1c,2e,3f)
Attributed to CHEPHREN

Fig. 386, Cat. 37, 38
(VIIIA2e,3f)

Fig. 387, Cat. 39d
(VIIIA1b,2c,3a)

Fig. 388, Cat. 39c (VIIIA1b,2a)
Attributed to CHEPHREN

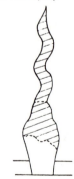

Fig. 389, Cat. 40
(VIIIA2e,3b)

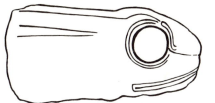

Fig. 390, Cat. 41b (VIIIA1a)   Attributed to CHEPHREN   Fig. 391, Cat. 41a (VIIIA2d)

Fig. 392, Cat. 42 (IIA4)   CHEPHREN   Fig. 393, Cat. 43 (IIE1)

Fig. 394, Cat. 44   Fig. 395, Cat. 45 (VIIIA1c,2e,3e)   Fig. 396, Cat. 46
(VIIIA2b,3d)   MYCERINUS   (VIIIA1b,2c,3d)

Fig. 397, Cat. 48a Fig. 398, Cat. 48b (IIE2) Fig. 399, Cat. 48c (IIE3) Fig. 400, Cat. 49
(IID2)   MYCERINUS   (IIE-2)

Fig. 401, Attributed to MYCERINUS, Cat. 47   Fig. 402, Attributed to SHEPSESKAF, Cat. 50
(VIIIA2c,3c)   (VIIIB1a,2a,3a)

DYNASTY IV OR LATER

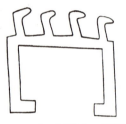

Fig. 403, Offering stand of Vizier SETHU Cat. 51 (VB)

DYNASTY V, c.2475-2345 B.C.

Fig. 404, Cat. 52 (VIIIA1b,2b,3g)   WESERKAF   Fig. 405, Cat. 53 (IIIB)

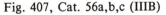

Fig. 406, Cat. 54 (VIIIA2b,3d)   SAHURA   Fig. 407, Cat. 56a,b,c (IIIB)

Fig. 408, Cat. 55 (IIIC)

Fig. 409, Cat. 57a (IIIA3)
SAHURA

Fig. 410, Cat. 57b (IIIA4)

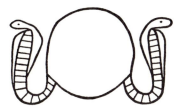

Fig. 411, Cat. 60a (IB1)

SAHURA

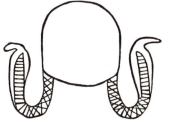

Fig. 412, Cat. 60, (IB1)

Fig. 413, Cat. 60a (IIA4)

Fig. 414, Cat. 61 (IIA5)
SAHURA

Fig. 415, Cat. 58, (IIA4)

   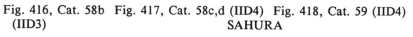

Fig. 416, Cat. 58b   Fig. 417, Cat. 58c,d (IID4)   Fig. 418, Cat. 59 (IID4)   Fig. 419, Cat. 61;
(IID3)   SAHURA   (IID2)

Fig. 420, Cat. 62 (IVA3)   SAHURA   Fig. 421, Cat. 59 (IVB2)

Fig. 422, Cat. 63   Fig. 423, Cat. 64 (VIIIA3f)   Fig. 424, Cat. 65
(VIIIA1c,2e)   NE-USER-RA   (VIIIA1c,2e,3g)

Fig. 425, Cat. 66a (VIIIA2e)   Attributed to NE-USER-RA   Fig. 426, Cat. 66b; (VIIIA2e,3f)

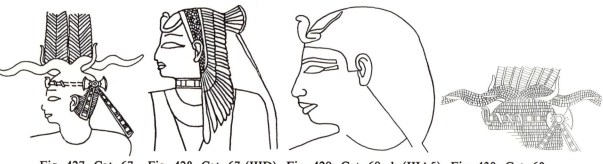

Fig. 427, Cat. 67   Fig. 428, Cat. 67 (IIID)   Fig. 429, Cat. 69a,b (IIIA5)   Fig. 430, Cat. 68
(IIIB)   NE-USER-RA   (IIIB)

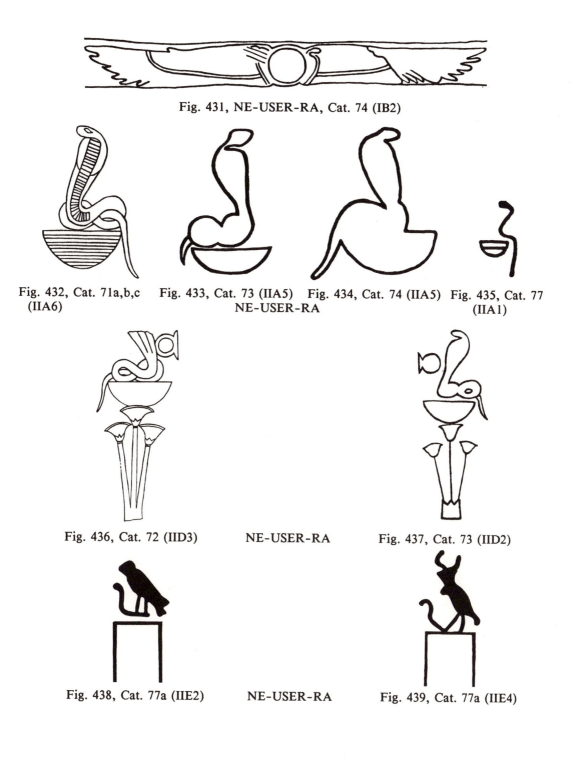

Fig. 431, NE-USER-RA, Cat. 74 (IB2)

Fig. 432, Cat. 71a,b,c
(IIA6)

Fig. 433, Cat. 73 (IIA5)
NE-USER-RA

Fig. 434, Cat. 74 (IIA5)

Fig. 435, Cat. 77
(IIA1)

Fig. 436, Cat. 72 (IID3)

NE-USER-RA

Fig. 437, Cat. 73 (IID2)

Fig. 438, Cat. 77a (IIE2)

NE-USER-RA

Fig. 439, Cat. 77a (IIE4)

Fig. 440, Cat. 75a-d (IVA3)

Fig. 441, Cat. 76a,b (IVA4)
NE-USER-RA

Fig. 442, Cat. 76c (IVA4)

LATE DYNASTY V

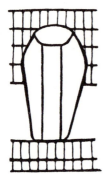

Fig. 443, Cat. 78 (VIIIC2a)

UNKNOWN KINGS

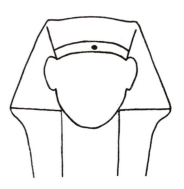

Fig. 444, Cat. 79 (VIIID1)

Fig. 445, Cat. 80 (IIIA1)

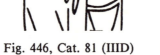
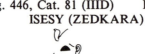

Fig. 446, Cat. 81 (IIID)
ISESY (ZEDKARA)

Fig. 447, Cat. 82a,b (IIA3)

Fig. 448, Cat. 85 (IIA5)

Fig. 449, Cat. 83 (IIIA4)
UNAS

Fig. 450, Cat. 85 (IID2)

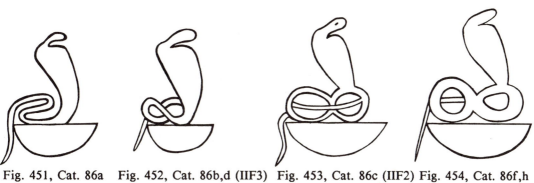

Fig. 451, Cat. 86a (IIF1)   Fig. 452, Cat. 86b,d (IIF3) UNAS   Fig. 453, Cat. 86c (IIF2)   Fig. 454, Cat. 86f,h (IIF5)

Fig. 455, Cat. 86g (IIF5)   UNAS   Fig. 456, Cat. 86e (IIF4)

Fig. 457, Attributed to UNAS, Cat. 84 (IID3)

Fig. 458, Obelisk of Vizier PTAH-HOTEP Cat. 87 (VB2)

DYNASTY VI, c.2345–2195 B.C.

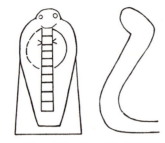

Fig. 459, Cat. 88 (VIIB)   TETY   Fig. 460, Cat. 88 (IIA2)

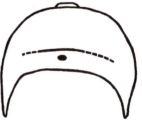

Fig. 461, Cat. 89a (IIID)   TETY   Fig. 462, Cat. 89b (IID3)

Fig. 463, PEPY I, Cat. 90 (VIIID1)   Fig. 464, PEPY I or MERNERA, Cat. 91 (VIIID2)

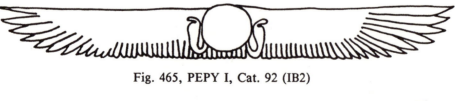

Fig. 465, PEPY I, Cat. 92 (IB2)

Fig. 466, PEPY I, Cat. 93 (IB2)

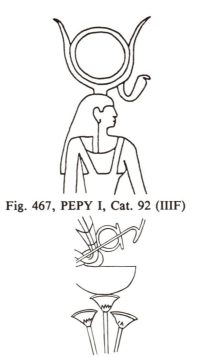

Fig. 467, PEPY I, Cat. 92 (IIIF)

Fig. 468, PEPY I or PEPY II?, Cat. 94 (IID3)

Fig. 469, Cat. 93 (IIA2)   Fig. 470, Cat. 92 (IIA3)   Fig. 471, Cat. 95 (IIE5)
                                      PEPY I

Fig. 472, Cat. 96 (VIIIA2f,3h)   PEPY II   Fig. 473, Cat. 97 (VIIIB2b,3b)

Fig. 474, Cat. 98, 99a (IIIC)   Fig. 475, Cat. 105a (IIIA3)   Fig. 476, Cat. 105b (IIIA4)
PEPY II

Fig. 477, Cat. 100b (IIID)   Fig. 478, Cat. 102a (IIID)   Fig. 479 Cat. 102b (IIID)
PEPY II

Fig. 480, Cat. 103 (IIIA2)   PEPY II   Fig. 481, Cat. 104 (IIIE)

Fig. 482, Cat. 99b (IIIF)   Fig. 483, Cat. 100a (IIIF)   Fig. 484, Cat. 101 (IIIF)
PEPY II

Fig. 485, PEPY II, Cat. 110 (IIE5)

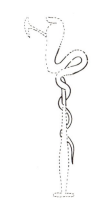

Fig. 486, Cat. 106b (IID4)   Fig. 487, Cat. 106a (IID4)   Fig. 488, Cat. 108 (IVB3)
PEPY II

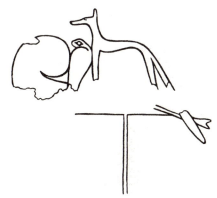

Fig. 489, Cat. 100a (VIA)   PEPY II   Fig. 490, Cat. 107 (IVA3)

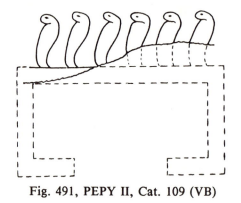

Fig. 491, PEPY II, Cat. 109 (VB)

LATE DYNASTY VI OR LATER

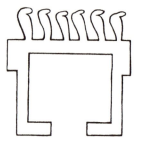

Fig. 492, Obelisk of VIZIER PRINCE TETY, Cat. 111 (VB)

LATE OLD KINGDOM ?

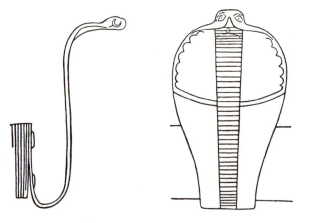

Fig. 493, Uraeus on GOLD-HEADED FALCON of HIERAKONPOLIS, Cat. 112 (VIIC)

12   URAEUS TYPE CHART

TYPE I.   WITH ANIMAL or DEITY SYMBOLS

A. WITH ELEPHANT

1. TWO INTERLACED URAEI

LATE PREDYNASTIC

Fig. 494, (Cat.1)   Fig. 495, (Cat. 2)   Fig. 496, (Cat. 3)

                           GERZEAN handles

2. SINGLE URAEUS

EARLY PREDYNASTIC

Fig. 497, AMRATIAN palette (Fig. 61)

LATE PREDYNASTIC

Fig. 498, (Cat. 4)   GERZEAN handles   Fig. 499, (Cat. 5)

B. WITH DEITY SYMBOL

1. WITH SUN DISK

DYNASTY V

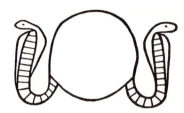

Fig. 500, SAHURA (Cat. 60a, b)

2. WITH WINGED SUN DISK

DYNASTY V

Fig. 501, NE-USER-RA (Cat. 74)

DYNASTY VI

Fig. 502, PEPY I (Cat. 92)

Fig. 503, PEPY I (Cat. 93)

TYPE II. IN DIVINE AND ROYAL NAMES

A. ON BASKET IN ROYAL *nbty* NAME

1. HIEROGLYPHIC *d̠*

DYNASTY I

Fig. 504, HOR AHA (MENES) (Cat. 6)   Fig. 505, QAY-A, (Cat. 13b)

DYNASTY V

Fig. 506, NE-USER-RA (Cat. 77a)

2. SINGLE COIL; HOOD IN PROFILE

DYNASTY I   DYNASTY VI

Fig. 507, SEMERKHET   Fig. 508, QAY-A   Fig. 509, TETY   Fig. 510, PEPY I
(Cat. 12a)   (Cat. 12b, 13a)   (Cat. 88)   (Cat. 93)

3. DOUBLE LOOP; HOOD FRONT VIEW

DYNASTY II   DYNASTY VI

KHASEKHEMUWY   PEPY I
Fig. 511, (Cat. 14a) Fig. 512, (Cat. 14b) Fig. 513, (Cat. 15)   Fig. 514, (Cat. 92)

**4.   DOUBLE LOOP;   HOOD FRONT VIEW;   TAIL THROUGH OR ACROSS
BACK LOOP FROM FRONT;   EYE, VENTRAL COLUMN, AND/OR OTHER
DETAILS**

DYNASTY III

Fig. 515, (Cat. 20)   ZOSER   Fig. 516, (Cat. 21, 22)

DYNASTY IV

Fig. 517, SNEFERU (Cat. 25)   Fig. 518,   CHEOPS (KHUFU) (Cat. 29a)   Fig. 519, (Cat. 29b)

Fig. 520, HETEP-HERES I Fig. 521, CHEOPS (Cat. 29c) Fig. 522, CHEPHREN (Cat. 42)
(Cat. 27)

DYNASTY V

Fig. 523, (Cat. 58a)   SAHURA   Fig. 524, (Cat. 60a)

5. SOLID LOOPS, WITHOUT DETAIL

DYNASTY V

Fig. 525, SAHURA (Cat. 61)   Fig. 526 , NE-USER-RA (Cat. 73)   Fig. 527, (Cat. 74)

Fig. 528, ISESY (Cat. 82a, b)   Fig. 529, UNAS (Cat. 85)

6. DOUBLE LOOP; TAIL THROUGH BACK LOOP FROM REAR

DYNASTY V

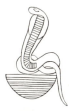

Fig. 530, NE-USER-RA (Cat. 71a-c)

B. DETAILED, HIEROGLYPHIC _d_ ABOVE FACADE

DYNASTY I

Fig. 531, ZET (WADJI) (Cat. 8)

C. DETAILED, DOUBLE LOOP ABOVE *nbw* and *šnw*

DYNASTY I

Fig. 532, DEN (WEDYMU) (Cat. 11)

D. WITH *w3s* SCEPTER AND *šnw* AND/OR NAME, WADJET

1. SOLID DOUBLE LOOPS WITHOUT DETAIL;

DYNASTY IV

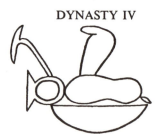

Fig. 533, HETEP-HERES I (Cat. 28a, b)

DYNASTY V

Fig. 534, NE-USER-RA (Cat. 74)

2.   SOLID DOUBLE LOOPS, WITH AND WITHOUT DETAIL; SUPPORTED BY PAPYRUS

DYNASTY IV

Fig. 535, MYCERINUS (Cat. 48)

DYNASTY V

Fig. 536, SAHURA (Cat. 61)   Fig. 537, NE-USER-RA (Cat. 73)   Fig. 538, UNAS (Cat. 85b)

3.   **DOUBLE LOOP; TAIL ACROSS, THROUGH, OR UNDER BACK LOOP FROM FRONT**

DYNASTY V

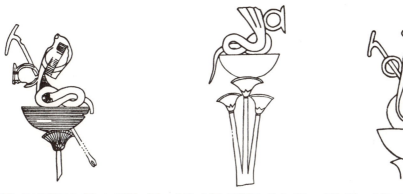

Fig. 539, SAHURA (Cat. 58b)   Fig. 540, NE-USER-RA (Cat. 72) Fig. 541, UNAS? (Cat. 84)

DYNASTY VI

Fig. 542, TETY (Cat. 89b)   Fig. 543, PEPY I (?) (Cat. 94)

4. DOUBLE LOOP; TAIL THROUGH BACK LOOP FROM REAR

DYNASTY V   DYNASTY VI

Fig. 544, SAHURA (Cat. 58c-d, 59)   Fig. 545, PEPY II (Cat. 106a, b)

E. WITH FALCON ABOVE HORUS NAME

1. BETWEEN TWO UNCROWNED BIRDS

DYNASTY IV

Fig. 546, CHEPHREN (Cat. 43)

2. WITH UNCROWNED FALCON

DYNASTY IV   DYNASTY V

Fig. 547, MYCERINUS   Fig. 548, NEFERIRKARE and NE-USER-RA
(Cat. 48, 49)   (Cat. 77a, b)

3. WITH WHITE CROWNED FALCON

DYNASTY IV

Fig. 549, MYCERINUS (Cat. 48)

4. WITH RED CROWNED FALCON

DYNASTY V

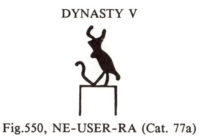

Fig.550, NE-USER-RA (Cat. 77a)

5. WITH FEATHER AND HORN CROWNED FALCON

DYNASTY VI

Fig. 551, PEPY I (Cat. 95)   Fig. 552, PEPY II (Cat. 110)

F. DETERMINATIVE IN NAMES OF COBRA GODDESS

1. BODY IN TWO CURVES ON BASKET IN IARWET

DYNASTY V

Fig. 553, UNAS (Cat. 86a)

2. DOUBLE LOOP BODY ON BASKET WITH TAIL THROUGH BACK LOOP
IN AKHET, RENNEWETET, NESRET (SOLID LOOPS),
IKHET-WETET

DYNASTY V

Fig. 554, UNAS (Cat. 86c, g)   Fig. 555, (Cat. 86f, h)

3. BODY OF DOUBLE COILS ON BASKET; TAIL HANGS FROM REAR
COIL IN IARWET

DYNASTY V

Fig. 556, UNAS (Cat. 86b, d)

4. WITHOUT BASKET; BODY IN THREE CURVES BEHIND BASE OF
HOOD IN SEBI

DYNASTY V

Fig. 557, UNAS (Cat. 86e)

TYPE III. ON ROYAL OR DIVINE HEADDRESS IN RELIEF

    A. ON FOREHEAD OF PLAIN HEADDRESS

        1. HOOD IN PROFILE HIGH ABOVE ROYAL HEAD

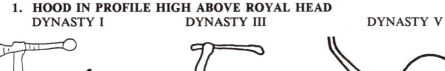

      DYNASTY I   DYNASTY III   DYNASTY V

Fig. 558, DEN (Cat. 10)   Fig. 559, ZOSER (Cat. 19)   Fig. 560, ISESY (Cat. 80)

        2. ON SHORT CAP OR WIG OF QUEEN MOTHER
                        DYNASTY VI

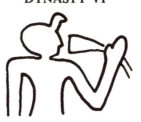

Fig. 561, ANKHNES-MERY-RA (Cat. 103)

        3. ON KING'S HEAD CARRIED ON STANDARD
          DYNASTY V   DYNASTY VI

Fig. 562, SAHURA (Cat. 57a)   Fig. 563, PEPY II (Cat. 105a)

        4. ON SHORT CAP OR WIG OF KING
          DYNASTY V   DYNASTY VI

Fig. 564, NEFIRERKARA   Fig. 565, UNAS (Cat. 83)   Fig. 566 Son of PEPY II
(Cat. 57b)   (Cat. 105)

5. ON *khat* **HEADDRESS**

DYNASTY V

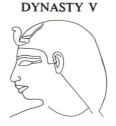

Fig. 567, NE-USER-RA (Cat. 69a, b)

B. ENTWINED ON DIADEM

DYNASTY IV

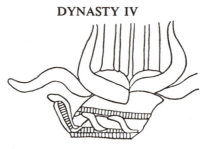

Fig. 568, SNEFERU (Cat. 26a, b)

DYNASTY V

Fig. 569, WESERKAF   Fig. 570, SAHURA (Cat. 56a-c)   Fig. 571, NE-USER-RA
(Cat. 53)   (Cat. 67, 68)

C. COILED ON KING'S HEADDRESS

DYNASTY V   DYNASTY VI

Fig. 572, SAHURA (Cat. 55) Fig. 573, NE-USER-RA (Cat. 70) Fig. 574, PEPY II(Cat.98,99a)

D. ON FEATHERED HEADDRESS OF GODDESS

DYNASTY V

Fig. 575, WADJET with NE-USER-RA (Cat. 67)   Fig. 576, WADJET with ISESY (Cat. 81)

DYNASTY VI

Fig. 577, WADJET in TETY relief   Fig. 578, WADJET with PEPY II, Fig. 579
(Cat. 89a)   (Cat. 100b)   (Cat. 102b)

E. ON FEATHERED HEADDRESS OF QUEEN

DYNASTY VI

Fig. 580, NEITH, Wife (?) of PEPY II (Cat. 104)

F. PENDENT FROM SUN DISK ABOVE DEITY

DYNASTY VI

Fig. 581 HATHOR with PEPY I (Cat. 92)   Fig. 582, Hathor with PEPY II (Cat. 99, 100a)

Fig. 583, FALCON-HEADED GOD with with PEPY II (Cat. 101)

TYPE IV. ON STANDARD

A. WEPWAWET STANDARD

1. URAEUS HEAD AND HOOD IN PROFILE FACING *šdšd*

DYNASTY I

Fig. 584, DEN (Cat. 10)

DYNASTY III

Fig. 585, SA-NEKHT (Cat. 17, 18)

2. DETAILED HOOD IN FRONT VIEW FACING *šdšd*; BODY BETWEEN LEGS OF CANINE

DYNASTY III

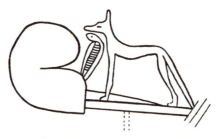

Fig. 586, ZOSER (Cat. 23a)

3. UNDETAILED HOOD IN FRONT VIEW FACING *šdšd*

DYNASTY V

DYNASTY VI

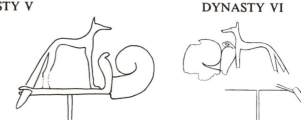

Fig. 587, SAHURA (Cat. 62) Fig. 588, NE-USER-RA (Cat. 75a-d) Fig. 589, PEPY II(Cat.107)

4. **NO** *šdšd*; **WITH AND WITHOUT BASKET-LIKE APPURTENANCE BELOW**

DYNASTY V

Fig. 590, NE-USER-RA (Cat. 76a, b)   Fig. 591, NE-USER-RA (Cat. 76c)

B. **WADJET STANDARD**

1. **UNDETAILED; HANGS IN THREE SOLID LOOPS (SIX CURVES) ON PAPYRUS STEM**

DYNASTY IV

Fig. 592, HETEP-HERES I (Cat. 28c)

2. **DETAILED; ENTWINED ON** *w3s* **SCEPTER IN SIX CURVES;** *'nḫ* **HANGS ON HOOD**

DYNASTY V

Fig. 593, SAHURA (Cat. 59)

3. WITH *w3s* SCEPTER ON PAPYRUS (?)

DYNASTY VI

Fig. 594, PEPY II (Cat. 108)

TYPE V. ARCHITECTURAL ELEMENT

A. ON A WALL

DYNASTY III

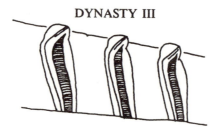

Fig. 595, ZOSER (Cat. 24)

B. IN RELIEF ATOP HIEROGLYPH, *t3yty*

DYNASTY IV(?)

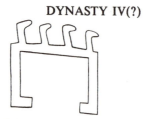

Fig. 596, Vizier SETHU offering stand (Cat. 51)

DYNASTY V

Fig. 597, Vizier PTAH-HOTEP obelisk in relief (Cat. 87)

DYNASTY VI

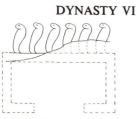

Fig. 598, PEPY II relief (Cat. 109)

DYNASTY VI or later

Fig. 599, Vizier Prince TETY obelisk (Cat. 111)

TYPE VI. ON ROYAL CLOTHING

DYNASTY VI

Fig. 600, PEPY II (Cat. 100a)

TYPE VII. SCULPTURE

A. IVORY

DYNASTY I   Attributed to DYNASTY II

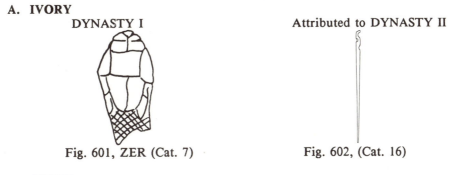

Fig. 601, ZER (Cat. 7)   Fig. 602, (Cat. 16)

B. STONE

DYNASTY VI

Fig. 603, TETY (Cat. 88)

C. GOLD

DYNASTY VI (?)

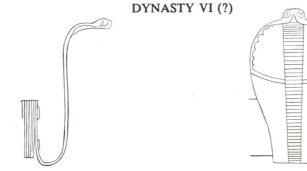

Fig. 604, Uraeus on GOLD-HEADED FALCON of HIERAKONPOLIS (Cat. 112)

TYPE VIII.   ON ROYAL HEADDRESS IN SCULPTURE

A.   ON NEMES

1. URAEUS HEAD

a. BROKEN OFF FROM GREAT SPHINX
DYNASTY IV

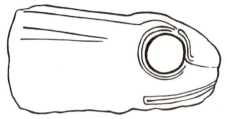

Fig. 605, CHEPHREN (?) (Cat. 41b)

b. REMAINS OF DAMAGED HEAD
DYNASTY IV

Fig. 606, RADEDEF   Fig. 607, CHEPHREN (Cat. 34, 39c,d)   Fig. 608, MYCERINUS
(Cat. 30)   (Cat. 46)

DYNASTY V

Fig. 609, WESERKAF (Cat. 52)   Fig. 610, NE-USER-RA (Cat. 65)

c. WORN OR UNFINISHED NODULE
DYNASTY IV

Fig. 611, CHEPHREN?   Fig. 612, CHEPHREN or MYCERINUS?   Fig. 613, MYCERINUS
(Cat. 35)   (Cat. 36)   (Cat. 45)

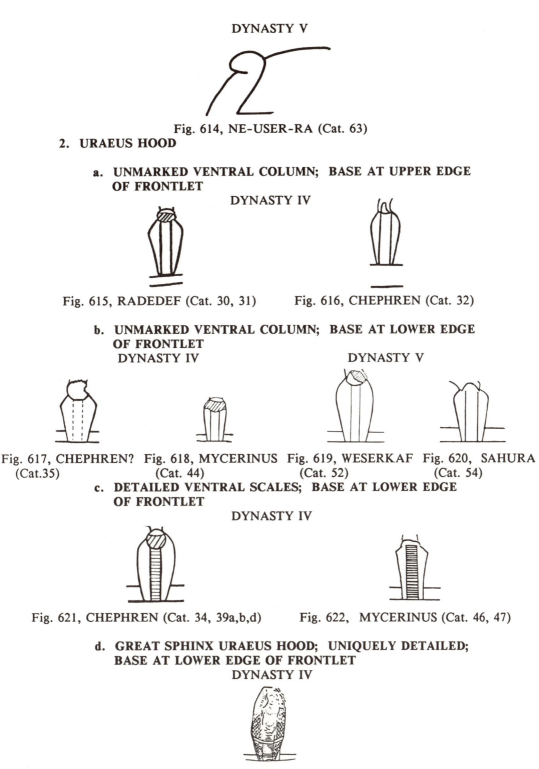

DYNASTY V

Fig. 614, NE–USER–RA (Cat. 63)

2. **URAEUS HOOD**

   a. **UNMARKED VENTRAL COLUMN; BASE AT UPPER EDGE
       OF FRONTLET**

DYNASTY IV

Fig. 615, RADEDEF (Cat. 30, 31)   Fig. 616, CHEPHREN (Cat. 32)

   b. **UNMARKED VENTRAL COLUMN; BASE AT LOWER EDGE
       OF FRONTLET**

DYNASTY IV   DYNASTY V

Fig. 617, CHEPHREN? Fig. 618, MYCERINUS Fig. 619, WESERKAF Fig. 620, SAHURA
   (Cat.35)   (Cat. 44)   (Cat. 52)   (Cat. 54)

   c. **DETAILED VENTRAL SCALES; BASE AT LOWER EDGE
       OF FRONTLET**

DYNASTY IV

Fig. 621, CHEPHREN (Cat. 34, 39a,b,d)   Fig. 622, MYCERINUS (Cat. 46, 47)

   d. **GREAT SPHINX URAEUS HOOD; UNIQUELY DETAILED;
       BASE AT LOWER EDGE OF FRONTLET**

DYNASTY IV

Fig. 623, CHEPHREN? (Cat. 41a)

**e. UNDETAILED; FLAT RELIEF; BASE AT LOWER EDGE
   OF FRONTLET**

DYNASTY IV

Fig. 624, CHEPHREN
(Cat. 33)

Fig. 625, CHEPHREN? (Cat. 36-38, 40)

Fig. 626, MYCERINUS
(Cat. 45)

DYNASTY V

Fig. 627, NE-USER-RA (Cat. 63-65)

Fig. 628, NE-USER-RA? (Cat. 66)

**f. APPARENTLY UNDETAILED, BADLY DAMAGED; BASE AT
   UPPER EDGE OF FRONTLET**

DYNASTY VI

Fig. 629, PEPY II (Cat. 96)

3. URAEUS BODY

a. FULL BODIED; THREE OPEN CURVES

DYNASTY IV

Fig. 630, RADEDEF (Cat. 30, 31)

Fig. 631, CHEPHREN (?) (Cat. 35)

b. SLIM BODIED; FOUR OPEN CURVES

DYNASTY IV

Fig. 632, CHEPHREN (Cat. 32, 33)

c. SLIM BODIED; FIVE OPEN CURVES

DYNASTY IV

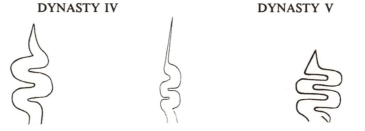

Fig. 633, MYCERINUS (Cat. 47)

d. FULL BODIED; FOUR SEMI-OPEN, CURVES

DYNASTY IV   DYNASTY V

Fig. 634, (Cat. 44) MYCERINUS, Fig. 635 (Cat. 46)   Fig. 636, SAHURA (Cat. 54)

e. FULL BODIED; SIX SEMI-COMPRESSED CURVES

DYNASTY IV

Fig. 637, CHEPHREN (Cat. 34)   Fig. 638, MYCERINUS (Cat. 45)

f. FLATTENED NODES ON TOP OF KING'S HEADS

DYNASTY IV   DYNASTY V

Fig. 639, CHEPHREN   Fig. 640, CHEPHREN or MYCERINUS   Fig. 641, NE-USER-RA
     (Cat. 38)   (Cat. 36)   (Cat. 64, 66b)

g. FULL BODIED; FIVE SEMI-COMPRESSED CURVES

DYNASTY V

Fig. 642, WESERKAF (Cat. 52)   Fig. 643, NE-USER-RA (Cat. 65)

h. SLIM BODIED; EIGHT SEMI-COMPRESSED CURVES
DYNASTY VI

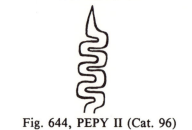

Fig. 644, PEPY II (Cat. 96)

B. ON SHORT CAP OR WIG

1. URAEUS HEAD

a. POINTED, EGG-SHAPED OVAL
DYNASTY IV

Fig. 645, SHEPSESKAF? (Cat. 50)

2. URAEUS HOOD

a. UNDETAILED, SHIELD SHAPE; BASE AT EDGE OF HORIZONTALLY STRIATED CAP OR WIG; FLAT RELIEF
DYNASTY IV

Fig. 646, SHEPSESKAF? (Cat.50)

**b. APPARENTLY UNDETAILED; BADLY DAMAGED; BASE
AT EDGE OF PLAIN CAP OR WIG**
DYNASTY VI

Fig. 647, PEPY II (Cat. 97)

3. URAEUS BODY

a. FULL BODIED; SIX SEMI-COMPRESSED CURVES
DYNASTY IV

Fig. 648, SHEPSESKAF? (Cat. 50)

b. SLIM BODIED; EIGHT SEMI-OPEN CURVES
DYNASTY VI

Fig. 649, PEPY II (Cat. 97)

C. ON DIADEM

2. URAEUS HOOD

a. UNDETAILED VENTRAL COLUMN, FAINTLY MODELED
Late DYNASTY V or early DYNASTY VI

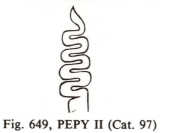

Fig. 650, UNKNOWN KING (Cat. 78)

D. CAVITY; URAEUS MISSING; FORM UNDETERMINED

    1. ON NEMES

Late DYNASTY V   DYNASTY VI

Fig. 651, UNKNOWN KING (Cat. 79)   Fig. 652, PEPY I (Cat. 90)

    2. ON SHORT CAP OR WIG; CORRODED NODES MAY INDICATE URAEUS BODY

DYNASTY VI

Fig. 653, PEPY I or PRINCE MERNERA (Cat. 91)

CONCORDANCE I - CHRONOLOGY

Objects with uraei cited in the HISTORY (CATALOG) section are listed below according to **CHRONOLOGY** (Time Period or King), Type, and Provenance with Catalog and Page Number.

TIME PERIOD OR KING	TYPE	PROVENANCE	CAT.	PAGE
EARLY PREDYNASTIC, c.4000 B.C.				
AMRATIAN				
Slate palette	IA2	Abadiyeh	Fig. 61	36
LATE PREDYNASTIC, c.3200-3000B.C.				
GERZEAN				
Knife handle	IA1	Abu Zeidan	1	39
Knife handle	IA1	Not known	2	42
Mace handle	IAI	Seyala	3	43
Comb handle	IA2	Not Known	4	44
Knife handle	IA2	Nagada?	5	45
EARLY DYNASTIC c.3000-2670 B.C.				
DYNASTY I, c.3000-2820 B.C.				
HOR AHA (MENES)	IIA1	Nagada	6	46
ZER	VIIA	Abydos	7	48
ZET (WADJI)	IIB	Abydos	8-9	49-51
DEN (WEDYMU)	IIIA1	Abydos?	10	52
DEN	IVA1	Abydos?	10	52
DEN	IIC	Abydos	11	54
SEMERKHET	IIA2	Abydos	12a	55
QAY-A	IIA2	Abydos	12b	55
QAY-A	IIA2	Abydos	13a	57
QAY-A	IIA1	Abydos	13b	57
DYNASTY II, c.2820-2670 B.C.				
PERIBSEN	IIA2	Abydos	13d	57
KHASEKHEMUY	IIA3	Abydos	14a	59
KHASEKHEMUY	IIA3	Saqqara	14b	59
KHASEKHEMUY?	IIA3	Gebelein	15	61
Ivory Pin	VIIA	Zawiyet el-Aryan	16	62

TIME PERIOD OR KING	TYPE	PROVENANCE	CAT.	PAGE

OLD KINGDOM, c.2670-2195

DYNASTY III, c.2670-2600 B.C.

TIME PERIOD OR KING	TYPE	PROVENANCE	CAT.	PAGE
SA-NEKHT	IVA	Sinai	17	63
SA-NEKHT	IVA	Gebelein	18	65
NETERKHET (ZOSER)	IIIA1	Sinai	19	66
ZOSER	IIA4	Saqqara	20-21	67-69
ZOSER	IIA4	Saqqara	22	70
ZOSER	IVA2	Saqqara	23	71
ZOSER	VA	Saqqara	24	73

DYNASTY IV, 2600-2475 B.C.

TIME PERIOD OR KING	TYPE	PROVENANCE	CAT.	PAGE
SNEFERU	IIA4	Dahshur	25	74
SNEFERU	IIIB	Dahshur	26a,b	75
HETEP-HERES I	IIA4	Giza	27	77
HETEP-HERES I	IID1	Giza	28a,b	79
HETEP-HERES I	IVB1	Giza	28c	79
CHEOPS	IIA4	Sinai	29a	81
CHEOPS	IIA4	Lisht	29b	81
CHEOPS	IIA4	Tanis	29c	81
RADEDEF	VIIIA1b,2a,3a	Abu Roash	30-31	83-84
CHEPHREN	VIIIA2a,3b	Giza	32	85
CHEPHREN	VIIIA2e,3b	Giza	33	86
CHEPHREN	VIIIA1b,2c,3e	Mit Rahina	34	87
Attributed to **CHEPHREN**	VIIIA1c,2b,3a	Giza	35	88
Attributed to **CHEPHREN** or **MYCERINUS**?	VIIIA1c,2e,3f	Mit Rahina	36	89
Attributed to CHEPHREN	VIIIA2e	Giza	37	90
Attributed to **CHEPHREN**	VIIIA2e,3f	Giza	38	91
Attributed to **CHEPHREN**	VIIIA2c	Giza	39a,b	92
Attributed to **CHEPHREN**	VIIIA1b,2a	Giza	39c	92
Attributed to CHEPHREN	VIIIA2c,3a	Giza	39d	92
Attributed to**CHEPHREN**	VIIIA2e,3b	Giza	40	94
Great Sphinx (**CHEPHREN**?)	VIIIA1a,2d	Giza	41a,b	95
CHEPHREN	IIA4	Near Bubastis	42	99
CHEPHREN	IIE1	Giza	43	100
MYCERINUS	VIIIA2b,3d	Giza	44	101
MYCERINUS	VIIIA1c,2e,3e	Mit Rahina	45	102
Attributed to **MYCERINUS**	VIIIA1b,2c,3d	Giza	46	103
Attributed to **MYCERINUS**	VIIIA2c,3c	Giza	47	105
MYCERINUS	IID2	Giza	48	106
MYCERINUS	IIE2	Giza	48	106
MYCERINUS	IIE3	Giza	48	106
MYCERINUS	IIE2	Not known	49	107
Attributed to **SHEPSESKAF**	VIIIB1a,2a,3a	Giza	50	108
Vizier Sethu	VB	Saqqara	51	110

TIME PERIOD OR KING	TYPE	PROVENANCE	CAT.	PAGE
DYNASTY V, 2475-2345 B.C.				
WESERKAF	VIIIA1b,2b,3g	Saqqara	52	111
WESERKAF	IIIB	Saqqara	53	112
SAHURA	VIIIA2b,3d	Koptos?	54	113
SAHURA	IIIC1	Abusir	55	114
SAHURA	IIIB	Abusir	56a,c	115
SAHURA	IIIA3	Abusir	57a	117
SAHURA	IIIA4	Abusir	57b	117
SAHURA	IIA4	Abusir	58a	118
SAHURA	IID3	Abusir	58b	118
SAHURA	IID4	Abusir	58c,d	118
SAHURA	IID4	Abusir	59	120
SAHURA	IVB2	Abusir	59	120
SAHURA	IB1	Abusir	60a,b	122
SAHURA	IIA4	Abusir	60a,b	122
SAHURA	IIA5	Abusir	61	124
SAHURA	IID2	Abusir	61	124
SAHURA	IVA3	Sinai	62	125
NE-USER-RA	VIIIA1c,2e	Mit Rahina	63	126
NE-USER-RA	VIIIA2e,3f	Karnak	64	127
NE-USER-RA	VIIIA1b,2e,3g	Not known	65	128
Attributed to **NE-USER-RA**	VIIIA1c	Byblos	66a	130
NE-USER-RA	VIIIA2e	Not known	66b	130
NE-USER-RA	IIIB	Abusir	67	131
NE-USER-RA	IIID	Abusir	67	131
NE-USER-RA	IIIB	Abu Ghurob	68	132
NE-USER-RA	IIIA5	AbuGhurob	69a,b	133
NE-USER-RA	IIIC1	Abusir	70	134
NE-USER-RA	IIA6	Abu Ghurob	71a-c	135
NE-USER-RA	IID3	Abu Ghurob	72	136
NE-USER-RA	IIA5	Abusir	73	137
NE-USER-RA	IID2	Abusir	73	137
NE-USER-RA	IB2	Sinai	74	138
NE-USER-RA	IIA5	Sinai	74	138
NE-USER-RA	IID1	Sinai	74	138
NE-USER-RA	IVA3	Abu Ghurob	75a-d	140
NE-USER-RA	IVA4	Abu Ghurob	76a-c	142
NE-USER-RA	IIA1	Not known	77a	144
NE-USER-RA	IIE2	Not known	77a-c	144
NE-USER-RA	IIE4	Not known	77a	144
UNKNOWN KING	VIIIC2a	Not known	78	145
UNKNOWN KING	VIIID1	Not known	79	146
ISESY (ZEDKARA)	IIIA1	Sinai	80	147
ISESY	IIID	Saqqara	81	148
ISESY	IIA3	Abusir	82a,b	149
UNAS	IIIA4	Saqqara	83	151
UNAS?	IID3	Saqqara	84	152
UNAS	IIA5	Saqqara	85a	153
UNAS	IID2	Saqqara	85b	153
UNAS	IIF1-5	Saqqara	86a-h	154

TIME PERIOD OR KING	TYPE	PROVENANCE	CAT.	PAGE
Vizier Ptah-hotep	VB	Saqqara	87	157
DYNASTY VI, c.2345-2195 B.C.				
TETY	IIA2	Not known	88	158
TETY	VIIB	Not known	88	158
TETY	IIID	Saqqara	89a	160
TETY	IID3	Saqqara	89b	161
PEPY I	VIIID1	Not known	90	162
PEPY I or **MERNERA**	VIIID2	Hierakonpolis	91	163
PEPY I	IB2	Tell Basta	92	164
PEPY I	IIA3	Tell Basta	92	164
PEPY I	IIIF	Tell Basta	92	164
PEPY I	IB2	Sinai	93	165
PEPY I	IIA2	Sinai	93	165
PEPY I?	IID3	Lisht	94	166
PEPY I	IIE5	Not known	95	167
PEPY II	VIIIA2f,3h	Not known	96	168
PEPY II	VIIIB2b,3b	Saqqara	97	170
PEPY II	IIIC	Saqqara	98	171
PEPY II	IIIC,F	Saqqara	99a	172
PEPY II	IIIF	Saqqara	99b	172
PEPY II	IIIF	Saqqara	100a	173
PEPY II	VI	Saqqara	100a	173
PEPY II	IIID	Saqqara	100b	173
PEPY II	IIIF	Saqqara	101	174
PEPY II	IIID	Saqqara	102a,b	175
PEPY II	IIIA2	Sinai	103	176
NEITH	IIIE	Saqqara	104	177
PEPY II	IIIA3	Saqqara	105a	178
PEPY II	IIIA4	Saqqara	105b	178
PEPY II	IIA6	Saqqara	106a	179
PEPY II	IID4	Saqqara	106a,b	179
PEPY II	IVA3	Saqqara	107	181
PEPY II	IVB3	Saqqara	108	182
PEPY II	VB	Saqqara	109	184
PEPY II	IIE5	Not Known	110	185
Vizier Prince Tety	VB	Saqqara	111	186
LATE DYNASTY VI?				
Diadem of Gold Falcon Head	VIIC	Hierakonpolis	112	187

CONCORDANCE II - TYPE

Objects with uraei cited in the HISTORY (CATALOG) section are listed below, first according to **TYPE** then by time Period or King, and Present Location with Catalog and Page Number.

TYPE	TIME PERIOD OR KING	PRESENT LOCATION	CAT.	PAGE£
IA2?	Amratian, c.4000 B.C.	Brussels MRAH E.7062	Fig. 61	36
IA1	LATE PREDYNASTIC,	Brooklyn 09.889.118	1	39
	c.3200 B.C.	New York MMA 26.7.1281	2	42
		Cairo JE 43883	3	43
		New York MMA 30.8.244	4	44
		London BM 68512	5	45
IB1	SAHURA	Abusir, *in situ*	60a	122
IB2	NE-USER-RA	Cairo JE 38570	74	138
	PEPY I	Cairo JE 72132	92	164
	PEPY I	Sinai, now destroyed	93	165
IIA1	HOR AHA	Cairo CG 14142	6	46
	QAY-A	New York MMA 01.4.20	13b	57
	NE-USER-RA	Brooklyn 44.123.30	77a	144
IIA2	SEMERKHET	London BM 32668	12a	55
	QAY-A	Philadelphia UPM E. 6880	12b	
IIA2	QAY-A	London BM 32672	13a	57
	TETY	New York MMA 26.7.1450	88	158
	PEPY I	Now destroyed	93	165
IIA3	KHASEKHEMUWY	London BM 35592	14a	59
	KHASEKHEMUWY	Cairo JE 55291	14b	59
	KHASEKHEMUWY?	Turin, cat. 12341	15	61
	ISESY	E. Berlin ÄMP 17933	82a	149
	ISESY	Brooklyn 64.148.2	82b	149
	PEPY I	Cairo JE 72132	92	164
IIA4	ZOSER	Cairo JE 49613	20	67
	ZOSER	Saqqara, *in situ*	21	69
	ZOSER	Cairo JE 52508	22	70
	SNEFERU	Cairo JE 89289	25	74
	HETEP-HERES I	Cairo CG 57711	27	77
	CHEOPS	Now destroyed	29a	81
	CHEOPS	New York MMA 22.1.19	29b	81
	CHEOPS	Tanis, *in situ*	29c	81
	CHEPHREN	New York MMA 07.288.24	42	99
	SAHURA	Berlin ÄMP 28613	58a	118
	SAHURA	Abusir, *in situ*	60a	122
	SAHURA	W. Berlin ÄM 343/67	60b	122

TYPE	TIME PERIOD OR KING	PRESENT LOCATION	CAT.	PAGE
IIA5	SAHURA	Cairo JE 39527	61	124
	NE-USER-RA	Cairo JE 38664	73	137
	NE-USER-RA	Cairo JE 38570	74	138
	UNAS	Cairo JE 35131	85	153
IIA6	NE-USER-RA	Not known	71a	135
	NE-USER-RA	Munich Gl 185	71b	135
	NE-USER-RA	Munich Gl 183	71c	135
	PEPY II	Not known	106a	179
IIB	ZET (WADJI)	Louvre E 11007	8	49
	ZET	London BM 32641	9a	51
	ZET	Cairo JE 47176	9b	51
IIC	DEN (WEDYMU)	London BM 35552	11	54
IID1	HETEP-HERES I	Cairo JE 72030	28a,b	79
	NE-USER-RA	Cairo JE 38570	74	138
IID2	MYCERINUS	Boston MFA 09.202	48	106
	SAHURA	Cairo JE 39527	61	124
	NE-USER-RA	Cairo JE 38664	73	137
	UNAS	Cairo JE 35131	85	153
IID3	SAHURA	E. Berlin ÄMP 28628	58b	118
	NE-USER-RA	Göttingen AIUZ.V.I-2t (1912)	72	136
	UNAS?	Saqqara, *in situ*	84	152
	TETY	Saqqara, *in situ*	89b	160
	PEPY I?	Montreal MFA 964.B.6	94	166
IID4	SAHURA	Strassburg, Germany	58c	118
	SAHURA	Not known	58d	118
	SAHURA	Abusir, *in situ*?	59	120
	PEPY II	Not known	106a,b	179
IIE1	CHEPHREN	Not known	43	100
IIE2	MYCERINUS	Boston MFA 09.202	48	106
	MYCERINUS	E. Berlin ÄMP 19999	49	107
	NEFERIRKARE and			
	NE-USER-RA	Brooklyn 44.123.30	77a	144
	NE-USER-RA	Brooklyn 44.123.31	77b	144
	NE-USER-RA	London UCL 11103	77c	144
IIE3	MYCERINUS	Boston MFA 09.202	48	106
IIE4	NE-USER-RA	Brooklyn 44.123.30	77a	144
IIE5	PEPY I	Brooklyn 44.123.32	95	167
	PEPY II	London BM 25422	110	185
IIF1	UNAS	Saqqara, *in situ*	86a	154
IIF2,5	UNAS	Saqqara, *in situ*	86c, f-h	154
IIF3	UNAS	Saqqara, *in situ*	86b,d	154
IIF4	UNAS	Saqqara, *in situ*	86e	154
IIIA1	DEN (WEDYMU)	London BM 55586	10	52
	ZOSER	Sinai, *in situ*	19	66
	ISESY	Sinai, now destroyed	80	147
IIIA2	ANKHNES-MERY-RA,			
	Mother of PEPY II	Sinai, now destroyed	103	176
IIIA3	SAHURA	Kalingrad, U.S.S.R.	57a	117
	PEPY II	Not known	105a	178

TYPE	TIME PERIOD OR KING	PRESENT LOCATION	CAT.	PAGE
IIIA4	Neferirkara	Hamburg, PC	57b	117
	UNAS	Not known	83	151
	Son of PEPY II	Not known	105b	178
IIIA5	NE-USER-RA	Not known	69a,b	133
IIIB	SNEFERU	Not known	26a,b	75
	WESERKAF	Cairo JE 56600	53	112
IIIB	SAHURA	Hamburg MKG 1925.63	56a	115
	SAHURA	Bonn ÄSU A 310	56b	115
	SAHURA	Formerly in Breslau	56c	115
	NE-USER-RA	E. Berlin ÄMP 16100	67	131
	NE-USER-RA	Not known	68	132
IIIC	SAHURA	Cairo JE 39533	55	114
	NE-USER-RA	E. Berlin ÄMP 17911	70	134
	PEPY II	Not known	98	171
	PEPY II	Not known	99a	172
IIID	NE-USER-RA with Wadjet	E. Berlin ÄMP 16100	67	131
	ISESY with Wadjet	Not known	81	148
	TETY with Wadjet	Saqqara magazine	89a	160
	PEPY II with Wadjet	Cairo CG 53836	100b	173
	PEPY II with Wadjet	Not known	102b	175
IIIE	NEITH (NITOKRIS)	Not known	104	177
IIIF	PEPY I with Hathor	Cairo JE 72132	92	164
IIIF	PEPY II with Hathor	Not known	99a,b	172
	PEPY II with Hathor	Cairo JE 62950	100a	173
	PEPY II with falcon-headed god	Saqqara, *in situ*?	101	174
IVA1	DEN (WEDYMU)	London BM 55586	10	52
	SA-NEKHT	Cairo CG 57101	17	63
	SA-NEKHT?	Cairo TL 20/1/21/7	18	65
IVA2	ZOSER	Saqqara, *in situ*	23	71
IVA3	SAHURA	Cairo JE 38569	62	125
	NE-USER-RA	Munich Gl 181	75a	140
IVA3	NE-USER-RA	Cairo JE 57110	75b	140
	NE-USER-RA	Cairo JE 57115	75c	141
	NE-USER-RA	Göttingen AIU Z.V.I-26 (1912)	75d	141
	PEPY II	Not known	107	181
IVA4	NE-USER-RA	Dresden SK A.745	76a	142
	NE-USER-RA	E. Berlin ÄMP 20078	76b	142
	NE-USER-RA	Not known	76c	142
IVB1	HETEP-HERES I	Cairo JE 72030	28c	79
IVB2	SAHURA	Abusir, *in situ*?	59	120
IVB3	PEPY II	Not known	108	182
VA	ZOSER	Saqqara, *in situ*	24	73
VB	Vizier Sethu	Cairo CG 1298	51	110
	Vizier Ptah-hotep	Cairo CG 1308	87	157
	PEPY II	Not known	109	184
	Vizier Prince Tety	Cairo JE 63404	111	186
VI	PEPY II	Cairo JE 62950	100a	173
VIIA	ZER	Cairo JE 34915	7	48
	DYNASTY II Ivory Pin	Boston MFA 11.2526	16	62

TYPE	TIME PERIOD OR KING	PRESENT LOCATION	CAT.	PAGE
VIIB	TETY	New York MMA 26.7.1450	88	158
VIIC	LATE DYNASTY VI?			
	Diadem of Gold Falcon	Cairo CG 52701	112	187
VIIIA1a	Great Sphinx(CHEPHREN?)	London BM 1204	41b	95
VIIIA1b	RADEDEF	Louvre E 12626	30	83
	CHEPHREN	Cairo CG 41	34	87
	MYCERINUS	Boston MFA 09.204	46	103
	WESERKAF	Cairo JE 52501	52	111
	NE-USER-RA	Munich ÄS 6794	65	128
VIIIA1c	CHEPHREN?	Leipzig ÄMKMU 1946	35	88
	CHEPHREN or MYCERINUS?	Cairo CG 39	36	89
	MYCERINUS	Cairo CG 42	45	102
	NE-USER-RA	Cairo CG 38	63	126
	NE-USER-RA?	Beirut MN B.7395	66a	130
VIIIA2a	RADEDEF	Louvre E 12626	30	83
	RADEDEF	Cairo JE 35138	31	84
	CHEPHREN	Cairo CG 14	32	85
	CHEPHREN?	Leipzig ÄMKMU(destroyed)	39c	92
VIIIA2b	CHEPHREN?	Leipzig ÄMKMU 1946	35	88
	MYCERINUS	Cairo JE 40704	44	101
	WESERKAF	Cairo JE 52501	52	111
	SAHURA	New York MMA 18.2.4	54	113
VIIIA2c	CHEPHREN	Cairo CG 41	34	87
	CHEPHREN?	Leipzig ÄMKMU 1950	39a	92
	CHEPHREN?	Leipzig ÄMKMU 1951	39b	92
	CHEPHREN?	W. Berlin ÄM 15048	39d	92
	MYCERINUS	Boston MFA 09.204	46	103
	MYCERINUS	Cairo JE 40705	47	105
VIIIA2d	GREAT SPHINX (CHEPHREN?)	Giza, in situ	41a	95
VIIIA2e	CHEPHREN	Cairo CG 15	33	86
	CHEPHREN or MYCERINUS?	Cairo CG 39	36	89
VIIIA2e	CHEPHREN?	Leipzig ÄMKMU 1945	37	90
	CHEPHREN?	Boston MFA 21.351	38	91
VIIIA2e	CHEPHREN?	Cairo JE 49692	40	94
	MYCERINUS	Cairo CG 42	45	102
	NE-USER-RA	Cairo CG 38	63	126
	NE-USER-RA	Rochester MAG 42.54	64	127
	NE-USER-RA	Munich ÄS 6794	65	128
	NE-USER-RA?	Beirut MN B.7395	66a	130
	NE-USER-RA?	Brooklyn 72.58	66b	130
VIIIA2f	PEPY II	Brooklyn 39.119	96	168
VIIIA3a	RADEDEF	Louvre E 12626	30	83
	RADEDEF	Cairo JE 35138	31	84
	CHEPHREN?	Leipzig ÄMKMU 1946	35	88

TYPE	TIME PERIOD OR KING	PRESENT LOCATION	CAT.	PAGE
VIIIA3a	CHEPHREN?	W. Berlin ÄM 15048	39d	92
VIIIA3b	CHEPHREN	Cairo CG 14	32	85
	CHEPHREN	Cairo CG 15	33	86
VIIIA3c	MYCERINUS	Cairo JE 40705	47	105
VIIIA3d	MYCERINUS	Cairo JE 40704	44	101
	MYCERINUS	Boston MFA 09.204	46	103
	SAHURA	New York MMA 18.2.4	54	113
VIIIA3e	CHEPHREN	Cairo CG 41	34	87
	MYCERINUS	Cairo CG 42	45	102
VIIIA3f	CHEPHREN?	Boston MFA 21.351	38	91
	CHEPHREN or			
	MYCERINUS?	Cairo CG 39	36	89
	NE-USER-RA	Rochester MAG 42.54	64	127
	NE-USER-RA?	Brooklyn 72.58	66b	130
VIIIA3g	WESERKAF	Cairo JE 52501	52	111
VIIIA3g	NE-USER-RA	Munich ÄS 6794	65	128
VIIIA3h	PEPY II	Brooklyn 39.119	96	168
VIIIB1a	SHEPSESKAF?	Boston MFA 09.203	50	108
VIIIB2a	SHEPSESKAF?	Boston MFA 09.203	50	108
VIIIB2b	PEPY II	Cairo JE 50616	97	170
VIIIB3a	SHEPSESKAF?	Boston MFA 09.203	50	108
VIIIB3b	PEPY II	Cairo JE 50616	97	170
VIIIC2a	UNKNOWN KING	E. Berlin ÄMP 14396	78	145
VIIID1	UNKNOWN KING	Athens NAM L.120 (4039 Rosovitz collection)	79	146
	PEPY I	Brooklyn 39.121	90	162
VIIID2	PEPY I or MERNERA?	Cairo JE 33035	91	163

CONCORDANCE III - PRESENT LOCATION

Objects with uraei cited in the HISTORY (CATALOG) section are listed according to **PRESENT LOCATION** with Registration or Accession Number when known, Time Period or King, Catalog and Page Numbers.

PRESENT LOCATION and REG. NO.		TIME PERIOD OR KING	CAT.	PAGE
Athens	NAM L. 120	UNKNOWN, LATE DYN. V		
	(4039) Rostoviz coll.)	or EARLY DYN. VI	79	146
Beirut	MN B.7395	NE-USER-RA?	66a	130
E. Berlin	ÄMP 15129	LATE GERZEAN	Fig. 65	38
E. Berlin	ÄMP 19999	MYCERINUS	49	107
E. Berlin	ÄMP 28613	SAHURA	58a	118
E. Berlin	ÄMP 28628	SAHURA	58b	118
E. Berlin	ÄMP 16100	NE-USER-RA	67	131
E. Berlin	ÄMP 17911	NE-USER-RA	70	134
E. Berlin	ÄMP 20078	NE-USER-RA	76b	142
E. Berlin	ÄMP 14396	UNKNOWN, DYN. V?	78	145
E. Berlin	ÄMP 17933	ISESY	82a	149
W. Berlin	ÄM 15048	CHEPHREN?	39d	92
W. Berlin	ÄM 343/67	SAHURA	60b	122
Bonn	ÄSU A.310	SAHURA	56b	115
Boston	MFA 11.2526	DYNASTY II	16	62
Boston	MFA 21.351	CHEPHREN?	38	91
Boston	MFA 09.204	MYCERINUS?	46	103
Boston	MFA 09.202	MYCERINUS	48	106
Boston	MFA 09.203	SHEPSESKAF?	50	108
Breslau?	Not known	SAHURA	56c	115
Brooklyn	61.87	LATE GERZEAN	Fig. 64	38
Brooklyn	09.889.118	LATE PREDYNASTIC	1	39
Brooklyn	61.20	DYNASTY XIX	Fig. 69	40
Brooklyn	72.58	NE-USER-RA?	66b	130
Brooklyn	44.123.30	NE-USER-RA	77a	144
Brooklyn	44.123.31	NE-USER-RA	77b	144
Brooklyn	64.148.2	ISESY	82b	149
Brooklyn	39.121	PEPY I	90	162
Brooklyn	44.123.32	PEPY I	95	167
Brooklyn	39.119	PEPY II	96	168
Brussels	MRAH E. 7062	AMRATIAN	Fig. 61	36

PRESENT LOCATION and REG. NO.		TIME PERIOD OR KING	CAT.	PAGE
Cairo	CG 14265	LATE PREDYNASTIC	Fig. 66	38
Cairo	JE 43883	LATE PREDYNASTIC	3	43
Cairo	CG 14142	HOR AHA, MENES	6	46
Cairo	JE 34915	ZER	7	48
Cairo	JE 47176	ZET (WADJI)	9b	51
Cairo	JE 55291	KHASEKHEMUWY	14b	59
Cairo	CG 57101	SA-NEKHT (NEBKA)	17	63
Cairo	TL 20/1/21/7	SA-NEKHT or ZOSER?	18	65
Cairo	JE 49613	NETERKHET (ZOSER)	20	67
Cairo	JE 52508	NETERKHET (ZOSER)	22	70
Cairo	JE 89289	SNEFERU	25	74
Cairo	CG 57711	HETEP-HERES I	27	77
(copy Boston	MFA 38.8743)			
Cairo	JE 72030	HETEP-HERES I	28	79
(copy Boston	MFA 39.746)			
Cairo	JE 35138	RADEDEF	31	84
Cairo	CG 14	CHEPHREN	32	85
Cairo	CG 15	CHEPHREN	33	86
Cairo	CG 41	CHEPHREN	34	87
Cairo	CG 39	CHEPHREN or MYCERINUS?	36	89
Cairo	JE 49692	CHEPHREN?	40	94
Cairo	JE 40704	MYCERINUS	44	101
Cairo	CG 42	MYCERINUS	45	102
Cairo	JE 40705	MYCERINUS?	47	105
Cairo	CG 1298	DYNASTY IV or LATER	51	110
Cairo	JE 52501	WESERKAF	52	111
Cairo	JE 56600	WESERKAF	53	112
Cairo	JE 39533	SAHURA	55	114
Cairo	JE 39527	SAHURA	61	124
Cairo	JE 39529	SAHURA	61	124
Cairo	JE 38569	SAHURA	62	125
Cairo	CG 38	NE-USER-RA	63	126
Cairo	JE 42003	NE-USER-RA	64	127
Cairo	JE 38664	NE-USER-RA	73	137
Cairo	JE 38570	NE-USER-RA	74	138
Cairo	JE 57110	NE-USER-RA	75b	140
Cairo	JE 57115	NE-USER-RA	75c	140
Cairo	JE 35131	UNAS	85	153
Cairo	CG 1308	DYNASTY V Obelisk	87	157
Cairo	JE 33035	PEPY I or MERNERA	91	163
Cairo	JE 72132	PEPY I	92	164
Cairo	JE 50616	PEPY II	97	170
Cairo	JE 62950	PEPY II	100a	173
Cairo	CG 53836	PEPY II	100b	173
Cairo	JE 63404	LATE DYNASTY VI	111	186
Cairo	CG 52701	LATE OLD KINGDOM?	112	187
Chicago	OIM 24119	A-GROUP	Fig. 63	37
Cleveland	MA 1018.81	GRAECO-ROMAN	Fig. 15	16
Dresden	SK A.745	NE-USER-RA	76a	142

PRESENT LOCATION and REG. NO.		TIME PERIOD OR KING	CAT.	PAGE
Göttingen	AIU Z.V.I-2t (1912)	NE-USER-RA	72	136
Göttingen	AIU Z.V.I-26(1912)	NE-USER-RA	75d	140
Hamburg	MKG 1925.63	SAHURA	56a	115
Hamburg	PC	SAHURA	57b	117
Kalingrad,U.S.S.R.	Not known	SAHURA	57a	117
Leipzig	ÄMKMU 1946	CHEPHREN?	35	88
Leipzig	ÄMKMU 1945	CHEPHREN?	37	90
Leipzig	ÄMKMU 1950	CHEPHREN?	39a	92
Leipzig	ÄMKMU 1951	CHEPHREN?	39b	92
Leipzig	Now destroyed	CHEPHREN?	39c	92
London	BM 68512	LATE PREDYNASTIC	5	45
London	BM 32641	ZET (WADJI)	9a	51
London	BM 55586	DEN (WEDYMU)	10	52
London	BM 35552	DEN (WEDYMU)	11	54
London	BM 32668	SEMERKHET	12a	55
London	BM 32672	QAY-A	13a	57
London	BM 49278	SEMTI, IRYNETJER	13c	57
London	BM 35556	PERIBSEN, RANEB, NY-NETJER	13d	58
London	BM 35592	KHASEKHEMUWY	14a	59
London	BM 1204	GREAT SPHINX	41b	95
London	BM 25422	PEPY II	110	185
London	BM 11103	NE-USER-RA	77c	144
Montreal	MFA 964.B.6	PEPY I	94	166
(formerly New York MMA 09.180.27)				
Munich	ÄS 6794	NE-USER-RA	65	128
Munich	Gl 185	NE-USER-RA	71b	135
Munich	Gl 183	NE-USER-RA	71c	135
Munich	Gl 181	NE-USER-RA	75a	140
New York	MMA 26.7.1281	LATE PREDYNASTIC	2	42
New York	MMA 30.8.244	LATE PREDYNASTIC	4	44
New York	MMA 01.4.20	QAY-A	13b	57
New York	MMA 22.1.19	CHEOPS	29b	81
New York	MMA 07.288.24	CHEPHREN	42	99
New York	MMA 18.2.4	SAHURA	54	113
New York	MMA 26.7.1450	TETY	88	158
New York	MMA 09.180.113	AMENEMHET I	Fig. 330	183
New York	MMA 08.200.10	AMENEMHET I	Fig. 331	183
Paris	Louvre E 27131	AMRATIAN	Fig. 62	37
Paris	Louvre E 11007	ZET (WADJI)	8	49
Paris	Louvre E 12626	RADEDEF	30	84
Philadelphia	UPM E. 6880	QAY-A	12b	55
Rochester	MAG 42.54	NE-USER-RA	64	127
Strassburg, Ger.	Unknown	SAHURA	58c	118
Turin	ME (cat.no. 12341)	KHASEKHEMUWY?	15	61
Saqqara	magazine	TETY	89a	160
Abusir	*in situ?*	SAHURA	59	120
Abusir	*in situ?*	SAHURA	60a	122
Giza	*in situ*	Great Sphinx (CHEPHREN?)	41a	95

PRESENT LOCATION and REG. NO.		TIME PERIOD OR KING	CAT.	PAGE
Saqqara	*in situ*	ZOSER	21	69
Saqqara	*in situ*	ZOSER	23	71
Saqqara	*in situ*	ZOSER	24	73
Tanis	*in situ*	CHEOPS	29c	81
Saqqara	*in situ*	UNAS	86a–h	154
Saqqara	*in situ*	UNAS	Fig. 1	9
Saqqara	*in situ*	TETY	89b	161
Saqqara	*in situ?*	PEPY II	101	174
Sinai	*in situ*	ZOSER	19	66
Sinai	Now destroyed	CHEOPS	29a	81
Sinai	Now destroyed	ISESY	80	147
Sinai	Now destroyed	PEPY I	93	165
Sinai	Now destroyed	PEPY II	103	176
Not known		SNEFERU	26	75
Not known		CHEPHREN	43	100
Not known		SAHURA	58d	118
Not known		NE-USER-RA	68	132
Not known		NE-USER-RA	69a,b	133
Not known		NE-USER-RA	71a	135
Not known		NE-USER-RA	76c	142
Not known		ISESY	81	148
Not known		UNAS	83	151
Not known		UNAS?	84	152
Not known		PEPY II	98	171
Not known		PEPY II	99a,b	172
Not known		PEPY II	102a,b	175
Not known		NEITH	104	177
Not known		PEPY II	105a,b	178
Not known		PEPY II	106a,b	179
Not known		PEPY II	107	181
Not known		PEPY II	108a,b	182
Not known		PEPY II	109	184

264

BIBLIOGRAPHY

ABUBAKR 1937
A. Abubakr. *Untersuchungen uber die ägyptischen Kronen.* Gluckstadt, 1937

ADAMS 1974
B. Adams. *Ancient Hierakonpolis.* Warminster, England, 1974.

ALDRED 1949
C. Aldred. *Old Kingdom Art in Ancient Egypt.* London, 1949.
ALDRED 1965
.... *Egypt to the End of the Old Kingdom.* London, 1965.
ALDRED 1968
.... *Old Kingdom Art in Ancient Egypt.* London, 1968.
ALDRED 1971
.... *Jewels of the Pharaohs.* New York, 1971.
ALDRED 1980
.... *Egyptian Art in the Days of the Pharaohs.* New York, 1980.

ALTENMULLER 1974
H. Altenmuller, "Zur Vergottlichung des Unas im Alten Reich", in *SAK* 1 (1974), pp. 6-8.

AMIET 1972
P. Amiet. *Glyptique susienne* I, II. Paris, 1972.

APPEL 1946
B. Appel. *Skin Beauty and Health.* Westfield, Mass., 1946.

ARCHEOLOGIE COMPAREE 1982
   Catalogue sommaire illustre des collections du Musée des Antiquités Nationales de Saint-Germain-en-Laye. Paris, 1982.

ARKELL 1933
A. J. Arkell, "The Signs ⸮ and ⸮ ", in *JEA* 19 (1933), pp. 175-76.

BADAWY 1954
A. Badawy. *A History of Egyptian Architecture I: From the Earliest Times to the End of the Old Kingdom.* Cairo, 1954.

BAER 1960
K. Baer. *Rank and Title in the Old Kingdom.* Chicago, 1960.

BAKRY 1969
S. K. Bakry, "A Stela from Heliopolis Dedicated to Edjo", in *RSO* 44 (1969), pp. 177-80, fig. 1, pl. 1.

BARSANTI 1901
A. Barsanti, "Sur les déblaiements opérés autour de la pyramide d'Ounas", in *ASAE* 2 (1901), pp. 244-57.

BARTA 1984
W. Barta, "Zur Bedeutung des Stirnband-Diadems šsd", in *GM* 72 (1984), pp. 7-8.

BATES 1917
O. Bates. *The Eastern Libyans*. London, 1917.

BAUMGARTEL 1955
E. J. Baumgartel, *The Cultures of Prehistoric Egypt*, I. Oxford, 1955.

BECKERATH 1971
J. von Beckerath. *Abriss der Geschichte des alten Ägypten*. Munich, 1971.
BECKERATH 1984
.... *Handbuch der Ägyptischen Königsnamen*. Munich, 1984.

BELTZ 1982
Walter Beltz. *Die Mythen der Ägypter*. Düsseldorf, 1982.

BÉNÉDITE 1905
G. Benedite, "La stèle dite du Roi Serpent", in *Mon. Piot* 12 (1905), pp. 87-105.
BÉNÉDITE 1918
..................., "The Carnarvon Ivory", in *JEA* 5 (1918), pp. 1-15, 2 pls.

BIANCHI 1979
R. S. Bianchi. *Ancient Egyptian Sculpture from The Brooklyn Museum*. Puerto Rico, 1979.

BISSING 1923
F. W. F. von Bissing and others. *Das Re-Heiligtum des Königs Ne-Woser-re̊ (Rathures)* II. Leipzig, 1923.
BISSING 1928
....III. Leipzig, 1928.

BMRAH 1935
Bulletin des Musées Royaux d'Art et d'Histoire, 3e serie, 7e année (nov.- dec. 1935).

BONNET 1952
H. Bonnet. *Reallexikon der Äegyptischen Religionsgeschichte*. Berlin, 1952.

BORCHARDT 1907
L. Borchardt. *Das Grabdenkmal des Königs Ne-user-re'*. Leipzig, 1907.
BORCHARDT 1909
.... *Das Grabdenkmal des Königs Nefer-ir-ke3-re'* I. Leipzig, 1909.
BORCHARDT 1910
.... *Das Grabdenkmal des Königs S'a3hu-re'* I. Leipzig, 1910.

BORCHARDT 1911
.... *Statuen und Statuetten von Königen und Privatleuten im Museum von Kairo* I.
  Berlin, 1911.
BORCHARDT 1913
.... *Das Grabdenkmal des Königs S'a3hu-re'* II. Leipzig, 1913.
BORCHARDT 1937
.... *Denkmäler des Alten Reiches* I. Berlin, 1937.

BOTHMER 1949
B. V. Bothmer, "Statuettes of *W3ḏ.t* as Ichneumon Coffins", in *JNES* 8 (1949), pp. 121-123, 3
  plates.
BOTHMER 1971
........................, "A Bust of Ny-user-ra from Byblos in Beirut, Lebanon", in *Kemi* 21 (1971),
  pp. ll-16, 2 plates.
BOTHMER 1974a
........................, "The Karnak Statue of Ny-user-ra (Membra Dispersa IV)", in *MDAIK* 30
  (1974), pp. 165-70, 6 plates.
BOTHMER 1974b
.... and J. L. Keith. *Brief Guide to The Department of Egyptian and Classical
  Art, The Brooklyn Museum.* Brooklyn, 1974.
BOTHMER 1978
........................, "On Photographing Egyptian Art", in *SAK* (1978), pp. 51-53, 12 plates.
BOTHMER 1982
........................, "On Realism in Egyptian Funerary Sculpture in the Old Kingdom", in *Exp.*
  24 (1982), pp. 27-39, 30 figs.

BREASTED 1905
J. H. Breasted. *A History of Egypt from the Earliest Times to the Persian Conquest.* London,
  1905.
BREASTED 1912
.... *The Development of Religion and Thought in Ancient Egypt.* New York,
  1912.

BROEKHUIS 1971
J. Broekhuis. *The Goddess Renenutet and Her Qualities.* (Pamphlet giving
  an abridged rendering of thesis, *De Godin Renenwetet*, Assen. 1971)

BROVARSKI 1982
E. Brovarski and others. *Egypt's Golden Age: The Art of Living in the New Kingdom, 1558-
  1085 B.C..* Boston, 1982.

BUDGE 1909
E. A. W. Budge. *A General Introductory Guide to the Egyptian Collections in The British
  Museum.* London, 1909.

CAPART 1905
J. Capart. *Primitive Art in Egypt.* (Translated by A. S. Griffith) London, 1905.
CAPART 1930
.... *Memphis à l'ombre des pyramides.* Brussels, 1930.

ČERNÝ 1955
J. Černý. *The Inscriptions of Sinai* II. London, 1955.

CHASSINAT 1921-1922
E. Chassinat, "A propos d'une tete en gres rouge du roi Didoufri", in *Mon. Piot* 25 (1921-1922), pp. 53-75, 2 pls.

CHRISTIE'S 1984
Christie, Manson, and Woods Ltd. *Fine Antiquities* (Sale Catalog)

CHURCHER 1984
C. S. Churcher, in W. Needler. *Predynastic and Archaic Egypt in The Brooklyn Museum.* Brooklyn, 1984.

CLARK 1978
R. T. R. Clark. *Myth and Symbol in Ancient Egypt.* London, 1978

COONEY 1949
W. Cooney. "Royal Sculptures of Dynasty VI" in *ACIO* Paris, 23-31 (July, 1948), pp. 74-76.

CURTO 1953
S. Curto. "Nota su un relievo proveniente da Gebelen nel Museo Egizio di Torino" in *Aegyptus* 33 (1953), pp. 105-124.

DAVIES 1982
W. V. Davies, "The Origin of the Blue Crown", in *JEA* 68 (1982), pp. 69-76, 16 figs., 1 pl..

DRIOTON 1959
E. Drioton. *Religions of the Ancient East.* (Translated by M. B. Loraine) New York, 1959.

DUKE U. 1965
Duke University. *A Survey of Egyptian Sculpture from the Old Kingdom.* Chapel Hill, N. C.

DUNHAM 1946
D. Dunham, "An Egyptian Diadem of the Old Kingdom", in *BMFA* 44 (1946), pp. 23-29, 13 figs..
DUNHAM 1958
.... *The Egyptian Department and Its Excavations.* Boston, 1958.
DUNHAM 1978
.... *Zawiyet el Aryan: The Cemeteries Adjacent to the Layer Pyramid.* Boston, 1978.

EATON-KRAUSS 1977
M. Eaton-Krauss, "The *khat* Headdress to the End of the Amarna Period", in *SAK* 5 (1977), pp. 21-39.
EATON-KRAUSS 1981
.........................., "The Dating of the 'Hierakonpolis Falcon'", in *GM* 42 (1981), pp. 15-18.

EDWARDS 1955
I. E. S. Edwards, "An Egyptian Bestiary of 5000 Years ago - From a Famous Flint Knife, Now Exhibited in The British Museum", in *ILN* (Dec. 17, 1955), p. 1061.
EDWARDS 1971a
.........................., "The Early Dynastic Period in Egypt", in *The Cambridge Ancient History* I, 2, pp. 1-59. Cambridge, England, 1971.

EDWARDS 1971b
.... and others. *General Introductory Guide to the Egyptian Collections in The British Museum.* Oxford, 1971.
EDWARDS 1976
.... *The Pyramids of Egypt.* Rev. ed., New York, 1976.

EMERY 1939
W. B. Emery. *Hor-Aha.* Cairo, 1939.
EMERY 1961
.... *Archaic Egypt.* Baltimore, 1961.

ENGELBACH 1928
R. Engelbach, "The So-called Hyksos Monuments", in *ASAE* 28 (1928), pp., 13-28, 4 pls..
ENGELBACH 1930
........................., "An Alleged Winged Sun-disk of the First Dynasty", in *ZÄS* 65 (1930), pp. 115-16, pl. VIII.

ERMAN 1966
A. Erman. *The Ancient Egyptians: A Sourcebook of Their Writings.* (Translated by A. M. Blackman, introd. by W. K. Simpson) New York, 1966.

EVERS 1929
H. G. Evers. *Staat aus dem Stein: Denkmäler, Geschichte und Bedeutung der Ägyptischen Plastik während des Mittleren Reichs* I, II. Munich, 1929.

FAKHRY 1954
A. Fakhry, "The Excavations of Sneferu's Monuments at Dahshur", in *ASAE* 52 (1954), pp. 563-85, pls. xi-xix.
FAKHRY 1959-1961
.... *The Monuments of Sneferu at Dahshur* I, II. Cairo, 1959, 1961.

FAULKNER 1933
R. O. Faulkner. *The Papyrus Bremner Rhind.* Brussels, 1933.
FAULKNER 1962
.... *A Concise Dictionary of Middle Egyptian.* Oxford, 1962.
FAULKNER 1969
.... *The Ancient Egyptian Pyramid Texts.* Oxford, 1969.

FAZZINI 1975
R. Fazzini. *Images for Eternity.* Brooklyn, 1975.

FIRTH 1929a
C. M. Firth. *Archaeological Survey of Nubia: Report 1910-1911.* Cairo, 1929.
FIRTH 1929b
........................, "Excavations of the Department of Antiquities at Saqqara", in *ASAE* 29 (1929), pp. 64-70, 2 plates.
FIRTH 1930
........................, "Report on the Excavations of the Department of Antiquities at Saqqara", in *ASAE* 30 (1930), pp. 185-89, 1 plate.
FIRTH 1935
.... and J. E. Quibell. *The Step Pyramid* I, II. Cairo, 1935.

FISCHER 1973
H. G. Fischer, "L'orientation des textes", in *Textes et langages de l'Égypte pharaonique* i, pp. 21-23. Cairo, 1973.
FISCHER 1976
........................, "Archaeological Aspects of Epigraphy and Palaeography", in *Ancient Egyptian Epigraphy and Palaeography*, by R. Caminos and H. Fischer, pp. 29-50, 6 figs. New York, 1976.
FISCHER 1977
........................, "Offering Stands from the Pyramid of Amenemhat I", in *Ancient Egypt in The Metropolitan Museum Journal,* 1-11 (1968-1976), p. 72, n. 5, fig. 5. New York, 1977.
FISCHER 1980
........................, "Hieroglyphen", in *LdÄ* III, pp. 1189-99. Wiesbaden, 1980.

FRANKFORT 1948
H. Frankfort. *Kingship and the Gods.* Chicago, 1948.

GARDINER - PEET 1917
A. H. Gardiner and E. T. Peet. *Inscriptions of Sinai* I. London, 1917.

GARDINER 1944
A. H. Gardiner, "Horus the Behdetite", in *JEA* 30 (1944), pp. 23-60.
GARDINER 1957
.... *Egyptian Grammar*, 3rd ed.. Oxford, 1957.

GARSTANG 1905
J. Garstang, "The Tablet of Mena", in *ZÄS* 42 (1905), pp. 61-64, 3 figs.

GOEDICKE 1971
H. Goedicke. *Re-used Blocks from the Pyramid of Amenemhet I at Lisht.* New York, 1971.

GOYON 1969
G. Goyon, "Le cylindre de l'ancien empire du Musée d'Ismailia", in *BIFAO* 67 (1969), pp. 147-57, 2 plates..

GRDSELOFF 1944
B. Grdseloff, "Notes d'epigraphie archaique: I. La tablette de Naqada et le roi Menes; II. Le nom du roi 'Serpent'; III. Le nom de *'Nisw.t-Bitj*'de l'Horus *Šmr-ḥt*.", in *ASAE* 44 (1944), pp. 279-88.

GRIFFITHS 1959
J. G. Griffiths, "Remarks on the Horian Elements in the Royal Titulary", in *ASAE* 56 (1959), pp. 63-86.

HABACHI 1957
L. Habachi. *Tell Basta.* Cairo, 1957.

HAENY 1984
G. Haeny. "Schientür" in *LdÄ* V (1984), pp. 564-574.

HALL 1913
H. R. Hall. *Catalogue of Egyptian Scarabs,... in The British Museum.* London, 1913.

HARRISON 1972
H. H. Harrison. *The World of the Snake*. Philadelphia, 1972.

HASSAN 1953
S. Hassan. *The Great Sphinx and Its Secrets: Giza* VIII. Cairo 1953.

HAYES 1947
W. C. Hayes, "Horemkha'uef of Nekhen and His Trip to It-towe", in *JEA* 33 (1947), pp. 6-ll.
HAYES 1953
.... *The Scepter of Egypt* I. New York, 1953.

HELCK 1954
W. Helck. *Untersuchungen zu den Beamtentiteln des ägyptischen Alten Reiches*. Gluckstadt, 1954.

HOFMANN 1970
I. Hofmann, "Zŭr Kombination von Elephant und Riesenschlange in Altertum", in *Anthropos* 65 (1970), pp. 619-32, 6 figs., 1 plate.

HÖLSCHER 1912
U. Hölscher. *Das Grabdenkmal des Königs Chephren*. Leipzig, 1912.

HOSTENS-DELEU 1971
R. Hostens-Deleu, "Review of *National Museum Cairo*", in **CdE** 46 (1971), p. 301.

JAMES 1974
T. G. H. James. *Corpus of Hieroglyphic Inscriptions in The Brooklyn Museum* I. Brooklyn, 1974.
JAMES 1982
..........................., "A Wooden Figure of Wadjet", in *JEA* 68 (1982), pp. 156-65, 2 pls.

JANKUHN 1974
D. Jankuhn. *Bibliographie der hieratischen und hieroglyphischen Papyri*. Wiesbaden, 1974

JÉQUIER 1927
G. Jéquier, "Rapport préliminaire sur les fouilles executées en 1926-1927 dans la partie méridionale de la nécropole memphite", in *ASAE* 27 (1927), pp. 49-61, 1 plate.
JÉQUIER 1929
.... *Tombeaux de particuliers contemporains de Pepi II*. Cairo, 1929.
JÉQUIER 1933
.... *Les pyramides des reines Neit et Apouit*. Cairo, 1933.
JÉQUIER 1934
..................., "Rapport préliminaire sur les fouilles executées en 1933-1934 dans la partie méridionale de la nécropole memphite", in *ASAE* 34 (1934), pp. 76-82, 2 plates.
JÉQUIER 1938-1940
.... *Le monument funéraire de Pepi II* II, III. Cairo, 1938-1940.

JUNG 1976
C. G. Jung. *Symbols of Transformation* (Translated by R. F. C. Hull from *Symbole der Wandlung*. Zurich, 1952)). Princeton, 1976.

JUNKER 1926
H. Junker. *Giza* I. Vienna, 1926.

JUNKER 1934
.... *Giza* II. Vienna, 1934.
JUNKER 1938
.... *Giza* III. Vienna, 1938.

KAISER 1971
W. Kaiser, "Die kleine Hebseddarstellung im Sonnenheiligtum des Neuserre", in *BABA* 12
    (1971), pp. 87-105.

KÁKÓSY 1981
Laszlo Kákósy, "The Astral Snakes of the Nile", in *MDAIK* 37 (1981), pp. 255-60, 1 plate.

KANTOR 1944
H. J. Kantor, "The Final Phase of Predynastic Culture, Gerzean or Semainean (?)", in *JNES* 3
    (1944), pp. 117-31, 13 figs.

KAPLONY 1980
P. Kaplony, "Horusname", in *LdÄ* III, pp. 59-60. Wiesbaden, 1980.
KAPLONY 1981
.... *Die Rollsiegel des Alten Reichs* II A, B. Brussels, 1981.

KEIMER 1947
L. Keimer. *Histoires de serpents dans l'Égypte ancienne et moderne.* Cairo, 1947.

KOZLOFF 1981
A. P. Kozloff. *Animals in Ancient Art: Cleveland Museum of Art.* Cleveland, 1981.

KRIÉGER 1960
P. Kriéger, "Une statuette du roi-faucon au Musée du Louvre", in *RdE* 12 (1960), pp. 37-58,
    23 figs..
KRIÉGER 1976
P. Posener-Kriéger. *Les archives du temple funéraire de Neferirkare-kakai* II. Cairo, 1976.

LABROUSSE, LAUER, LECLANT 1977
A. Labrousse, J-P. Lauer, J. Leclant. *Le temple haut du complexe funéraire du roi Ounas.*
    Cairo, 1977.

LAUER 1939
J-P. Lauer, "Fouilles du service des antiquités a Saqqarah: secteur de la pyramide à degrés,
    (Novembre 1938 - Mai 1939), in *ASAE* 39 (1939), pp. 452-54.
LAUER 1962
.... *Histoire monumentale des pyramides d'Égypte, I: les pyramides à degrés.* Cairo,
    1962.
LAUER 1976
.... *Saqqara: The Royal Cemetery of Memphis; Ecavations and Discoveries since
    1850.* (English translation) London, 1976.

LAUER - LECLANT 1972
J-P. Lauer et J. Leclant. *Le temple haut du complexe funéraire du roi Teti.* Cairo, 1972.

LECLANT 1971
J. Leclant, "Fouilles et travaux en Egypte et en Soudan", in *Orientalia* 40 (1971), pp. 232-33.

272   Bibliography

LEHNER 1982a
M. Lehner, "The ARCE Sphinx Project; A Preliminary Report", in *NARCE* 112 (Fall, 1980), pp. 3-33, 12 figs..
LEHNER 1982b
...................., correspondence with the author.

LILLESØ 1975
E. K. Lillesø, "Two Wooden Uraei", in *JEA* 61 (1975), pp. 137-46, 1 fig., 1 plate.

LURKER 1980
M. Lurker. *The Gods and Symbols of Ancient Egypt.* London, 1980.

MARTIN 1985
K. Martin, "Uraus", in *LdÄ* VI, pp. 864-868. Wiesbaden, 1985.

MASPERO 1890
G. Maspero and others. *Le musée égyptien* I. Cairo, 1890.

MINTON and MINTON 1969
S. A. Minton, Jr. and M. R. Minton. *Venomous Reptiles.* New York, 1969.

MORGAN 1897
J. de Morgan, "Le tombeau royal de Negadah", in *Recherches sur les origines de l'Égypte: ethnographie préhistorique.* Paris, 1897.
MORGAN 1926
.... *La préhistoire orientale* II. Paris, 1926.

MORENZ 1973
S. Morenz. *Egyptian Religion* (Translated by A. E. Keep). Ithaca, 1973.

MOUSA 1985
A. M. Mousa, "Excavations in the Valley Temple of King Unas at Saqqara (II)" in *ASAE* 70 (1985), pp. 9-10, fig. 1, pls. i-ii.

MÜLLER 1938
H. Müller. *Die formale Entwicklung der Titulatur der ägyptischen Könige.* Gluckstadt, 1938.

MÜLLER 1978
M. Müller. "Oberteil einer Königstatuette", in *Geschenk des Nils.* Basel, 1978, p. 53, cat. no. 173.

MUNDKUR 1983
B. Mundkur. *The Cult of the Serpent: An Interdisciplinary Survey of Its Manifestations and Origins.* Albany, 1983.

NEEDLER 1984
W. Needler. *Predynastic and Archaic Egypt in The Brooklyn Museum.* Brooklyn, 1984.

PETRIE 1896
F. Petrie and J. E. Quibell. *Naqada and Ballas, 1895.* London, 1896.
PETRIE 1900
.... *The Royal Tombs of the First Dynasty* I. London, 1900.

PETRIE 1901a
.... *Royal Tombs of the Earliest Dynasties* II. London, 1901.
PETRIE 1901b
.... *Diospolis Parva.* London, 1901
PETRIE 1902-1904
.... *Abydos* I, II, III. London, 1902, 1903, 1904.
PETRIE 1903
.... *A History of Egypt* I. London, 1903.
PETRIE 1906
.... *Researches in Sinai.* New York, 1906.
PETRIE 1917
.... *Scarabs and Cylinders with Names.* London, 1917.
PETRIE 1925
.... *Tombs of the Courtiers.* London, 1925.

PIANKOFF 1968
A. Piankoff. *The Pyramid of Unas.* Princeton, 1968.

PM 1934
B. Porter and R. Moss. *Topographical Bibliography of Ancient Egyptian Hieroglyphic Texts, Reliefs, Paintings IV: Lower and Middle Egypt.* Oxford, 1934.
PM 1951
.... *Topographical Bibliography...VII: Nubia, the Deserts, and Outside Egypt.* Oxford, 1951.
PM 1974
.... *Topographical Bibliography ...III: Memphis; pt. 1 Abu Rawash to Abusir,* 2nd ed. rev. and augmented by J. Malek. Oxford, 1974.
PM 1977
.... *Topographical Bibliography...III: Memphis; pt. 2 fasc. 1, Saqqara to Dahshur,* 2nd ed. rev. and augmented by J. Malek. Oxford, 1977.
PM 1978
.... *Topographical Bibliography...III: Memphis; pt. 2 fasc. 2, Saqqara to Dahshur,* 2nd ed. rev. and augmented by J. Malek. Oxford, 1978.
PM 1981
.... *Topographical Bibliography...III: Memphis; pt. 2 fasc. 3, Saqqara to Dahshur,* 2nd ed. rev. and augmented by J. Malek. Oxford, 1981.

POSENER 1962
G. Posener. *A Dictionary of Egyptian Civilization,* (English translation). London, 1962

QUIBELL 1900
J. E. Quibell. *Hierakonpolis* I. London, 1900.
QUIBELL - GREEN 1902
.... and F. Green. *Hierakonpolis* II. London, 1902.
QUIBELL 1905
.... *Archaic Objects (CG nos. 11001-12000 and 14001-14754).* Cairo, 1905.
QUIBELL 1908
.... *Excavations at Saqqara, 1906-1907.* Cairo, 1908.
QUIBELL 1909
.... *Excavations at Saqqara, 1907-1908.* Cairo, 1909.
QUIBELL 1923
.... *Excavations at Saqqara, 1912-1914: Archaic Mastabas.* Cairo, 1923.

REDFORD 1983
D. B. Redford, "Notes on the History of Ancient Buto", in *BES* 5 (1983), pp. 67-94, pls. 1-6 and map.

REISNER 1931
G. Reisner. *Mycerinus: The Temples of the Third Pyramid at Giza* . Cambridge, MA, 1931.
REISNER 1932
................, "The Bed Canopy of the Mother of Cheops", in *BMFA* 30 (1932), pp. 56-60, 13 illus.
REISNER 1942
.... *A History of the Giza Necropolis* I. Cambridge, Mass., 1942.
REISNER - SMITH 1955
.... and W. S. Smith. *A History of the Giza Necropolis* II: *The Tomb of Hetepheres.* Cambridge, Mass., 1955.

RICKE 1944
H. Ricke. *Bermerkungen zur Baukunst des Alten Reiches* I. Zurich, 1944.
RICKE 1970
................, "Der Harmachistempel des Chefren in Giseh", in *BÄBA* 10 (1970), pp. 1-43, 20 figs., 17 pls., 4 plans.

ROMANO 1983
J. Romano, "Head and Bust of A King" and "King Pepy II and His Mother", in *Neferut Net Kemit: Egyptian Art from The Brooklyn Museum.* Brooklyn, 1983, cat. nos. 12, 15.

RÖSSLER-KÖHLER 1978
U. Rössler-Köhler, "Zür Datierung des Falkenbildes von Hierakonpolis (CGC 17717)", in *MDAIK* 34 (1978), pp. 117-25, 3 plates.

RUSSMANN 1974
E. Russmann. *The Representation of the King in the XXVth Dynasty.* Brooklyn, 1974.

SCAMUZZI 1963
E. Scamuzzi. *Egyptian Art in the Egyptian Museum of Turin* (English translation). Turin, 1963.

SCHÄFER 1904
H. Schäfer, "Zür Geschichte des Uraus am Kopfschmucke des Königs", in *ZÄS* 41 (1904), pp. 62-65, 2 figs.
SCHÄFER 1910
.... *Ägyptische Goldschmiedearbeiten.* Berlin, 1910.
SCHÄFER 1928
.... *Ägyptische und heutige Kunst und Weltgebaude der alten Ägypter.* Berlin, 1928.
SCHÄFER 1933
................, "Der Reliefschmuck der Berliner Tür aus der Stufenpyramide und der Königstitel *Ḥ-nb*", in *MDAIK* 4 (1933), pp. 1-17, 18 figs.
SCHAFER 1974
.... *Principles of Egyptian Art* (Translated by J. Baines). Oxford, 1974.

SCOTT 1968
J. and L. Scott. *Egyptian Hieroglyphs.* New York, 1968, p. 17.

SETHE 1935-1962

K. Sethe. *Ubersetzung und Kommentar zu den altägyptischen Pyramiden-Texten.* Hamburg, 1935-1962.

SHARPE 1862
S. Sharpe. *Egyptian Antiquities in the British Museum.* London, 1862.

SHENNUM 1977
D. Shennum. *English-Egyptian Index of Faulkner's Concise Dictionary of Middle Egyptian.* Malibu, 1977.

SMITH 1946
W. S. Smith. *A History of Egyptian Sculpture and Painting in the Old Kingdom.* Boston, 1946.
SMITH 1960
.... *Ancient Egypt as Represented in the Museum of Fine Arts, Boston,* 4th ed., rev. Boston, 1960.

SMITH - SIMPSON 1981
.... *The Art and Architecture of Ancient Egypt,* 2nd integrated ed., rev. by W. K. Simpson. New York, 1981.

SPENCER 1980
A. J. Spencer. *Catalogue of Egyptian Antiquities in the British Museum V: Early Dynastic Objects.* London, 1980.

SPIEGEL 1973
J. Spiegel. *Die Götter von Abydos.* Wiesbaden, 1973.

SPIEGELBERG 1896
W. Spiegelberg, "Ein neues Denkmal aus der Frühzeit der ägyptischen Kunst", in *ZÄS* 35 (1896), pp. 7-ll.

STADELMANN 1984
L. R. Stadelmann. *Die Ägyptischen Pyramiden.*

STIDWORTHY 1971
J. Stidworthy. *Snakes of the World.* New York, 1971.

STRUDWICK 1985
N. Strudwick. *The Administration of Egypt in the Old Kingdom.* London, 1985

VANDIER 1952
J. Vandier. *Manuel d'archéologie égyptienne* I, 3 pts.. Paris, 1952.
VANDIER 1958
.... *Manuel d'archéologie égyptienne* III, 2 pts.. Paris 1958.

VERNER 1982
M. Verner, "The False-door of Khekeretnebty", in *ZÄS* 109 (1982), pp. 72-75, fig. 3.
VERNER 1985
............, "Les sculptures de Reneferef decouvertes à Abousir" in *BIFAO* 85 (1985), pp. 267-281, 16 plates.

VERNIER 1927
E. Vernier. *Bijoux et orfevreries (CG nos. 52001-53855)* I, II. Cairo, 1927

VERGOTE 1961
J. Vergote, "Le nom du roi 'Serpent'", in *Orientalia* 30 (1961), pp. 355-65.

VYSE 1842
H. Vyse. *Appendix to Operations Carried on at the Pyramids of Giza in 1837*. London, 1842.

WB
A. Erman and H. Grapow. *Wörterbuch der Ägyptischen Sprache* I-V. Leipzig, 1926-1931.

WEEKS 1983
K. R. Weeks, "The Berkeley Map of the Theban Necropolis, Report of the Fifth Season, 1982", in *NARCE* 121, Supplement (Spring 1983), pp. 1-17.

WESTENDORF 1978
W. Westendorf, "Uraus und Sonnenscheibe", in *SAK* 6 (1978, **Festschrift Hans Wolfgang Müller**), pp. 201-25, 22 figs..

WHITFIELD 1984
P. Whitfield, ed.. *Animal Encyclopedia*. New York, 1984.

WILDUNG 1984
D. Wildung. *Ni-user-re, Sonnenkönig - Sonnengott*. Munich, 1984

WOLF 1957
W. Wolf. *Die Kunst Ägyptens*. Stuttgart, 1957.